THE MOURNING
OF JOHN LENNON

THE MOURNING
OF JOHN LENNON

ANTHONY ELLIOTT

UNIVERSITY OF CALIFORNIA PRESS
BERKELEY   LOS ANGELES   LONDON

University of California Press
Berkeley and Los Angeles, California

University of California Press, Ltd.
London, England

© 1999 by
Anthony Elliott

Library of Congress Cataloging-in-Publication Data

Elliott, Anthony, 1964–
    The mourning of John Lennon / Anthony Elliott.
      p.   cm.
    Includes bibliographic references, discography, and index
    ISBN 0-520-21548-6 (alk. paper).—ISBN 0-520-21549-4
    (alk. paper)
      1. Lennon, John, 1940–1980.   2. Rock musicians—
    England—Biography.   I. Title.
  ML420.L38E45   1998
  782.42166′092—dc21   98-3637 CIP

Printed in the United States of America
9 8 7 6 5 4 3 2 1

To the memory of
Albert J. Paolini
and
Séan H. Geraghty-Elliott

You don't know what you got
Until you lose it.

John Lennon

There is no imagination that is not, overtly or
secretly, melancholy.

Julia Kristeva

I can't remember anything
without a sadness
So deep that it hardly
becomes known to me.

John Lennon

World is suddener than we fancy it.

Louis MacNeice

It's fear of the unknown. The unknown is what
it is. And to be frightened of it is what sends
everybody scurrying around chasing dreams,
illusions, wars, peace, love, hate.

John Lennon

Imagine all the people
Living life in peace.

John Lennon

Contents

Acknowledgments

It is a pleasure to acknowledge the help I received while researching and writing this book. Jon Wiener supported the project from the beginning, offering encouragement at the right moments and terrific advice throughout. I am much indebted to him, both for helpful comments on chapters and for assistance with research when I visited Los Angeles. Elliot Mintz was also extremely helpful, and I am grateful to him for taking the time to discuss with me his memories of Lennon, his thoughts on Lennon's music, and his friendships with Lennon and Yoko Ono. I also thank Allan Kozinn, who gave much helpful advice on Lennon and The Beatles.

My debts to the late Albert Paolini are great indeed. He provided me with intellectual and emotional support throughout my research; discussed with me in detail Lennon's life and art; raised many important critical issues concerning my interpretation of Lennon; and read various versions of the manuscript. In studying Lennon and Ono's films, especially *Rape* and *Fly,* I drew liberally from his keener analytical mind. That he is not here to see the finished product causes me intense sadness.

Nick Stevenson lived up to his reputation as an outstanding sociologist of culture, and I am grateful for his wise reflections on various aspects of the book. I am also thankful for his help on our trip to Liverpool in December 1995 to conduct research on Lennon and The Beatles. He may have listened to more Beatles music on that trip than he cared to, but our evenings spent at The Philharmonic must surely have served as some sort of compensation. His friendship and loyalty have been vital throughout.

Research assistance was provided by Andrew Newton, with whom it has been my good fortune to work. I would also like to acknowledge the support of the following colleagues, who in a variety of ways contributed, either directly or indirectly, to this book: Tony Giddens, John Thompson, Stephen Frosh, Jeffrey Prager, Charles Spezzano, Simon Prosser, Jane Flax, Jessica Benjamin, Bryan Turner, and Tim Kendall.

The book was written with the assistance of several institutions. I was awarded an Australian Research Fellowship by the Australian Research Council, which provided the financial support for the project. I was also the recipient of an Australian Research Council Research Grant, and this grant proved of vital importance in the final stages of writing. The bulk of the work on the manuscript was undertaken at the Department of Political Science at the University of Melbourne, and I must thank in particular departmental members Michael Crozier, Ann Capling, Mark Considine, and Leslie Holmes, and departmental staff Rita De Amicis, Wendy Ruffles, and Natalie Madaffari. The Department of Psychology at Birkbeck College, University of London—where much of the research and writing on the reunion of The Beatles was undertaken—kindly appointed me Visiting Honorary Fellow in December 1995. I am indebted to Stephen and Judith Frosh for their kind hospitality during my stay in London.

Special thanks are due to William Murphy at the University of California Press, who proved to be a model editor. His critical comments on an earlier draft of the manuscript came just at the right time, and his suggestions on how to bring biography and theory into a more reflective encounter were particularly helpful. I would also like to thank Naomi Schneider, who supported the project throughout; her assistance and guidance have been greatly appreciated. Carlotta Shearson, who copyedited the book, made many stylistic comments that helped transform the text. Many other people at the University of California Press—especially Amber Teagle Thompson and Jeanne Park—and at Melbourne University Press—especially Susan Keogh and Teresa Pitt—have helped, at one stage or another, in the preparation of this book for publication.

An earlier, more theoretically elaborated, version of chapter 5 appeared as "Celebrity and Political Psychology: Remembering Lennon" in *Political Psychology* 19, no. 4 (December 1997).

Then there are family and friends who have offered suggestions, advice, support, and love: Jean Elliott, Keith Elliott, Nick Maxwell,

Alex Maxwell, Gus Geraghty, Grace Geraghty, Davida Geraghty, Naomi Geraghty, and Delwen Geraghty. Deborah Elliott Maxwell deserves particular acknowledgment (or blame), for it was she who introduced me to John Lennon's *Plastic Ono Band,* thus setting me on a largely unconscious search to work out the meanings of an album (and shared experience) that meant so much. It is my hope that she finds in this book a kind of rewind to the mystery and puzzle of an intensely invested, and shared, musical awakening. Thanks also to Carmel Meiklejohn, Cameron Barnett, Grant Parsons, Taren McCallen, Lina Paolini, Judith Linnane, and Ann Houlihan. Special thanks to Kriss McKie, Anthony Moran, Fiore Inglese, and Simone Skacej, to whom I owe so much—for their support, generosity, and kindness over the last few years especially, I thank them.

I am, above all, indebted to Nicola Geraghty for encouraging me to write this book. She has been marvelously insightful in helping me conceptualize the project, commenting illuminatingly on particular chapters. Acknowledgments that thank loved ones for tolerating research and writing commitments can, I know, verge on the nauseating. Yet it is surely imaginable that there is some kind of limit to how often one might want to listen to Lennon's records ("I really have to hear 'Dig a Pony' once more"), watch *The Beatles Anthology,* or read biographies of Lennon. For involving herself in all that, I thank her: eternally, always.

Ja guru deva—om!

Anthony Elliott
Melbourne, 1998

The Mourning of John Lennon

Pain is the pain we go through all the time. You're born in pain. Pain is what we're in most of the time. And I think the bigger the pain, the more gods we need.

John Lennon

I want people to love me. I want to be loved.

John Lennon

The loss of a love object is an excellent opportunity for the ambivalence in love-relationships to make itself effective and come into the open.

Sigmund Freud

Since his tragic death in 1980 at the age of forty, John Lennon has become strangely representative of loss in our culture—an object of mourning, of fantasy, of intense feelings of hope and dread. Lennon is for many a figure of idealization. Inside the myth of the Fab Four, the moptops, Lennon reigns supreme. He is championed as musician, poet, avant-garde artist, political radical, and world peace activist. Outside the myth, Lennon sometimes elicits a more negative response: he is seen as a fraud or phony, a man who claimed to advance peace but was often violent toward himself and others. At once idolized and denigrated, Lennon does not fit into the standard categories by which we make sense of celebrities. More than any other cultural icon, ambivalence pervades our memory of him.

Lennon provokes. He is adored, canonized, deified. It is easy to see why. The Beatles were the most influential group in the history of popular music, the most talented, the most successful, the most worshipped. ("I was in the greatest show on earth, for what it was worth," Lennon wrote sarcastically in his 1973 song "I'm the Greatest"). The songwriting partnership Lennon-McCartney signals genius; theirs was the most important musical coupling of the twentieth century. The Beatles' success overwhelms: from the rise of Beatlemania in Britain to their first American performance, on *The Ed Sullivan Show* in front of an audience of seventy-three million people; from the chart topping experimentation of *Sgt. Pepper's Lonely Hearts Club Band* to the first global satellite broadcast of "All You Need Is Love," which reached an estimated four hundred million people. Everybody knows The Beatles. Everybody knows their music. Everybody feels their influence on our culture. That influence is, it seems, equated with permanence. "When you get to the top," writes poet Philip Larkin, "there is nowhere to go but down, but The Beatles could not get down. There they remain, unreachable, frozen, fabulous."[1]

There is something special, something peculiar even, about Lennon's Beatle fame. What is so remarkable, perhaps, is that the man not only created but also personifies The Beatles. He takes pop music into new realms of the autobiographical and the political with songs such as "Help!," "Strawberry Fields Forever," "I Am the Walrus," and "Revolution." His wit is unique. At the 1963 Royal Variety Show, when introducing "Twist and Shout," he implores, "Will all the people in the cheaper seats clap your hands. All the rest of you, if you'll just rattle your jewellery!" At press conferences, he gently mocks. "The French seem not to have made up their minds about The Beatles. What do you think about them?" asks a BBC reporter in Paris in 1964. "Oh, we like The Beatles," answers Lennon casually. His inexhaustible fascination with language redefines the connections between high and popular culture. Critic Jack Kroll likens Lennon's magisterial "A Day in the Life" to T. S. Eliot's *The Waste Land*.[2] That guardian of high seriousness, the *Times Literary Supplement*, claims Lennon's poetry is "worth the attention of anyone who fears for the impoverishment of the English language."[3]

Lennon's post-Beatles fame equally resonates down the years. As Jann Wenner came to reflect: "If John's songs with The Beatles forever altered the landscape of popular music, his solo work gave voice to the John Lennon the world remembers: the evolutionary utopian who dug for the truth within himself as fiercely as he demanded it of the world."[4] What was remarkable was how Lennon, in a move that brilliantly redefined public relations, used his fame to advance the cause of world peace. Not all his attempts to fuse art and social comment were successful, however. A flirtation with New Left politics led to the rapid deterioration of Lennon's music in the early 1970s, as well as to the commercial and critical disaster *Some Time in New York City.*

Lennon disturbs. He is rebellious, recalcitrant, dangerous. At the height of Beatlemania, he makes the blasphemous comment that his group is more popular than Jesus. A few years later, toward the end of the 1960s, he effectively turns his back on the group that inspired such messianism in favor of his personal and artistic relationship with Yoko Ono. Deconstructing the Fab Four's charming public image, Lennon writes of his addiction to heroin in "Cold Turkey" and records the song with his new group, The Plastic Ono Band. He returns his MBE (Member of Order of the British Empire) medal, proclaiming, "Your Majesty, I am returning this MBE in protest against Britain's involvement in the Nigeria-Biafra thing, against our support of America in Vietnam, and against 'Cold Turkey' slipping down the charts. With Love, John Lennon of Bag."[5] This gesture outraged the political establishment, which was, of course, the whole point. He wanted to shock. For several years, he and Ono lived their lives in terms of a radical political aesthetic: bed-ins and bag-ins for peace, performance art, electronic music, avant-garde films.

There is always ambivalence with John Lennon. Ambiguity defines our relation to Lennon the man, the performer, the songwriter, the artist, the political utopian. He wanted to fracture the barriers between art and entertainment, between culture and politics. "I feel," Lennon told *Rolling Stone,* "I want to be all of them—painter, writer, actor, singer, player, musician."[6] This sentiment is perhaps less a symptom of megalomania than a reflection of his desire to transcend boundaries, artistic and political. It is, in part, because of his strong commitment to these different facets of life that Lennon remains a figure of extraordinary paradoxes and elusive contradictions. Lennon, says biographer Ray Coleman, is "both a butterfly and a bee."[7] "Brilliant, hilarious and inspired," writes biographer Philip Norman, "but also indolent and vague. Rebellious and anarchic, but also self-doubting and cautious. Ruthless, exploitative, sometimes unspeakably callous and vicious, but also considerate, decent and kind."[8] The impact of this ambivalence on our memory of John Lennon is one topic of this book.

WE HAVE BEEN TOLD that John Lennon "is the spirit of a generation."[9] As transcendent hero, Lennon haunts our culture. He is always already there. His image is everywhere. He is known. But what is known about Lennon is largely filtered through the oppressive ideology of celebrity, the dreary constraint of myth. Lennon himself told us that for much of his life he had managed to exist as a fantasy or dream about what he thought he might be. Shortly before his death, he discussed with journalist David Sheff some of the more personal difficulties that encircled him as an ex-Beatle: "I was stuck in the feeling that one did not—was not justified in being alive unless one was fulfilling other people's dreams, whether they were contractual dreams or the public's dreams, or fulfilling my own dreams and illusions about what I thought I was *supposed* to be, which, in retrospect, turned out to not be what I am."[10] The fantasy "John Lennon, Beatle," had left illusory traces that he sought to deconstruct during his time as a househusband in the late 1970s. For Lennon, fantasy functioned not only as psychic constraint but also as an essential ingredient for reflective thought and an examined life.

Lennon lived many lives—as a Beatle, as an ex-Beatle, as a musician, as a writer, as a painter, as a political activist, as a husband, as a lover, and as a father. As a Beatle, he lived an intensely public life. As an ex-Beatle—particularly when he retired from the music business to be with his wife, Yoko Ono, and to raise his son Sean—he lived a very private life. In an interview, Elliot Mintz, one of Lennon's closest friends, discussed with me these different identities, the division between the public and the private Lennon.[11] According to Mintz, Lennon had, over the course of many years, come to grips with the burdens of his worldwide celebrity. He had long felt trapped by his identity as a Beatle and wanted to prevent the marks of fame from harming his self-understanding. Lennon, said Mintz, wanted to reclaim his self for himself. Tellingly, in his semiretirement years, Lennon turned inward, to his inner self and to his beloved wife and child. What he discovered was a free and engaging space for personal pleasure, a new sense of authenticity, another way of being, another way of living. His semiretirement was more than mere respite from the world of entertainment: it was the fashioning of a new balance between the private and the public worlds. "John once commented on the need to outlive our biographers," Mintz explained. What Lennon was trying to do, it seems, was to live life on his own terms, to be someone other than who he imagined himself to be, to be someone other than who the public imagined him to be. To outlive his biographers was, in effect, to push the limits of conventional thinking.

Lennon offers no consistent image or vision of life, despite the efforts of his biographers to impose consistency—a problem which I will address in chapter 1. Lennon confronts us, as Mintz has helped me see, with the always provisional, precarious tensions between public and private life, between identity and its presentation, between celebrity and ordinary life. To deconstruct his public facade was not enough for Lennon. He wanted, indeed needed, more. He hungered for self-understanding, for something real. His search for authenticity was relentless, driven by his desire to come to terms with the loneliness and pain that had marked his life from the earliest years. Paul McCartney reflected on Lennon's emotionally insecure childhood thus: "He was very focused, very witty, very sensitive, and one of my theories is that he was that way because he'd come from the school of hard knocks. If you look at his life . . . his dad leaving him when he was two, his mum getting killed by a car driven by an off-duty policeman who didn't get brought to book . . . he went through some terrible things."[12] Lennon carried the emotional wounds of lost love, coupled with a deep sense of lovelessness, from his childhood through celebrity and beyond. His is a heroic story, if only because of the unfailing honesty and emotional courage with which he responded to these personal difficulties, and there were many.

The interplay between loss and mourning is a key to understanding Lennon. The intimate psychological connections between loss, mourning, and artistic creativity hold a central place in psychoanalytic theory. According to Freud, loss and grief trigger the work of imagination and support it as much as they threaten and disfigure it. Creative work is integral to the process, often unconscious, of mourning lost love. Without mourning there can be no self-development, understanding, or change. Without mourning we are psychically ill-equipped for creative living. Without mourning we are hampered in preparing for our own loss, as it were, in death. Lennon was ahead of his time in his artistic response to, and creative elaboration of, mourning. He not only took the imprint of lost love into himself and created brilliant and spectacular art but also created a powerful form of aesthetic self-commentary on mourning as a whole. It is one of the rich ironies of Lennon's life that he experienced so much loss and mourning and then came to represent mourning, came to symbolize the struggle to mourn, at the level of our general culture.

Anguish, pain, and lost love permeate much of Lennon's oeuvre. He wrote about the pain of loss, as well as about the emotional problems of dealing with loss. In songs like "I'm a Loser," "Help!," "Nowhere Man," "Isolation," and "I'm Losing You," Lennon created an aesthetic vocabulary of loss, pain, and loneliness that is private and popularist in equal measure. To the extent that I have concentrated upon the impact of loss upon Lennon's world, I have engaged in the kind of dialogue with my subject that underscores the primacy of emotion, affect, and desire. Whatever the limitations of my perspective, such a focus must surely hold a central place in any interpretation of Lennon's life; his artistic work places emotion center stage within the broader context of a reinvention of human existence. My purpose, however, is not to suggest that Lennon's life and art can be understood simply in terms of loss; all artistic creativity, after Freud, is at root a culturally sophisticated form of grief.[13] Rather, I have tried to suggest that Lennon's most creative work represents a kind of container for the shadow of despair which affected the very core of his emotional life. *The Mourning of John Lennon* seeks to convey the ex-Beatle's personal complexity and artistic irreducibility in such a way as to reveal the importance of the human experience of loss for an understanding of our general culture.

Lennon confronts us with the split in our culture between personal and public worlds, with the inherent social contradictions of art, and with the difficult cultural problem of representation itself. From the linguistic instability of "Strawberry Fields Forever" to the emotive directness of "Woman," from the celebratory emotion of "All You Need Is Love" to the primal screaming of "Mother," Lennon experiments with words and phrases to reveal complex, multiple forms of meaning. He presses language against itself to uncover the cultural repressed. In this typically modernist search to discover how identity excludes otherness, Lennon is matched in contemporary music perhaps only by Bob Dylan, who also uncouples style and form but in a manner that often produces complete dislocation. Both share a desire to discover the strange at the very heart of the familiar. Both strongly distrust the idea that language can represent the world as it is, as well as the conventional distinctions between norm and pathology. (Lennon wrote a superb parody of Dylan's linguistic excesses, entitled "Stuck inside of Lexicon with the Roget's Thesaurus Blues Again.")[14] Yet if Dylan destabilizes meaning by taking narrative to the breaking point, Lennon assaults the aesthetic dimension of music itself. Lennon uncovers key differences between the commercial and aesthetic dimensions of music, showing how the former often rests upon a degraded sense of the latter. What he presents us with is music reconciled to its own contradictions, ambivalences, and ambiguities.

For Lennon, music lies at the intersection of the private and public realms. Beyond entertainment, music is that which trades on desire and fear. It is from such a conception of the sociological value of music that Lennon uses the medium in an attempt to arrest and restructure the political imagination. Lennon's music addresses the nature of personal freedom ("Across the Universe"), psychic pain ("Yer Blues"), sexual inequality ("Woman Is the Nigger of the World"), political resistance ("Power to the People"), the links between love and daily life ("Whatever Gets You thru the Night"), political change ("Revolution"), sexual repression ("You've Got to Hide Your Love Away"), and the possibility of alternative futures ("Imagine").

THIS BOOK IS not another biography of Lennon. Instead, I use a range of biographical studies that propose to reveal the real John Lennon in order to reconsider the relationship between his life and his art. Above all, I seek to unravel the cultural and ideological meanings invested in, and provoked by, Lennon. In doing so, my aim is to uncover some of the implications Lennon's assault on the ideology of celebrity carries for our personal and political lives. It might be said, then, that this book aims to be metabiography, to dip into our collective imaginings of Lennon and sift through them for what they can tell us about contemporary society, to loop biography and culture around politics in its broadest sense. It is precisely from such an interweaving of the personal and the political that I seek to contribute something new to our understanding of Lennon. I draw on a rich and diverse literature in social theory and cultural studies, biography and biographical theory,

psychoanalysis and studies of celebrity. Although my central focus is
Lennon, my aim is also to consider the relationship between celebrity
and contemporary culture more generally. This is not to say that cultural theory can simply be applied to Lennon in order to reveal
broader social dynamics. Although theoretical reflection can illumi-
nate issues of biography, selfhood, culture, and politics (and their in-
terrelations), the central figure of this story profoundly problematizes
the uses of theory. In this book, therefore, I explore the way that
Lennon's life enables us to comprehend how celebrity affects our personal and political lives, as well as the way that Lennon's life raises
questions about the adequacy of contemporary social thought.

Two major traditions of thought inform this study: contemporary
critical theory and psychoanalytic theory. While these theoretical traditions overlap in complex and shifting ways throughout the book (and,
thus, any reader in search of an integrated, slick theory will be disap-
pointed), I want to comment briefly on this conceptual interlock. I
have tried to bring to bear on Lennon the language of critical social
theory, with its emphasis on the intertwining of identity, power, and social relations. My aim is to place Lennon at the intersection of the personal and the social, to develop ways of connecting lived experience
with a theory of culture. My attempt to rescue the complexity of
Lennon is strongly driven by critical-cultural issues. Chapters 4, 5, and
6 highlight the importance of these issues by examining the challenge
that his blending of art and politics presents to society; by reflecting
upon the cultural need to mourn, as well as to deny grief, after his
death; and finally by considering the "reunion" of The Beatles in the
1990s, in which John Lennon magically returned from the dead for the
recording of "Free as a Bird" and "Real Love." Throughout, I question
the cultural forms in and through which contemporary society creates,
invests, and remembers its most important celebrities.

Freud currently occupies a central place in biographical theory and
practice, and it is my view that developments in psychoanalytic theory
are of paramount importance for the analysis of identity and social relations alike.[15] Psychoanalytic theory complicates conventional thinking about narratives of the self, biographical self-continuity, and the
symbolic thread of life, and thus it is a powerful tool for rethinking the
relations between celebrity and contemporary culture. Psychoanalysis
forces us to confront dislocation and fracturing when thinking about
the rich, imaginary textures of human experience. Especially relevant

to my concerns here are the interconnections between fantasy and culture—in particular, the ways in which celebrities are imagined and, thereby, symbolically "used" by people in their everyday lives. Chapters 2 and 3 deploy psychoanalysis by reading Lennon's life and music in terms of his deeper emotional conflicts and looking at the way his music connects to our wider cultural and political world.

It is instructive in this context to recall that, for Freud, the practice of biography is itself shaped by an unconscious wish for certainty and order. The biographer has a desire to get things straight, a desire that if not taken into account can undermine intellectual imagination and knowledge. "Anyone who writes a biography," writes Freud, "is committed to lies, concealments, hypocrisy, flattery and even to hiding his own lack of understanding, for biographical truth does not exist, and if it did we could not use it."[16] While some ultimate biographical truth about Lennon may not exist, what can be reclaimed is the emotional investment at work in each interpretation, an appreciation of the importance of fantasy in shaping cultural fictions and myths. I seek to use psychoanalytic theory in a manner that illuminates contemporary cultural forms and mass culture. In particular, I examine the ways that celebrity provokes, inflects, displaces, and confuses individual and collective fantasies.

Lennon's life and art are, of course, well-charted terrain already, and it is partly for this reason that my account of the ex-Beatle ranges freely across various aspects of his life—personal, artistic, political—without much regard for chronology. Although I consider many of Lennon's finest Beatles compositions and his contribution to the band, my predominant interest lies in his post-Beatles years: his solo music; the tensions and reconciliations of his marriage to Yoko Ono; the identity crisis he underwent, and worked through, in the 1970s; his time as a househusband and father; his musical comeback; and his death and its cultural consequences. I have chosen to focus on this period of Lennon's life not only because it represents the period in which he most successfully linked his personal and political concerns but also because it has rarely received the sort of serious attention it deserves. His withdrawal from public life in the late 1970s notwithstanding, my contention is that during his post-Beatles years Lennon devised more, not fewer, constructive solutions to psychic conflict through his music, essays, poetry, and painting, as well as through his intimate and familial relationships. I look afresh at the personal crisis

of Lennon's "lost weekend"; consider the broader cultural implications of his desire to withdraw from celebrity and its lifestyle; and examine his artistic endeavors during his seclusion. In doing so, I seek to
challenge dominant conceptions of how we have come to see Lennon
in wider cultural terms.

Because I focus attention upon Lennon's post-Beatles years, there
are consequently some omissions in this book which I should perhaps
explain. First, I rarely analyze his relationships with Paul McCartney,
George Harrison, and Ringo Starr. There are, it is true, many works
that chart the rise of The Beatles; although a volume that did so pre-
dominantly from Lennon's vantage point would be welcome indeed.
Engaging with the early Beatles years of, say, Liverpool or Hamburg
would have resulted in another book on the Fab Four and would have
been a diversion from the kind of research embodied in this book
about Lennon and contemporary culture. The second omission, perhaps more irritating for those who know Lennon's biographical details
well, is that, in the interests of matching my biographical and theoretical concerns, certain of Lennon's friends and colleagues have not
received the full attention they deserve. My analysis of Lennon's intimate relationships in chapter 3, for example, concentrates primarily
on Cynthia Powell, Yoko Ono, and May Pang. Although I originally
conceived of the chapter as a kind of doubled enquiry which would
also trace Lennon's friendships with Pete Shotton, Stuart Sutcliffe,
and Elliot Mintz, space limitations prevented this approach—it is
something which might be taken up in some future study.

There is an autobiographical dimension to this book. Lennon, as
cultural icon, was an intimate companion throughout my childhood.
The Beatles became a global phenomenon in the year that I was born,
and so it was not until some years later that I discovered the musical
pleasures of "Twist and Shout," "A Hard Day's Night," "Lucy in the Sky
with Diamonds," and "I'm So Tired." When I eventually discovered
The Beatles' music, it functioned as a kind of "transitional space," permitting me to explore my feelings and allowing me to imagine a kind
of self-transcendence through an identification with the celebrity of
Lennon. It seemed to me, or at least this is how I have come to think
of it, that Lennon offered an image of utopian possibility, of life lived
as self-determined and other-directed in equal measure. Perhaps I

simply sensed that Lennon spoke his mind freely with little regard for social convention. Or, perhaps my fascination arose from something more emotive: there is, for me, something haunting about his singing. "He has a voice," said The Beatles' producer, George Martin, "which sends shivers down the spine."[17]

However, my identification with Lennon was assaulted—and irrevocably so—when he was shot dead in December 1980. I vividly recall watching television when the news broke that he had been murdered. Shock, confusion, and horror gripped me. My mother and grandmother, who were with me at the time, expressed their concern for me. Their concern, their recognition that something important to me was now lost, surprised me. My driving impulse, I remember, was to be alone. I went to my bedroom, turned on the radio (all stations, it seemed, were playing Lennon), and, eventually, cried. I wept for some time, although I was not sure for exactly whom I was crying.

I have drawn on my own experience of Lennon—reactions provoked in me by his life and music—throughout this book. No doubt such reflectiveness has something to recommend it in these postmodern times. But my self-reflectiveness here—the manner in which I call up certain memories, fantasies, images, and dreams—runs deeper than the current postmodern fascination with private ambiguity and ambivalence. Rather, I attempt to incorporate an emotional awareness generated by these memories into my critical reading of Lennon. Nowhere is this attempt more obvious, perhaps, than in my deployment of the concept of mourning. In grieving over Lennon's death, I recognized the cultural importance of loss. Through my grief, I came to wonder about how loss connects to the broader dynamics of culture. For whom, exactly, is the mourner mourning? Are we mourning some aspect of ourselves? How might mourning of the self relate to cultural mourning? How does contemporary culture mourn? How does the cultural field seek to evade the pain of mourning?

The interplay between loss and mourning is a central dynamic in Lennon's own life. In researching the ways in which Lennon's death is at once recognized and displaced in our general culture, I became increasingly aware of the importance of loss in the life of Lennon. Of course, there might be some element of theoretical projection here: study the dynamics of a particular phenomenon for long enough and you are bound to find it almost everywhere you look. I do not mean to say that Lennon in any sense mastered loss. On the contrary, one of the reasons Lennon remains a figure of such fascination is that, while loss pervaded his life, he never sought to make it entirely his own. Profoundly aware of the emotional trials and tribulations that loss generates, Lennon's art uncovers the otherness of mourning, sadness, absence. In a 1961 poem, Lennon wrote,

I can't remember anything
without a sadness
So deep that it hardly
becomes known to me.[18]

1

Mind Games

Identity Trouble

As for show biz, it was never my life.
John Lennon

Shattered beings are best represented by bits and pieces.
Rainer Maria Rilke

The Beatles spent 1964 colonizing the world under the sign of Beatle-mania. Having seized Britain in 1963, they expanded their 1964 touring schedule to include Denmark, Holland, Sweden, Hong Kong, Australia, and New Zealand. But by far the most important country they visited that year was the United States. By late 1963, within weeks of its American release, The Beatles had sold more than two million copies of their new single, "I Want To Hold Your Hand"—a feat which took the record straight to number one and gave them an unprecedented six singles in the American top 100.[1] *Introducing the Beatles*, the band's first album released in the United States, was also rapidly climbing the charts. In fact, all things Beatle began flooding the marketplace: buttons, mugs, wigs, T-shirts, notebooks, and dolls. To ensure the success of their American trip, Capitol Records initiated a seventy-thousand-dollar publicity campaign; Americans everywhere read signs and stickers that said "The Beatles Are Coming!"

On the eve of their departure from Britain, John Lennon was asked if The Beatles were taking the same act to the United States that they performed throughout Europe. "No," he said, speaking in the 1988 film *Imagine*, "we haven't really got an 'act.' So, we'll just do what we do." Lennon's retort inevitably spawned incredulity in media circles.

After all, The Beatles were the hottest band in Britain, and they were about to take the United States by storm. More than that, the Fab Four were transforming themselves from a musical smash into a cultural phenomenon. Against this backdrop, Lennon's comment is interesting precisely because it reveals his tendency to mock the world of show business. He is less concerned, one might argue, with observing the protocols of celebrity than with undermining them. His comment drives at something else as well: it reflects his concerns about authenticity and substance, and his questioning of the limits of entertainment.

Lennon was in equal measure attracted and repelled by the cult of celebrity. He dreamed of "making the big time." He hungered for its rewards: wealth, fame, success. "When The Beatles were depressed," he said in *Imagine*, "thinking the group was going nowhere and this is a shitty deal and we're in a shitty dressing room, I'd say, 'Where are we going, fellas?' And they'd go, 'To the top, Johnny.' And I'd say, 'Where's that, fellas?' And they'd say, 'To the toppermost of the poppermost.'" Their years of musical apprenticeship in Liverpool and Hamburg had pushed Lennon's dream to the limit. Now that they had gone through the dream, success was their reality—and on a scale unheard-of for a pop group. Lennon knew the value of his fame; he celebrated and enjoyed it. "I dug," said Lennon, "the fame, the power, the money and playing to big crowds. Conquering America was the best thing."[2]

But, for Lennon, the thrills of Beatlemania soon turned to boredom, engendering a sense of suffocation and dread—especially during the group's world tours of 1965 and 1966. He came to see celebrity more in terms of its burdens than its rewards. For the most part, the routine of touring consisted of riotous airport greetings, media interviews, ecstatic crowds outside The Beatles' hotels, and performances at which the screams of hysterical fans drowned out the music. It was a lifestyle in which "there was no switching off," he said. "The elevator man wanted a little piece of you on your way back to the hotel room, the maid wanted a little piece of you back at the hotel—I don't mean sexually, I mean a piece of your time and your energy."[3] No matter how much energy Lennon put into performing, it was never enough; somebody always wanted something more. "The bigger we got, the more unreality we had to face," he said of Beatlemania.[4] In time, he came to regard the cult of celebrity as debasing, in part because its cultural forms seemed at once socially spellbinding and politically gratuitous.

Lennon's response to this dilemma was to deconstruct the entire opposition between art and entertainment. He did this, in his early years as a Beatle, by distancing himself from the group's commercial, respectable image. Dressed in the suits that conservative manager Brian Epstein insisted upon, the moptops sang "whoa yeah!" to the delight of young people everywhere, notching up hits such as "Please Please Me," "From Me to You," and "She Loves You." But Lennon sought to debunk and, in time, subvert the whole moptop image. "I used to try and get George to rebel with me," he said. "I'd say to him, 'Look, we don't need these fuckin' suits. Let's chuck them out of the window.' My little rebellion was to have my tie loose with the top button of my shirt undone."[5] Though his little rebellion was hardly a giant step toward overthrowing the image of stardom which dominated pop at the time, he made a good deal about it in later years, seeing it as suggestive of his dissatisfaction with showbiz.

The most significant challenge Lennon made to the entertainment industry was, however, in his songwriting. Bored with the romantic formula of boy meets girl and falls in love, he began experimenting with a more autobiographical prose—the beginnings of which can be detected in "If I Fell" and "I'm a Loser." These songs mark the emergence of Lennon's more introspective, confessional mode of songwriting, in which lyrics are no longer thought of as a decorative supplement to the music but rather as a concrete content in some more formal sense. A privileged place is still accorded to romantic love, but unlike the cute refrains of "From Me to You" or "She Loves You," Lennon's reflections on desire and loss pertain to questions of identity and culture in general. Indeed, Lennon developed this mode of composition brilliantly in such intensely reflective Beatles songs as "In My Life," "Help!," and "I'm So Tired" and during his solo years in "Mother" and "I'm Losing You." Lennon's originality here is in his mesmerizing exploration of the dynamics of emotional life through the medium of popular culture.

The more successful Lennon became, the more he worked against the oppositions which pervade the realm of celebrity—private and public, individual and history, self and image—in his music, painting, performances, and political commitments. Indeed, Lennon's mature work, Wulf Herzogenrath argues, "addresses the media reception of fame itself."[6] This is particularly evident in his last Beatles single, "The Ballad of John and Yoko," which documents the trials and tribulations that celebrity imposes on his relationship with Yoko Ono, their decision to get married, and the bed-in for peace which they staged during their honeymoon in Amsterdam. The song is a biting critique of the media's double standards, as well as of their flagrant disregard for the psychological well-being of their victims. He underscores the media's hounding of him and his new wife in the strongest possible terms: "Christ you know it ain't easy, you know how hard it can be / The way things are going, they're gonna crucify me." At the same time, however, he ironically mocks the press's representation of itself—the ways in which it erases distinctions between real life on the one hand and mere appearance on the other. Lennon makes no secret of his distaste for the viciousness of the media attacks upon him and Ono; and in this song he seeks to capture the way the media ignore, or pass over in silence, their dependence on the very celebrities they chastise, castigate, and demolish.

Caught the early plane back to London
Fifty acorns tied in a sack
The men from the press said, "we wish you success"
"It's good to have the both of you back."

In all of this we find Lennon at once underscoring and mocking how the media create, invest, and reproduce fame.

"I cannot live up to other people's expectations of me because they're illusionary," Lennon commented in his last *Rolling Stone* interview, in 1980. He wanted, he said, to distance himself not only from the public's imaginings about his fame but also from his own conceptions. "The hardest thing," he continued, "is facing yourself. It's easier to shout 'Revolution' and 'Power to the people' than it is to look at yourself and try to find out what's real inside you and what isn't."[7] In a culture accustomed to the illusions of celebrity, it is perhaps not surprising that Lennon's effort to distance himself from his own image should be associated with fear—a fear that is, above all, a fear of the unknown. Lennon is, for many people, strongly associated with this fear, not only because he challenges the private/public split in our sexual and cultural worlds but also because his contradictions (personal, artistic, political) are often too scandalous for contemporary culture to contemplate. This has been especially true of biographies of Lennon, in which narrative and emotion come together either as idealization or denigration. Yet the gap between praise and put down turns out, in a familiar irony, to be less than imagined: the ideal serves to protect against the abject, just as vilification is one way to give the slip to that sorrow which unmet expectations generate. It is precisely these interacting tropes of idealization and denigration that figure prominently in biographical plottings of Lennon's life.

How have we come to understand John Lennon in contemporary culture? How have we remembered, responded to, and talked about Lennon's identity and celebrity? In answering these questions, I am concerned primarily with tracing what Lennon's biographers have looked for in studying his life, and this tracing will necessarily involve reflecting on the worst that has been done biographically to Lennon. Albert Goldman's *The Lives of John Lennon* deserves particular consideration. Published in 1988, the book became a bestseller largely on the basis of its claim to reveal the shocking truths about Lennon's private life, particularly his sexual life. Widely dismissed by many—Paul McCartney described it as trash—it reveals powerfully, if somewhat grotesquely, the fears and fantasies with which Lennon has been invested. Ray Coleman's two-volume biography, *John Lennon,* functions in many ways as culturally inverse to Goldman's symbolic attack, idealizing its subject in the act of defining the "real" John Lennon. Coleman and Goldman are thus mirror opposites—there are many structural similarities in their work. Each seeks a high degree of certitude in his biographical portrait of Lennon; and each, in his own way, generates a willed manipulation of Lennon as cultural icon.

ALBERT GOLDMAN'S *The Lives of John Lennon* begins in the late 1970s: Lennon's "lost years" of semiretirement, of personal introspection, of living as a househusband and raising his son Sean. The book wastes no time, however, in informing the reader of Lennon's severe psychic turmoil, described as a blending of anxiety, depression, and obsessional neurosis.

John Lennon comes to consciousness before dawn in a pool of light cast by two spots above the polished dark wood of his church-pew headboard. These lights are never extinguished because John has a horror of waking in a dark bedroom. Darkness to him is death. The first thing he looks for with his feeble eyes are the fuzzy red reflections in the big oval mirror above his bed. These smudges assure him that his life-support system is working, for night and day he lives buffered by its soothing sounds and flickering images, like a patient in a quiet room. . . .

Lennon has confined himself to this room for the past three years. Save for summer holidays in Japan, he rarely leaves his queen-size bed, to which he clings like a sailor aboard a raft. Much of the time he sleeps, perhaps half the day, in two- to four-hour spells. The balance of the day he spends sitting in the lotus position, his head enveloped in a cloud of tobacco or marijuana smoke, reading, meditating, or listening to tapes. . . .

Though he is lying in the bosom of his family, John could not be much more removed even if he spent his life out on the road. The only times he sees them are for an hour or two in the morning and during supper and a little thereafter, when Daddy, as he likes to call himself, watches TV with his little boy, Sean. All the rest of the day Lennon is back here in his room, alone and silent.[8]

In the book's introduction, Goldman develops a disturbing portrait of complete psychopathology. Not only does Goldman confine the ex-Beatle to his bedroom for three years (sleeping the day away, unable to face the wider world), but he recasts Lennon as delusional through and through.

According to Goldman, an obsessional neurosis lies at the heart of Lennon's inner world. Lennon is obsessed, Goldman argues, with cleanliness. He refuses physical contact with others (his wife and son included) and takes up to a dozen baths a day.[9] The reclusive celebrity obsessed with cleanliness is, of course, a stereotype, and Goldman pushes this theme to the nth degree. Lennon is cast as a victim, leaving his bedroom only to confront "his surgically clean bathroom" with its "big old-fashioned tub only he is permitted to scrub."[10] Note how this reference to the surgically clean is located firmly in relation to Lennon. It is Lennon himself, not his staff, who maintains the desired standard of cleanliness. Goldman links such obsessiveness with a desire for self-mastery or narcissistic perfection. The focus of this self-control concerns his body, which is malnourished. The ex-Beatle is anorexic: he would love to "pig out on junk food," but with grim determination he "starve[s] himself to perfection," wishing to "recover the body image he presented at nineteen." With Lennon shielded from the world and wasting away (mentally and physically), the stage is now set for Goldman's introductory verdict: "John Lennon no longer resembles himself."[11]

But if Goldman's Lennon is a man deeply at odds with himself, this
is largely because Goldman's portrait is a kind of caricature. That is,
Goldman takes up the staple diet of pop music biographies—the triad
of sex, drugs, and rock 'n' roll—and turns it upon Lennon with a
vengeance. Goldman rehashes stories, for instance, about The Beatles' frenzied wanderings through various countries while on tour,
mixing the familiar cocktail of booze and pills, wild sex orgies, and lack
of sleep. But these stories are less shocking revelation than a rehash of
Lennon's own disclosures about life on the road as a Beatle. According to Lennon,

The Beatles tours were like the Fellini film *Satyricon.* We had that image.
Man, our tours were something else, if you could get on our tours you were
in. They were Satyricon, all right. Wherever we went, there was always a
whole scene going, we had our four separate bedrooms. We tried to keep
them out of our rooms. [The other] rooms were always full of junk and
whores and who-the-fuck-knows-what, and policeman with it. . . . They did-
n't call them groupies then, they called it something else and if we couldn't
get groupies, we would have whores and everything, whatever was going.[12]

Lennon himself has provided the raw material for Goldman's framing
of "the shocking truth." However, Goldman's book promises scandalous revelations about Lennon, and to deliver Goldman must shift
the theme of sex up a gear into full-blown erotic violence. In Goldman's diagnosis, Lennon is always on the lookout for scapegoats in
order to displace his inner destructiveness; he attacks those he loves
as much as he attacks outsiders. Goldman documents a history of
youthful rage. He argues that, in Hamburg, Lennon mugged and
killed an English sailor simply to get some money. Likewise, he alleges that Lennon beat up his best friend, Stuart Sutcliffe (the first
bass player of The Beatles). Lennon, writes Goldman, knocked Sutcliffe to the ground in a violent outburst, repeatedly kicking him in
the head while "wearing cowboy boots with hard, pointy toes."[13] Sutcliffe subsequently died of a brain tumor, and Lennon, writes Goldman, lived thenceforth with the guilt of murder on his mind.

If murderous rage defines the broader contours of pathology, this is
no less than a primordial violence that threatens to undercut all that
Lennon says and does. Goldman's book begins with specific scenarios
of destructiveness (culminating in murder) and attributes to Lennon
a chronic violence that penetrates to the core of his psyche. What

Goldman's attribution of chronic violence means, in effect, is that Lennon is forever at war with himself. Nowhere is this more obvious, in Goldman's view, than in the sham of his marriage to Yoko Ono. Goldman writes, almost compulsively, of "the myth of John and Yoko." Ono, says Goldman, was certainly at Lennon's side most of the time. But he finds their inseparability a sign less of love or commitment than of the codependence of two vain, narcissistic celebrities who are fascinated only with their public image. Their intense absorption in each other was one great public relations scam fabricated for the media. "When the camera was switched off or the tape recorder stopped rolling," writes Goldman, "the stars sank back into their normal selves and exhibited a marked indifference to each other."[14] Why? Tellingly, Goldman is silent on this score; nowhere does he discuss what Lennon's motive might have been in living such a lie. Instead, he concentrates on linking Lennon's troubled celebrity to deeper problems of psychological insecurity or disturbance. Drugs are fundamental in this respect; heroin, cocaine, hashish, LSD, marijuana, and Biphetamine pills are consumed by Lennon and Ono throughout the book. But, again, Goldman appears less concerned with Lennon's stated reasons for turning to drugs, or indeed with examining the effect of drugs upon Lennon's inner world, than with hitting home the point that the ex-Beatle was addicted to such substances because he could not face the painful realities of his life.[15]

The Lives of John Lennon generated a great deal of media controversy at the time of its publication and in particular raised important issues about the ethical limits of investigative biography. Though the book clearly fell short in revealing anything of substance, Goldman's reviewers carefully documented the many factual errors in his account of Lennon's life. Several reviews called into question Goldman's key sources.[16] Luc Sante, in the *New York Review of Books,* described Goldman's book as "pathography." *Rolling Stone* ran a detailed rebuttal to Goldman. And *Newsweek* ran an issue dealing with the stakes of cultural rememberings of Lennon, indicting Goldman for his savage attack.[17] In addition, many celebrities felt it necessary to comment on Goldman's work. The surviving Beatles, Elton John, Mick Jagger, and Cilla Black all urged fans to boycott the book. That their dismissive comments were subsequently deployed by Bantam Books to publicize the paperback edition of the book is in itself a useful index of postmodern culture: the negative terms used to describe Goldman's book—"rubbish" and "trash"—actually became part of the symbolic economy which they were meant to discredit.

These efforts to protect the memory of Lennon were repeated elsewhere. There were, for example, various academic bids to assess the critical strength of popular biography in general and the symbolic damage that Goldman had done to Lennon in particular. Jon Wiener, a professor of history and the author of a political biography of Lennon, *Come Together*, put forward the following argument:

> According to Goldman, Lennon in 1979 was a rock 'n' roll Howard Hughes— he suffered from malnutrition, seldom got out of bed, took a dozen baths a day, and avoided touching anyone including his 4-year-old son Sean. The problem with this picture is that Howard Hughes didn't do what Lennon did: get up one morning, record a number-one album (*Double Fantasy*), and talk about his life in a series of interviews that were often brilliant and moving.[18]

Wiener underscores Lennon's personal and artistic achievements to discredit the disturbing narrative which Goldman writes. Indeed, the interviews to which Wiener refers, in which Lennon's sardonic humor is as captivating as ever, provide a useful foil for debunking the embarrassingly infantile fantasizing of Goldman.

One might, in fact, argue that these interviews can be read as an advance rebuttal of Goldman, as if Lennon anticipated the worst of what our culture might do to him. Consider, for example, Lennon's comments made to *Playboy* in late 1980:

> Nobody controls me. I'm uncontrollable. The only one who controls me is me and that's just barely possible. . . . Listen, if somebody's gonna impress me, whether it be a Maharishi or a Yoko Ono, there comes a point when the emperor has no clothes. There comes a point where I will *see*. So for all you folks out there who think that I'm having the wool pulled over my eyes— well, that's an insult to me. Not that you think less of Yoko, because that's your problem; what I think of her is what counts! But if you think you know me or you have some part of me because of the music I've made, and then you think I'm being controlled like a dog on a leash because I do things with her, then screw you. Because—fuck you brother and sister, you don't know what's happening. I'm not here for you. I'm here for me and here for the baby![19]

Shifting the focus from others to himself ("the only one who controls me is me"), Lennon argues that self-control is a contradiction in terms (something that is "just barely possible"). In an ironic twist, the control of the self actually weakens that which it is meant to strengthen, the ego, because the latter becomes intimately bound up with restriction, constraint, closure. Against such images of self-constraint, Lennon says that far from finding family life crippling he finds it enriching. What is perhaps most remarkable is that he constructs what is life-enhancing in direct opposition to that which culture idealizes, namely, celebrity and stardom ("I'm not here for you. I'm here for me").

Returning to Goldman, I would argue that *The Lives of John Lennon* is an important document insofar as it is primarily about its author, Goldman (as representative of the worst excesses of popular biography), rather than about its object of analysis, Lennon. Reconsidering the book from this perspective should shed light on the extraordinary power of celebrity in contemporary culture and, in particular, on the challenges that John Lennon presents to ideologies of fame and stardom. For Goldman's diagnosis of Lennon has, in my view, everything to do with maintaining the illusions of stardom.

Time and again, sexuality is Goldman's central reference point. *The Lives of John Lennon* claims to uncover the secrets of Lennon's sexual life, to provide an in-depth biographical plotting of his erotic pleasures and amorous delights. But Goldman's book speaks less of the erotic or emotional than of misconduct and mischief. It is less a question of psychological subtleties than a question of moral transgression. Goldman informs the reader about, for instance, the "girlie mags" that Lennon kept in a box beside his bed. Goldman's point, it seems, is that there is a secretive dimension to Lennon's sexuality; indeed, Goldman constructs sexuality as a metaphor for perversion and guilt throughout the book.

According to Goldman, Lennon either evaded or displaced his deepest sexual longings in order to avoid the terrible truths and unacceptable actions of his past. Lennon remained radically cut off from his self, in a splitting from which the "forbidden" was projected onto something outside and other. That otherness takes a variety of forms throughout the book, but Goldman fixes it time and again to homosexuality. Lennon, he writes, enjoyed a homosexual affair with The Beatles' manager, Brian Epstein, and also experienced homoerotic desires for his close friend Stuart Sutcliffe. If it is hard to see Lennon's evasion of feeling or impulse here, it is perhaps easier after Goldman introduces the theme of guilt. For according to Goldman, Lennon could not accept his homosexual desires; he evaded them by acting out some sort of hyperheterosexuality.[20] He was compulsively driven to engage in episodic sexual encounters (read conquests), the effects of which were self-loathing and misogyny. Such sexual conquests, because of the tightening grip of sexual repression, were typically aggressive in nature, permitting Lennon to avoid any close emotional contact with women.[21]

Goldman thus constructs Lennon's sexuality as a kind of return of the repressed: the denial of homosexual desire, its displacement onto women as substitute objects, and the escalation of guilt and consequent denigration of self. Repression is understood here not in the Freudian sense of a mysterious past which haunts psychic life but rather in terms of certitude. As a result, any sense of mystery in Lennon's life is eradicated. Working from the unproven premise that Lennon could not accept his homosexual passions or fantasies, Goldman proceeds to read his subject's loves and losses in the light of this. In fact, Goldman sees denial as fueling all of Lennon's worldly ambitions—especially his desire for fame. For while Lennon might have registered his own suspicion of the media and the cult of celebrity, his public image was nonetheless carefully constructed for general consumption. Lennon, in Goldman's reckoning, brilliantly orchestrated the media to invest him with complete power and omnipotence: he presented himself as the leader of The Beatles, as an artist working at the cutting edge, as a spokesperson for political and social causes, and the like. But what the media obscured here, says Goldman, is the paranoia and destructiveness, driven by repressed desire, of Lennon himself. Both Lennon and the celebrity industry had a vested interest in maintaining this illusion, even though it meant that Lennon repressed his sexual desires and maintained a violent and, at times, hateful relationship to himself and others.

Goldman makes a further transposition to Lennon's sexual identity which is worth considering, principally because it highlights the symbolic violence done in the search for biographical certitude. Goldman holds that Lennon's sexuality was not only radically cutoff from reflective self-knowledge but also given expression in and through the acting out of various erotic perversions. The key term here is "forbidden sex." Goldman alleges that Lennon loved to transgress sexual boundaries and that he regularly engaged in anxiously controlling forms of sex. Again, the semiretirement years figure strongly here, if only because it seems logical to suppose that Lennon must have gone beyond the reaches of his family life to feed these perverse sexual appetites. Here is Goldman on a stopover trip that Lennon made to Bangkok in 1976:

When John walked out of the world-famous Oriental Hotel on the banks of the Chao Phraya River, he would have been accosted by steerers, who would have presented him with their comically garbled cards, reading, "You haven't had your job blown until one of our girls does it."

Stepping into the first parlour that caught his fancy, he would have found a room stacked on the one side with bleachers on which were lined up the girls, each one holding in her hands a placard with a big number. When he had picked the best numbers, the girls would check out the job with the mama-san and then lead him to a private room. Here they would disrobe, revealing themselves as tiny, undeveloped creatures with small breasts and virtually no pubic hair, very shy, very softly spoken, talking almost in whispers, and utterly compliant. Having sex with these girls is the closest thing in the world to legally sanctioned child abuse, which is why Thai whores are the favourites of jaded men.

John's girls would be reluctant to do anything kinky but would be eager to whack him off, blow him, or have intercourse. The cost of the toss was about the price of a movie ticket. John might have also indulged himself with a Thai boy, who enjoys precisely the same reputation among sophisticated homosexuals as do the girls with straight men.[22]

Note how this passage generates its own pornographic unfolding: "John would have been," "he would have found," "John might have also indulged." It is as if the speculative nature of Goldman's prose is somehow informed by the promissory dimension of pornography: anything you want, everything is permissible. Note also the racial stereotypes in which Goldman trades when thinking forbidden sex: in relation to white superior men, the Thai girls are "utterly compliant," "talking almost in whispers." Devoid of subjectivity, these girls function as sexual objects to the extent that they permit a fusion of violence and eroticism. Indeed, eroticized violence is associated with the dislocation of sexual difference itself: a boy is traded for a girl, since both share the "same reputation" as degraded sexual objects. And eroticized violence, Goldman insists, is Lennon's key sexual fetish.

By emphasizing so insistently the perversity of the sexual scenarios in this passage, Goldman uses Lennon to express a predictable misogyny of the psychic economy of the pornographic. Bewitched by the notion of sex as battle, Goldman produces an image of fixed gender assignment: an active, controlling male violating the passive feminine object. This sexual distribution of roles is inserted, neatly and without remainder, into the battle of gender hierarchy, into the spacings of domination and submission. As a consequence, the scenario also opens a path to sexual omnipotence: to satisfy his desires, Lennon (so it is imagined) could have women or men whenever he wanted, in whatever perverse ways he wanted. Psychoanalysis recognizes in Goldman's portrayal of Lennon the psychic operation of projection, whereby unwanted feelings are expelled from the self and put into another person or thing. Projection so understood is a very primitive defense, a defense which relocates unwanted parts of the self in an imagined external space. Used in this way, projection contributes to a world that is dangerously concrete, a world in which things simply are as they are, a world in which there is really nothing to think about because the facts always speak for themselves.[23] In this connection, it is important to highlight the impersonal and objectified tone of Goldman's writing; his mode of writing takes no account of its own inevitable prejudices and emotional investments. Figures of idealization, such as political leaders, rock stars, and other celebrities, provide blank screens for such projected feelings. As screens, celebrities are used in various ways to express and transfer fantasies of the inner life of the biographer (Goldman here) onto cultural objects of fiction (in this case, Lennon). I would argue then that at the same time that Goldman writes Lennon's sexuality, he also writes his own inner world of fantasy. In psychoanalysis, the boundary between self and other is radically fluid. The self may seek to keep inside and outside apart; but at the level of the unconscious one is inserted into the other, and they become all mixed up and tangled.

Projection is not, however, simply an operation for getting rid of unwanted states of feeling. It is also—and this is crucial—a means by which the individual can fantasize that he or she fully possesses and controls the object. Psychoanalyst Melanie Klein describes one specific elaboration of this mechanism as "projective identification," whereby in the fantasized projection of split off parts of the self the individual attempts to control and injure the object from within. In projective identification, an individual deals with anxiety by relating to other people through persecutory fear. The intensity of such anxiety, says Klein, is so dangerous that the self fears persecution within the realm of the other and thus must struggle to deny any emotional involvement or personal connection.[24]

I think that Klein's account of projective identification is instructive for understanding Goldman's ruthless objectification of Lennon. Klein's account is especially instructive if we recall that projective identification not only transfers fantasies of danger and catastrophe onto the other person but also maintains hatred and anxiety in a form of internal check; projective identification locks the self, so to speak, into repetition. What Klein's account implies here, then, is that Goldman, as biographer, makes his subject, Lennon, in and through the unwitting repetition of unconscious fantasies. Goldman creates Lennon as the carrier for a range of fantasies about desire and sexuality, fantasies which, once projected onto Lennon, can be (re)presented as dangerous, threatening, and disturbing. By charging perversity (repressed homosexuality, sexual violence, the thrill of transgression), bisexuality, and even hints of child sexual abuse, Goldman unleashes his fantasies on Lennon in order to both "know" his subject and establish control.

Moreover, Goldman's idea of investigative biography seems to function as a form of psychic protection. He makes much of the "six years of intense research conducted all around the world" in the writing of his book; he stresses that he and his staff undertook twelve hundred interviews with Lennon's family and friends.[25] His idea is the familiar one that through interviews and recollections it is possible to find the real Lennon, the man behind the mask, stripped of the Beatles mystique, revealed for all to see. However, Goldman's raw material, his independent research and interviews, serves an important ideological purpose here: it functions to deny Goldman's imaginary relation to Lennon and thus maintains one of the key fictions of investigative biography: that clarity, objectivity, and certitude can be achieved. By underscoring this "investigative research," Goldman is able to pass off his imaginative speculations about Lennon's Bangkok trip ("John would have been," "John would have found") as objective reality.

IF GOLDMAN'S BOOK IS considered extremist (the second assassination of Lennon?), this is because it is propelled by a powerful and disturbing anxiety in its construction of him, an anxiety which Goldman seeks to deny at all costs. Despite—might it really be because of?—

Lennon's death, certain critics of Lennon have continued to attack the ex-Beatle and his artistic work. In this vilification, it is clear that rage and fear operate at the biographical level concerning Lennon both as a person and as a celebrity. In one way or another, other portions of Lennon's written life have acquired the same interplay of fantasy and anxiety present in Goldman's demolition job. Yet, unlike Goldman, these other critics often fail to document even the basic details of Lennon's personal and professional achievements; instead, these biographical plottings of Lennon are hostile, ill-tempered, and vitriolic.

For example, Frederic Seaman presents, according to the jacket description of his memoir *The Last Days of John Lennon* (1991), a catalog of "startling revelations" about the ex-Beatle's wild passions and eccentricity. Seaman was one of Lennon's personal assistants between 1979 and 1980, and in performing his duties he came into contact with his employer on a daily basis. Seaman seeks to seductively draw the reader into the inner, private world of Lennon; Seaman was, we are told, "John's trusted friend and confidant."[26] This opening rhetorical move allows Seaman to pass off a deeply personal attack on Lennon as part of the biographical business of disclosing the personality of a performer. The startling revelations include

Lennon's virtual imprisonment in the Dakota;

His obsession with food and sex;

The Lennons' colossal shopping sprees in New York and Palm Beach;

John and Yoko's fascination with the occult;

The collapse of the Lennons' sex life;

John's ongoing rivalry with former Beatles Paul McCartney and George Harrison;

John's premonition of his violent death.

The Last Days of John Lennon thus seeks to show that "the world's greatest rock star" was beset with painful insecurities, unfulfilled desires, and crippling self-doubt.[27]

Seaman's disclosures concentrate, predictably enough, on Lennon's motives for withdrawing from music and celebrity, his reclusiveness, and his relationship with Ono. Seaman, having recently commenced his position as a private secretary, sketches his impressions of his employers:

John rarely saw anyone outside of the family and staff, and he took virtually no phone calls, except over the intercom. When he did use the phone, it was always with the conviction that the FBI was listening. Thus, his insulation from the outside world seemed nearly complete. . . . It did not take me long to see that John and Yoko's relationship was anything but the mythical romance they had fashioned for the media. Slowly, I came to understand that John and Yoko did not have much of a relationship.

Yoko lived at a frantic pace—submerging herself in round-the-clock meetings in her office with a steady stream of visitors during the day, and spending much of the night on the phone. John lived in slow motion, killing time in the bedroom, the White Room, and the kitchen. He lived upstairs. She lived downstairs.

As a result, all communications within the confines of the Dakota were conducted in a most peculiar fashion. There were telephones everywhere, each connected to an elaborate intercom system that enabled Yoko to keep tabs on John at all times. . . . But if John wanted to talk to Yoko, he would sometimes call me first, to ask as if she appeared busy, because if she had been on the phone or tied up in a meeting and refused to talk to him, or if she were brusque with him, it might ruin his day. Calling me first was his defense. It made me sad, maybe even a little angry sometimes, that the great John Lennon was in the humiliating position of having to call me, a virtual stranger, to ask if his wife were "available" for lunch or a chat on the phone.[28]

Note how Seaman plays on our cultural idealization of the ex-Beatle ("the great John Lennon") only to render him a victim or fool ("in the humiliating position"). The dichotomies are also depressingly familiar: Yoko Ono the manipulative, conniving woman; John Lennon the recluse utterly dependent upon Ono—helpless and paranoid (he even fears the telephone!).

If Seaman's "bittersweet memoir" —a memoir which is very bitter indeed—sounds reminiscent of Goldman's work, this is because Seaman collaborated with Goldman in the latter's vicious rewriting of Lennon's life.[29] Seaman's reasons for doing so sprang from Simon and Schuster's cancellation of his own book contract after he was convicted of the theft of Lennon's personal diaries. (In passing a sentence of five years' probation, the presiding judge prohibited Seaman from ever revealing the contents of Lennon's journals for profit; hence, his collaboration with Goldman.) Seaman's own memoir, published a few years after Goldman's book, trades on the extraordinary drama of the stolen diaries without contravening the court order concerning the disclosure of their contents. In fact, in the prologue, Seaman claims that he was badly beaten up by officers of the New York Police Department before being charged with the theft of the diaries. He defended his theft by claiming that Lennon had asked him to pass the diaries to Lennon's son Julian. Elliot Mintz, in a public denouncement of Seaman, argued that this defense is absurd. He pointed out that, had Lennon wanted Julian to have his diaries, he would have instructed his attorney, or asked Ono, to give them to Julian. Mintz ironically noted: "even if John's last wish to Fred if anything happened to him was to take the journals and bring them to Julian, why didn't he? He had travelled to Wales to see Julian. He had gone out to Cold Spring Harbor to spend some time with Julian. He had the journals in his possession for over a year and made no attempt to get them to Julian because that was not his intent."[30] Instead, Seaman stole Lennon's diaries, I believe, to corner the gossip market on the ex-Beatle.

A number of other employees and associates have sought to cash in on Lennon and his story. John Green, Yoko Ono's tarot reader for a time, was inspired in 1983 to write *Dakota Days*. Like Seaman, Green attempts to seduce by emphasizing his intimate knowledge of Lennon. According to the book jacket, "In a room of the Dakota apartments overlooking Central Park, John Lennon broods on his past and struggled to find his lost muse. His adviser, confidant and friend during those dark days was tarot reader John Green." Green seeks to strip the myth of Lennon. Focusing on a conversation with Ono concerning the family's summer holiday of 1979 and the need to keep Lennon away from public scrutiny because of an alleged breakdown, Green recalls giving the following advice:

"If you can't find a way to make John want to go, then just make the reservations and take him. Order him. He is still lackadaisical enough to be unlikely to put up any genuine resistance. So just tell him that all the plans are set and paid for and that's all there is to it."

So it was that John was carted off for yet another summer on an extensive journey that, according to the theory, was for his own good.[31]

Green writes of his admiration for Lennon, but the book seeks throughout to uncover the psychological disturbances at the heart of Lennon's inner world. He speculates about the state of Lennon's marriage, Lennon's inability to work, and the depression he claims

Lennon underwent during the last five years of his life. More than that, Green takes credit for supplying the myth of the happy house-husband, a myth designed to keep the public from knowing the painful truth about Lennon's mental breakdown. Lacking in personal agency and creative energy, Lennon was controlled not only indirectly but also directly. There is, therefore, no need to strip the mask away: Lennon's subjectivity is rendered equivalent to a mask itself.

The thematic interpretation of Lennon developed by Ray Cole-man in his two-volume biography, *John Lennon*, is very different from the interpretations of Seaman and Goldman.[32] Coleman, a British music journalist who knew Lennon, wrote these volumes after interviewing Cynthia Powell and Yoko Ono, and hence his bi-ography has a certain semiauthorized quality about it. The first vol-ume describes Lennon's childhood, his school days and friendships, his romance with Cynthia Powell, the formation and rise of The Beatles, Beatlemania, the pressures of stardom, and, finally, the breakdown of his first marriage. The second volume begins with Lennon divorcing Powell and charts the breakup of The Beatles, Lennon's marriage to Yoko Ono, their campaign for peace, their move to the United States in the early 1970s, and Lennon's final years of seclusion. This painstaking chronological reconstruction lends the book a certain kind of objectivism: Lennon's life is con-structed as a series of actions and events. Unlike Goldman, Coleman is not seeking to unmask Lennon; he instead prefers to let the facts speak for themselves.

A close reading of Coleman's biography, however, reveals that it conceals as much as it exposes: what is left unsaid (or what is implicit throughout the text) is perhaps just as significant as the chronicled events. Lennon's life history is documented in some considerable de-tail but always in terms of stardom and success, with an eye on society's reception and evaluation of his artistic work. Records are made, concerts are performed, relationships are initiated and termi-nated, artistic projects are completed, and Lennon's remarkable cre-ativity is continually underlined. What inevitably intrudes into Cole-man's biographical framing of Lennon, however, is something more personal, something more human. Lennon's very successes and achievements point to a psychological or emotional motivation that outstrips the documented life history. Coleman writes, for instance, that Lennon "was brilliant, warm, tender, sensitive, generous. He was also infuriating, tough, aggressive, naive and woundingly abrasive."[33] Despite the enumeration of these emotional traits, though, the complexity of Lennon's lived experience is flattened into a one-dimensional portrait, perhaps as part of the familiar grab for the broad audience of popular biography. Indeed, it is as if Lennon as an individual is written out of the narrative, only to be replaced by Lennon the celebrity.

Consider Coleman's account of the impact of celebrity and drugs on Lennon's first marriage: "The stress of life with this agitated, extraordinary pop star who darted in and out of their home took a heavy toll on their marriage" and "Drugs entered their marriage, and contributed to its eventual collapse, quite innocently."[34] It is difficult not to find Coleman's logic humorous; although humor is presumably the last thing he intended in writing the chapter, entitled "Drugs," from which these quotations are taken. Despite Coleman's admiration for his subject, these quotations show Coleman operating with a logic similar to that of the biographers considered thus far. We are told that Lennon, the "extraordinary pop star," was essentially relegated to a defensive position as regards the impact of fame and drugs. In short, his personal agency was outstripped by drugs; so too was his marriage derailed. Amazingly, Lennon appears not to have been involved in any of this, for it all happened "quite innocently."

I think Coleman believes that by insisting on Lennon's innocence he is protecting Lennon from a more critical assessment of his drug use. What he is actually trying to do, however, is maintain an ideal image of Lennon. Coleman seeks to romanticize fame and stardom, so that Lennon is untarnished by the personally destructive consequences of drug use. But through such denial Lennon is transformed into an unrepresentative biographical subject. Freud points out some of the dangers of biographical idealization:

Biographers are fixated on their heroes in a quite special way. In many cases they have chosen their hero as the subject of their studies because—for reasons of their personal emotional life—they have felt a special affection for him from the very first. They then devote their energies to a task of idealization, aimed at enrolling the great man among the class of their infantile models—at reviving in him, perhaps, the child's idea of his father. To gratify this wish . . . they smooth over the traces of [the subject's] life struggles with internal and external resistances, and they tolerate in him no vestige of human weakness or imperfection. They thus present us with what is in fact a cold, strange, ideal figure, instead of a human being to whom we might feel ourselves distantly related.[35]

Coleman does, in fact, tolerate the occasional sign of imperfection in his subject. But the shift from the ordinary to the extraordinary happens all too easily, and when it does idealization appears to soothe the unbearableness of psychic complexity. At such points, Coleman attempts to "smooth over" Lennon's inner struggles as well as his conflicts with others. Indeed, his biography offers a drastic cleaning up of the messiness of lived experience.

It is thus that Coleman founds the identity of Lennon. He implies that Lennon, notwithstanding an interest in alternative lifestyles and different cultures, kept a strong grip on himself, even during the most difficult stages of his career, because he had a solid sense of his own identity. But this implication raises the difficult question, What does Coleman mean Lennon's identity to be identical to? The answer to this question depends on whether identity is fixed to the pole of sameness or the pole of difference. That an either/or logic haunts the biographical framing of Lennon is established by commentators such as Coleman and Goldman, who have drastically simplified him, suggesting either that he was a man of consistent commitments and passions or that he was a man without self-understanding. Interestingly enough, both Coleman and Goldman describe Lennon's lasting cultural importance in terms of his astounding artistic creativity. Yet both are troubled by the loose ends of his life: Coleman attempts to tidy up the mess, and Goldman ceaselessly rewrites it as a sign of moral lapse. What neither of them sees, however, is that Lennon, in effect, opens up the significance of imagination to the whole substance of living—not only music and art but also the pleasures and constraints of individual living and interpersonal relationships, cultural invention and social refashionings, and political association in its broadest sense.

BY EXAMINING THE WRITINGS of Goldman and Coleman on Lennon, we can discern a general movement from public image to private life, from historical myth to revised personality, from constructed celebrity to original identity. These biographies, notwithstanding their different intentions and values, reduce Lennon's artistic endeavors and creative achievements to mere effects of his personal circumstances. They also split Lennon into all good or all bad; they deploy a kind of schizoid investment to keep at bay the ambivalence and ambiguity of individual subjectivity. Goldman, for instance, makes little of Lennon as an individual; he is instead fascinated by the "creative genius" of Lennon's Beatle and post-Beatles artistic output. But when Goldman explores Lennon's artistic inventiveness it is only to denigrate him, to write a pathological drama about celebrity and its consequences. The name "Lennon" is continually referenced, but the man is lost, replaced almost entirely with random sexual sufferings, drug addictions, and personal neuroses. What we find in Goldman is less a reflective engagement with a complicated character than a cynical amalgam of rationalized envy and moral indignation. Coleman, by contrast, occasionally recognizes the awkward proximity of genius and eccentricity; yet such awareness is generally foreclosed through his idealization of Lennon. In this respect, Lennon's "complex personality" becomes little more than shorthand for moodiness or depression, feelings which must be left to one side for fear that they may overwhelm (and hence destroy?) our rememberings of Lennon as a cultural icon.

A difficult biographical question remains. In what sense does biography necessarily entail making assumptions about observer and observed, life and text, experience and fantasy? The explicit purpose of popular biography (as with Goldman and Coleman) is to restate, reconstruct, reinterpret, and thus retrieve what is of special interest in a particular life. Biographers, by necessity, construct a master plot about their subject's world. Richard Holmes reflects on what should go into the ideal biography:

"Biography" meant a book about someone's life. Only, for me, it was to become a kind of pursuit, a tracking of the physical trail of someone's path through the past, a following of footsteps. You would never catch them; no, you would never catch them. But maybe, if you were lucky, you might write about the pursuit of that fleeting figure in such a way as to bring it alive in the present.[36]

The biographer constructs a life as a series of achievements and failures, desires and obsessions, fortunes and misfortunes, as a linear narrative which traces the biographical subject from origin to finality. This approach to biography is oftentimes connected to psychological or social factors; there is some residual recognition that biography is also of necessity the cultural history of a particular era. No doubt this recognition arises because popular biography is strongly wedded to empirical research: there is nowhere to go but the historical record (read facts) for the plotting of a life story. This constructive aspect of biography, however, always contains the risk of distortion or falsity. "The possibility of error," writes Holmes, "is constant in all biography."

But one can talk about the "possibility of error" only as long as biography is conceived as the restating of a life. For the "recovered past" which popular biography strives to achieve is recovered only to the extent that it is actively shaped and created by the biographer. The biographer, as Erik Erikson argues, "must try to acknowledge the inescapable fact that his interpretation is subject to the mood of his own life, and heir to a given lineage of conceptualisation."[37] The inescapable fact which Erikson points to is the murky dividing line between biography and autobiography, the crossover in which biography slips into clandestine autobiography. It can be argued that all biography is intimately bound up with the cultural reproduction of identity. Popular biographical writing fashions a consistent and unified "I," as the inner and outer lives of the subject are transformed into myth, fiction, fantasy. Life becomes a literary fiction; but, through a curious inversion, that fiction is itself passed off as reality. "Reading lives," as biographer Graham McCann argues, "creates our image of the subject; even though the historical figure dies, the biography continues her presence—in itself a mythic, phoenix-like activity, re-creating and perpetuating the self."[38]

The realist trappings of popular biography (the conceptualization of identity in terms of origins and finalities) do not sit well with a critical approach to relations between self and society. It was Nietzsche who spoke of "all the learned dust of biography,"[39] in one stroke underscoring the drastic biographical limiting of life stories. Nietzsche multiplied our ways of thinking about identity: the ways in which our memories of the past push for expression in fragments, thus making us aware of the multiplicity of lives lived by any human subject. In recent decades, the practice of biography has been further challenged by continental traditions of social thought: primarily, poststructuralist and postmodernist theory. The poststructuralist challenge to biography, in particular, stems from notions of the "death of the author," as articulated by Roland Barthes, and the "death of man," as articulated by Michel Foucault.[40] Critical biography influenced by poststructuralist and postmodernist thought assumes that every life may be read as a text, as a complex network of meanings in which text and context cross. The texts of a life (diaries, autobiographies, novels, songs) are analyzed in terms of a broader discursive framework. This framework necessarily involves other texts (social, cultural, economic, political, and philosophical) through which the texts of the biographical subject are read and interpreted. This emphasis on textuality, perhaps not surprisingly, makes for a very different understanding of the nature of selfhood in particular and human experience in general from that portrayed in popular biographies. The core aim in this respect is to trace the genealogy of the biographical subject, the emergence of the self within discursive formations, rather than to presume the preexistence of personal identity. This is not to say that poststructuralist authors read texts in a manner which renders superfluous the notion of the human subject but to highlight that at the center of this approach there lies a decentering of subjectivity—a decentering of the self, identity, and human agency.[41]

In pointing out the contrasts between popular and critical biography, I do not intend to locate Lennon within some privileged field of concepts, conjectures, framings, knowledges. Both popular and critical biography are genres of self-telling, framings or probings of a life story. One operates through construction, the answering of questions about our lives and the ways in which life stories should be recounted, and the other through deconstruction, the dismantling of our ideological assumptions about the plotting of life. I write about John Lennon at the border between these genres. Reading biographical accounts of Lennon with and against each other, in an attempt to discern other images and representations, I seek alternative imaginings of the ex-Beatle. My close attention to popular biographies is vital because they are core texts in and from which cultural representations of "John Lennon" are framed, reconstituted, translated. I examine these biographies, then, with a view to producing a kind of biography of biography, seeking to uncover the ways in which we make meaning with Lennon. In addition, I look in detail at Lennon's own texts—his songs, performances, films, interviews, and books—in order to comprehend how his personal and artistic concerns have become both enmeshed with and transgressive of cultural representations of the ex-Beatle.

To approach Lennon—as I do—through the lenses of psychoanalysis, the sociology of culture, social theory, and postmodernism is, among other things, to invent new ways of approaching the complexity of identity and biography; it is a means of asserting, in effect, that the creation of cultural rememberings of Lennon should be viewed as an open-ended process of invention and reinvention.

As an example, consider Lennon's fascination with human deformity. As a child, Lennon was, by his own reckoning, at once drawn to and repulsed by cripples and spastics. At school, he was constantly writing and drawing in an exercise book which he dubbed *The Daily Howl;* its contents ranged from obscene verse to poetry to caricatures. Pete Shotton, Lennon's close friend, remembers *The Daily Howl* thus: "John by this time had developed quite a fascination with the physically handicapped—such as dwarfs, blind men, and cripples—whom he rather cruelly impersonated at every opportunity. Many of the characters in his drawings sported grotesquely long necks, one leg—or three—or two heads."[42] As a youngster in Liverpool, Lennon often insulted invalids ("How did you lose your legs? Chasing the wife?"). Deformities abound in his drawings from *In His Own Write* and *A Spaniard in the Works.*

As a Beatle, Lennon routinely deployed this kind of cruel humor to distance himself from the turbulence of Beatlemania. He developed an uncanny ability to mock public and media receptions of the band's work, determined as he was to underscore the hiatus between performance and product, art and commercialism. When exhausted by the pressures of performing, he would often pull grotesque faces and imitate cripples and spastics. It was his way of ridiculing what he saw as the absurdities, indeed the pathologies, of the entertainment business. While McCartney encouraged the audience to clap their hands or stamp their feet, Lennon lampooned such suggestions by turning his body inside out in violent contortions. His spastic imitations were especially cruel in this context given that front-row seats were oftentimes reserved for the disabled. Lennon spoke about his personal unease in having to deal with disabled people during the height of Beatlemania:

You want to be alone and you don't know what to say, because they're usually saying "I've got your record," or they can't speak and just want to touch you. And it's always the mother or nurse pushing them on you. They would just say hello and go away but they would push them at you like you were Christ or something, as if there were some aura about you which will rub off on them. It just got to be like that.

We were very sort of callous about it. It was just dreadful. You would open up every night and instead of seeing kids there you would just see a row full of cripples along the front. . . . It seemed that we were surrounded by cripples and blind people all the time, and when we would go through corridors they would all be touching us. It got like that, it was horrifying.[43]

Personal recollections by friends stress Lennon's intense dislike of deformity or weakness of any kind. George Harrison saw in Lennon's reactions a deep psychological fear of the human condition. Paul McCartney spoke of Lennon's spastic imitations as a means of debunking the cult of celebrity.[44] I see no final resolution here, only provocative questions. How did Lennon's denigration of the disabled enter into a contradiction with itself? Did it, for example, mirror his feelings about life as a Beatle? Or did it reflect his feelings about fame and his relation to the adoring masses? Did it, perhaps, connect to his fraught and painful relationship with his mother? All of these possibilities cross and tangle, and indeed Lennon himself spoke on various occasions of feeling crippled inside by both his childhood and his fame. The point here is not simply that internal experience comes to find some prop at a societal or cultural level; that would be the reductive version of my argument. My point is rather that in Lennon's attitudes and reactions to deformity we find multiplex fusions of the psychic and the cultural.

THE CENTRAL PURPOSE of this opening chapter has been to consider how John Lennon is constituted and contested as a subject of biography. By considering the major biographical portraits, this chapter highlights that cultural rememberings of Lennon divide his personality between the acceptable and the unacceptable, and interpret his life in terms of the compulsive banality of a binary opposition of good or evil. However different their approaches, Goldman and Coleman have a common intention, which is to present in a clear and comprehensible light the personality and work of an artist who is too often seen as unapproachably complex, elusive, and recalcitrant.

Whereas these biographical portraits view as unproblematic the relationship between Lennon's life and artistic work on the one hand and the culturally mediated process of remembering on the other, I see this relationship as overdetermined, intensely invested with passion and desire. I have offered psychoanalytic theory as a means of juxtaposing biographical constructions with a more open and questioning attitude to the multiplicities, ambivalences, and contingencies that make a life. Psychoanalysis adds to the wealth of biographical life framings by showing that stories of continuity conceal other life framings; it deconstructs the relationship between biography and theory as mediated by desire.

In the chapters that follow, I will draw on psychoanalysis and contemporary theory to prize open new interpretative possibilities for approaching Lennon and his inscription in contemporary culture. I seek to disrupt biographical constructions that privilege continuity, and instead to examine the multiple plots of Lennon's life. In psychoanalytic terms, such disruption and examination require detailed attention to instances of psychic conflict. The versions of Lennon I present seek to show the centrality of psychic conflict and division, not only in his own life but also in the cultural construction of memory.

2

Mother

Paths of Loss

I soon forgot my father. But I did see my mother now and
again. I often thought about her.

John Lennon

What child is not supposed to prefer its mother to everything in the world?

Nathalie Sarraute

In December 1970, two weeks before Christmas, John Lennon released his first solo album since the breakup of The Beatles.[1] Titled
John Lennon/Plastic Ono Band, the album is a haunting excavation
of the psychic dimensions of personal crisis, its songs taking up the
tensions between adulthood and childhood, the present and the past,
art and life. Richly autobiographical, *Plastic Ono Band* finds Lennon
abandoning his Beatles imagery of walruses and glass onions and instead declaring a preference for experience over illusion: "I was the
Walrus / But now I'm John."

The album's candid lyrics and sparse musical arrangements signaled,
in fact, a profound self-exorcism.[2] The minimalism of *Plastic Ono Band*
inverts the lush sounds and symphonic melodies of *Abbey Road,* the
final masterpiece from The Beatles. There were important reasons for
this contrast. Lennon had opposed McCartney's long medley of song
fragments for the second side of *Abbey Road.* He thought the idea con-
trite and preferred the straight rock 'n' roll sound of the "Get Back" sessions. Lennon explained: "I always liked simple rock and nothing else.
And I was influenced by acid and got psychedelic, like the whole generation, but really, I like rock and roll and I express myself best in
rock." *Plastic Ono Band* finds Lennon not only returning to rock but
also breaking from the linguistic excesses and rhetorical flourishes of
the 1960s, an artistic sensibility that he had helped to shape. "I started
trying," says Lennon, "to shave off all imagery, pretensions of poetry,

illusions of grandeur, what I call à la Dylan. . . . As they say, Northern people are blunt, right, so I was trying to write like I am."[3]

For Lennon, this newly recovered sense of bluntness necessitated a radical dismantling of the past. He was now an ex-Beatle, and it seemed an opportune time to set the record straight about his musical history. In a 1970 interview with *Rolling Stone* editor Jann Wenner, conducted to promote *Plastic Ono Band,* Lennon commented that The Beatles had been "the biggest bastards on earth." This was an amazing comment—no Beatle had dared talk about the band in such terms. But there was more. "One has to completely humiliate oneself," said Lennon, "to be what The Beatles were, and that's what I resent." The psychic costs of being a Beatle had been too high, and the experience had left Lennon angry. He felt that The Beatles had succumbed to the commercial pressures of the music industry, simply churning out product for its own sake since the death of manager Brian Epstein in 1967. On a more personal level, he blamed the band for his addiction to heroin. He claimed that he had turned to the drug because of "the shit thrown at me and at Yoko, especially at Yoko."[4] Lennon's "Cold Turkey," written in the latter half of 1969, was a testament to the psychic pain he and Ono experienced in trying to break their addiction. "Cold Turkey," which culminates in harrowing screams of pain, found Lennon feverish from withdrawal yet fiercely determined. The song had been considered for *Abbey Road* but was rejected by the other Beatles as too personal, intense, honest. It did not fit the myth of the Fab Four, a myth that Lennon was now determined to deconstruct.

Speaking to Wenner about The Beatles, Lennon made it abundantly clear that he regarded that part of his life as finished. "I don't believe," he said, "in The Beatles myth. 'I don't believe in The Beatles'—there is no other way of saying it, is there? I don't believe in them whatever they were supposed to be in everybody's head, including our own heads for a period."[5] On *Plastic Ono Band,* in which Lennon declares that "the dream is over," his repudiation of the myth of The Beatles is tied to a thorough confrontation with the illusions of self-identity, especially clichéd fantasies which locate identity as idyllic or devoid of conflict. Instead, Lennon connects identity with pain. "Pain," comments Lennon, "is the pain we go through all the time. You're born in pain. Pain is what we're in most of the time."[6] Lennon analyzes pain through various optics on *Plastic Ono Band.* From the reflective ambivalence of "Look at Me," in which everyday assumptions about identity are displaced by questions like "Who am I supposed to be?" to the bleakness of "Working Class Hero," in which the capitalist order keeps the individual "doped with religion and sex and TV," Lennon casts identity as both psychic symptom and social role.

This basic tension between desire and society is at its most disturbing when Lennon confronts childhood. *Plastic Ono Band* is a harrowing exploration of childhood pain, from the opening song ("Mother")

Mother, you had me, but I never had you
I wanted you, but you didn't want me

to the closing refrain ("My Mummy's Dead")

I can't explain
So much pain
I could never show it
My Mummy's dead.

By naming maternal absence as the foundation of pain, Lennon sets up a powerful link between loss and identity. He represents self-constitution as interwoven with rupture, rupture of the relation of child and mother. So painful is this rupture that it both brings identity into being and threatens to overwhelm, or perhaps even destroy, the self. A subtle interplay between self-constitution and self-disintegration is the primary stuff of *Plastic Ono Band,* and Lennon charts the interplay's various manifestations by recollecting his own childhood, his career with The Beatles, and his relationship with Yoko Ono.

Plastic Ono Band is also Lennon's "primal scream" record. This description captures his seething anger, but it also refers to his encounter with Dr. Arthur Janov's primal therapy.[7] Janov, a Californian psychologist and author of the cult book *The Primal Scream,* argued that children routinely suffer psychological disturbance when first encountering human sexuality. Janov called this first encounter the "primal scene" and regarded it as a profoundly traumatic event. From a therapeutic perspective, he argued that this trauma needs to be reintegrated into consciousness, and his primal therapy was designed to facilitate the psychic restructuring of such pain. Patients were encouraged to regress into childhood memories of anger and humiliation, to make contact with repressed feelings through primal screaming, and thereby to undo the terror and hatred of their parents.

Lennon became fascinated with Janov's book in early 1970. The linking of childhood trauma and adult rage in *The Primal Scream* struck a chord with his own experience, especially the bitterness and animosity he felt toward his own parents. Lennon arranged for the psychotherapist to visit him at his new home, Tittenhurst Park, in England. Janov asked that Lennon, and also Ono, write down their memories and feelings about their own childhoods. He also recommended that they abstain from alcohol and drugs of any kind. Lennon found primal therapy grueling but rewarding. Indeed, he drew from the despair and pain uncovered in these therapeutic encounters for the *Plastic Ono Band* album. The treatment proved sufficiently beneficial that the following month Lennon and Ono flew to Los Angeles to continue primal therapy at Janov's Primal Institute. The central focus of the therapy remained Lennon's past, the traumas of parental neglect in particular. But his current emotional difficulties were also dealt with; and this was especially important given that Ono miscarried for a second time with Lennon after arriving in Los Angeles. They remained in Los Angeles for a few months, undergoing treatment with Janov and writing music for their new albums. However, Lennon and Ono broke off treatment after Janov attempted to film a group therapy session. Years later Lennon reflected, "He just happened to be filming the session with John and Yoko in it."[8]

Lennon described *Plastic Ono Band* as "terribly uncommercial, it's so miserable in a way and heavy." Critics thought much the same. "The overwhelming feeling of the album is one of sadness," writes Ray Coleman, a construction which in itself indicates that sadness can be reacted to as overwhelming. Another critic, Stephen Holden, describes *Plastic Ono Band* as an album of "monumental self-centeredness."[9] Most striking here is the implication that despair cancels out not only positive emotion but also engagement with the wider world. The self is rounded back upon itself—without the logics of mind or society—in a destructively narcissistic moment of self-centeredness. In all of this it is possible to detect an assumption that anger can spoil or destroy, that positive emotion can be wiped out by the very presence of bad feelings.

It might be said, then, that Lennon's *Plastic Ono Band* works on the edge of emotional danger, pushing feelings of sadness and despair to their limit and breaking down conventional distinctions between the present and the past. This is not to suggest that Lennon masters the anxieties and fears which he has unlocked with the help of Janov's primal therapy; and this point is, perhaps, especially important given that primal therapy encodes cultural fantasies about doing away with sadness and hatred once and for all. It is, however, to claim that Lennon raises important issues about self-constitution: the horror implicit in the awareness that identity frames a sense of otherness, the fear of that which is excluded or repressed. The opening song on *Plastic Ono Band*, "Mother," works precisely at this intersection of identity and difference, sameness and otherness; and it is, in many ways, a profound personal commentary on the emergence of identity as interwoven with the loss of other people. The song culminates in Lennon repetitively screaming "Mother, don't go / Daddy come home."

In all of this, we find the shadow of despair in the drafting of the self. Lennon drew from such intimate experience of despair throughout his life and especially in his creative, artistic work. From the sad despondency of "I'm a Loser" to the grievous pain of "Mother," Lennon casts loss as intrinsic to identity. What follows is an exploration of the pain and despair brought out in Lennon's song "Mother" in terms of what it might tell us about the connections between loss and identity. I subsequently consider Lennon's exploration of the interplay between identity and otherness in such Beatles classics as "Strawberry Fields Forever" and "I Am the Walrus." As a frame for my discussion, I raise the issue—against the backdrop of Lennon's psychic economy—of whether fear of loss addresses the ambivalence of identity in general, or whether that fear concerns instead a fear of losing oneself as such.

JOHN LENNON WAS BORN on 9 October 1940 at Oxford Street Maternity Hospital in Liverpool. Like many babies at that time, he was delivered on an evening when Hitler's air force bombed the city and port with a vengeance.[10] Alfred Lennon, his father, and Julia Stanley, his mother, had married in 1938. Lennon would be their only child, and there can be little doubt that his relationship with his parents involved much pain, sadness, and anger. Lennon's father, known to friends and family as Freddie, worked on a shipping line, a job which required him to be away at sea for long periods. He was thus effectively separated from both his son and his wife. Married to an absent husband, Julia at first attempted to raise her son in her parents' house at 9 Newcastle Road, near Penny Lane. On Newcastle Road, Julia enjoyed a close relationship with her four sisters—Anne, Elizabeth, Harriet, and Mary—and they helped her to care for her new baby. "There were five women," Lennon reflected in 1980, "that were my family. Five *strong, intelligent, beautiful* women, five sisters. One happened to be my mother. My mother just couldn't deal with life. She was the youngest. And she had a husband who ran away to sea and the war was on and she couldn't cope with me and I ended up living with her elder sister."[11]

Julia Stanley seems to have experienced her son as an unwelcome intrusion; she felt that the boy interfered with her private and social life. Seeking to break permanently from her husband and forge a new life, Julia often left her son in the care of her sister Mary (Lennon's Aunt Mimi). In 1945, Julia gave birth to a daughter, Victoria, out of wedlock but gave the child up for adoption. Sometime later, she fell in love with another man, John Dykins, with whom she subsequently lived and had two daughters, Julie and Jacqueline. The difficulties Julia experienced in reorienting her life with Dykins were immense, and she decided that it would be best for her son to be brought up by her sister. Mary and her husband, George Smith, were childless and eagerly embraced the prospect of raising John Lennon as their own. Accordingly, Lennon went to live with the Smiths at Menlove Avenue in Woolton, Liverpool (which they called Mendips). He continued to see his mother sporadically; she now lived with Dykins in Allerton, a short distance away. Pete Shotton, Lennon's closest childhood friend, recollects: "John must have felt somewhat disorientated by his real mother's ongoing visits to Mendips. The youthful, carefree Julia would unexpectedly appear at Mimi's door to engage her son's love and attention, then vanish once more for weeks on end. Until his early adolescence, John never realized that his mum was living only a few miles away."[12]

Major emotional upheavals took place when Freddie Lennon dramatically reentered his son's world in 1945. Arriving unexpectedly one afternoon at the Smiths' house, he asked permission to take his son for a day's outing to Blackpool. Neither Julia Stanley nor Mimi Smith were aware, however, that Freddie Lennon had a half-baked plan to leave England permanently and begin life anew in New Zealand. During the next couple of weeks, Lennon remained with his father in

Blackpool. Meanwhile, Julia searched frantically for her son. Upon discovering their whereabouts in Blackpool, she told her husband she wanted her son back. Unable to sort out their competing claims, they put the predicament to the five-year-old Lennon. The boy was told that he had to decide with whom he wanted to live. Lennon, frightened and tearful, chose at first to stay with his father. Julia asked him whether he was absolutely sure. Again, Lennon responded in favor of his father. However, when his mother attempted to leave, Lennon shouted, "Mummy, Mummy, don't go, don't go."[13] Thus it was that Lennon went back with his mother to Liverpool, where he continued to live with Aunt Mimi and to see his mother at irregular intervals.

This parceling out between his mother and his aunt produced in Lennon a lifelong ambivalence over creativity and conventionality, desire and self-control, an ambivalence rooted in the different personal styles of these two women, both of whom were central to Lennon's emotional development. Mary Smith was a reserved woman who believed that unrestrained desires threatened personal well-being and social order. Smith attempted to raise Lennon with a proper respect for self-discipline, order, and work; and she instilled in him the value of both independence and conventionalism. Julia Stanley, by contrast, was individualistic, unconventional, and easygoing. She attempted to avoid the more stultifying conventions of social life and in her contact with her son conveyed the importance of emotion, passion, intuition, and empathy. Crucially, she introduced him to music by teaching him the banjo. Julia and Mimi's differing personal styles and understandings of the place of the individual within society were deeply impressed upon Lennon's emerging sense of self.

Such emotional trials left deposits that Lennon evaded, by his own reckoning, for years; he would recapture these repressed emotional longings in music and poetic imagination later in life. Ever since Blackpool, or what in Freudian terms might be called the "family romance" of Blackpool, Lennon had been left with something unrepresentable, a pain unnameable.[14] Lennon's mind was made up of these things: his young, vivacious mother withdrawing and returning her love in equal measure; his returned father, determined to make up for his absence, offering a new life in a faraway country; his devoted aunt offering the promise of protection and safety from the ravages of the outside world. Lennon's inner world was profoundly shaped by these bewildering familial demands, demands which, not surprisingly, he found extremely difficult to reconcile. Nevertheless, it seems that the most painful demand was the impossible choice between mother and father, between desire and protection, a choice so confusing that a kind of nothingness is the hidden face of its very affirmation. Further trauma occurred when Lennon's mother tragically died in 1958; she was run over by a car after leaving her sister's house one evening. Physical loss, as Lennon himself commented, followed psychic loss: "She got killed by an off-duty cop who was drunk. She was just at the bus stop and he ran her down in a car. So that was another big trauma for me. I lost her twice. Once as a five-year-old when I moved in with my auntie. And once again at fifteen when she actually, physically died. And that was *very* traumatic for me."[15]

To CONSIDER FURTHER the impact of loss upon Lennon's psychic economy, we must take a brief detour through psychoanalytic theory, since it offers an approach which makes loss central to the inner world of the self. The theoretical preoccupation with loss in various versions of psychoanalysis concerns, above all, the pain of loss. Psychoanalysts from Freud to Melanie Klein to Julia Kristeva have argued that the individual establishes a relation to the self and other people through loss: the loss of loved ones, the loss of selves, the loss of pasts. When I speak of loss from a psychoanalytic point of view, then, I mean to stress that people create themselves through forgetting and remembering their losses.

Freud argued quite early in his writings that self-experience begins with the experience of loss. Although Freud developed only a rudimentary account of the impact of maternal desire upon the fantasy world of children, and of how such longings are carried over into adulthood, he locates the loss of mother as the child's first and most significant loss. Through her absence, the infant comes to recognize that mother is different from itself. For it is only through the mother's absence, says Freud, that the infant comes to desire her presence. This moment of separation is both frightening and exciting, and in order to cope the infant creates fantasies about the mother that compensate for her painful absence. In other words, the infant reacts to the absence of the mother in reality by imagining her present in fantasy. In its capacity for imagination, writes Freud, the infant has "created an object out of the mother."[16]

It is worth considering what the denial of loss might mean at the level of the inner world, given the emphasis on repression in psychoanalysis. In his 1915 essay "Mourning and Melancholia," Freud reconstructs the connections between love and loss on the one hand and the limits of identification and identity on the other. "The loss of a love object," writes Freud, "is an excellent opportunity for the ambivalence in love-relationships to make itself effective and come into the open."[17] The loss of a loved person, he suggests, brings into play ambivalence and aggression. Under such circumstances, both one's passion and one's anger for lost love come to the fore. Since the other person is loved, the self incorporates some aspect of the loved other into itself in order to maintain the emotional tie. However, because the other person is also hated, this incorporated aspect of the other now becomes something despised within the self.

On this basis, Freud distinguishes between "normal mourning" and the "complex of melancholia." Freud considers mourning a normal response to the loss of a loved person. In normal mourning, the self incorporates aspects of the other person and then gradually detaches itself from the lost love. By acknowledging the pain of absence, the mourner emotionally draws from the lost love; he or she borrows personality traits and feelings associated with the loved person and in so doing is able to work through these feelings of loss. In the complex of melancholia, the individual fails to break from the lost love, keeping hold of the object through identification. Unable to mourn, the melancholic cannot express love and hate directly toward the lost love and instead denigrates his or her own ego. Freud describes this melancholic process as an "open wound": the melancholic is caught in a spiraling of identifications, a spiraling in which hatred rounds back upon the self, "emptying the ego until it is totally impoverished."[18] Whereas the mourner gradually accepts that the lost love no longer exists, the melancholic engages in denial in order to protect the self from loss.

Another way of putting all this is to say that selfhood is drafted against the backdrop of an individual's willingness or unwillingness to mourn loss. If the pain of loss can be tolerated, the individual subject can set about relinquishing primary involvements. If the pain of loss cannot be tolerated, the subject grafts sadness onto the lost object itself, a reaction which transforms mourning into melancholia.[19]

Language plays a central role in an individual's negotiation of loss. Words, for Freud, are the means to figure out loss. Language fills in for what has been lost. Words are a stopgap, helping to close up the pain of lost love.[20] As Kristeva writes, "The child . . . becomes irredeemably sad before uttering his first words: this is because he has been irrevocably, desperately separated from the mother, a loss that causes him to try to find her again, along with other objects of love, first in the imagination, then in words."[21] The possibilities of language, and of the symbolization it encodes, come to represent, among other things, the cultural means of managing loss. As wounded beings, we dwell within a body that transmutes itself as a work of mourning.

In turning to psychoanalytic theory to consider the complexities of Lennon's reflections on loss, my purpose is to raise some questions concerning how we talk about grief in contemporary culture. To consider Lennon's speculations about loss and in particular his negotiation of grief is not to treat him as a pathological case, although psychoanalysis has certainly been put to this purpose by some critics. English professor David Aberach, for example, has commented on the disastrous psychic consequences for Lennon of his parents' separation, noting that the "enormous numbers of styles and faces with which he experimented testify to the insecurity of his self-image."[22] No attempt at ambiguity here. Aberach takes a normative self, secure and stable, as the psychoanalytic guideline from which to consider deviance and pathology. In this approach, however, the very contingencies and ambivalences of object-loss as they affect self-organization are lost from view. As Adam Phillips, a psychoanalytic critic, writes of Aberach's diagnosis of Lennon:

All the normative versions of psychoanalysis generate nostalgic bad faith by implying that one's life could have been better if only one had been born into a different family. John Lennon's life would not have been better if his parents hadn't separated, because it wouldn't have been his life. And a self-image is always exactly that—an image. It is a fundamentally useful Freudian insight that we are never coincident with—the same as—the images we have of ourselves. And in a certain sense there are no selves, only families of images that we sometimes choose to think of, or collect, as a self-image.[23]

I agree with Phillips that the idea of a self-identical subject is a fiction (an illusion designed to keep at bay the pain of loss), and instead of using psychoanalysis to diagnose, I will focus upon the contingencies at play between loss and identity. Such contingencies concern the ways in which we think of ourselves and the sorrows that haunt our lives. If loss is pivotal to emotional development, then the imprint of loss is in ongoing relation to the negotiation of daily life.

In what ways does loss manifest itself in Lennon's art? How does Lennon construct the connections between loss and identity? Is there a characteristic manner in which he approaches loss and its consequences? To grasp the significance of loss in Lennon's artistic work let us return to "Mother," a song which powerfully restages his own childhood anguish and emotional darkness. "Mother" begins with the sound of an old church bell chiming four times. Lennon commented that in using the sound of bells, he intended to convey "the death knell of the mother/father, Freudian trip."[24] While he may have sought to write an obituary for the Freudian field, the imaginative reach and emotional intensity of "Mother" can in fact be fleshed out with reference to psychoanalytic theory in illuminating ways. After the chimes fade, Lennon's vocal cuts in with a sharpness and urgency suggestive of psychic rupture—the fracturing of present and past, the dislocation of love and loss. Hurt, regret, and lost love permeate the song, which is underpinned by the compelling directness of Lennon's lament for his dead mother. Yet if the song points back to the lost paradise of the mother-child relation, imaginary plenitude, and primary narcissism, it also moves toward the fear of object-loss and separation and toward the anxiety implicit in self-differentiation. Lennon's replay of the pain of loss—("Mother, you had me / But I never had you")—captures the psychic refusal to let go of lost love. From this angle, repetition holds in check the working out of loss within the psyche: the most Lennon can do is repeat (in words and in music) the memory of pain occasioned by maternal absence. Yet it can also be argued that Lennon's attempt to acknowledge the impact of loss—("I wanted you / You didn't want me")—displaces the grip of lost love upon the psyche. That is, "Mother" is less a repetition of impossible desire than a replay of the suffering *and* relief in negotiating object-loss. At this level, loss is figured out through negation and in language. "Signs," writes Kristeva, "are arbitrary because language starts with a negation of loss, along with the depression occasioned by mourning."[25] Lennon's words are suffused with emotion, replete with sadness and uncertainty, bitterness and anger.

It is not hard to see in all this the influence of mourning, the hungering for lost love, coupled with the attempt to outflank the pain of loss. Artistically, Lennon had been experimenting with the themes of

pain and loss for some time. In Beatles compositions like "I'm a Loser,"
"Nowhere Man," and "Help!" Lennon strikes a mournful tone. "Help!"
for example, which Lennon acknowledged as strongly autobiographical,[26] finds him in 1965 looking back to an earlier time of content-
ment, to a past life that he compares favorably with the perplexing
present (in which "life has changed in oh so many ways"). He is
"down," in need of emotional connection and understanding: "Won't
you please, please help me?" During this period, his self-proclaimed
"Fat Elvis" period, he thought himself overweight, and he was increasingly reliant on alcohol and drugs, emotionally disconnected
from his family, and fed up with the life of celebrity. But his cry for
help was not rooted in external sources only. It also came from within.
Unconscious fears and anxieties were pressing for expression, and
Lennon articulated this confusion about his personal life with special
force on the "White Album" in 1968. His inner turmoil is perhaps best
captured in the song "Julia," a maudlin plea to his dead mother. The
only Beatles song recorded solo by Lennon, "Julia" identifies the importance of emotional longing in the wake of loss ("Half of what I say
is meaningless / But I say it just to reach you"). The minor chords
throughout "Julia" also summon feelings of sadness. Lennon's psychic
fragility is held in check by another love: "Ocean child calls me" is a
reference to his blossoming love for Yoko, whose name means "ocean
child" in Japanese.

If Lennon's "Julia" is a maudlin longing for lost love, "Mother" is an
altogether more desperate affair. It is as if having reflected upon the
pain of loss in all its complexity, Lennon is attempting to emerge
somewhere on the other side. In fact, Lennon is grappling in
"Mother" with an enigmatic paradox: the complex interplay of mourning and melancholia. The losses that Lennon mourns are stark: loss is
cast as that which overwhelms the self; it threatens to wipe out con-
sciously perceived identity. The tonality of Lennon's voice evokes
such pain: there is something compelling about his singing as he
deepens the loss to include his absent father ("Father, you left me / I
never left you"). Lennon's "Mother" dramatizes the way we live with
loss, capturing the ambivalence of mourning in such a way that every
line in the song perpetually threatens to dissolve into melancholy. He
explicitly acknowledges his grief by revealing his inner desires: "I
wanted you / You didn't want me." In writing of frustrated desire, he
identifies his own struggle against pain, a struggle against imagined

psychic catastrophe. Lennon touches on the emotional paradox that each of us must negotiate: the psychic refusal to let go of our primary involvements, coupled with the triumph over the pain of loss achieved in self-differentiation.

In the middle of the song, however, the tempo suddenly changes. "Mother" becomes more frantic as the sense of fragility touched upon in the verses turns to angst. Lennon endlessly repeats "Mama don't go / Daddy come home" as his singing turns into screams of pain. At times, these screams are almost unbearable. Lennon's agony, one might speculate, connects to the terrors of being alive to loss. He reacts to the terrors of loss with horror. It is here, in this psychic space of fright and anger, that Lennon most skillfully questions the way in which we manage loss. In fact, Lennon's screams of pain touch on the thorny issue of the *object* of loss—of what it is that has actually been lost. In "Mother," loss is being figured out, enacted and repeated, through the medium of poetic language, of music. In this figuring of loss, the psychic boundaries of pain are rendered uncertain and ambiguous. To say this is to argue that Lennon moves back and forth across the spacings of loss, from object-loss to loss of self. Lennon's screams of pain burst forth as a redoubling of loss, reopening the gap between the lost maternal body and self-differentiation.

In her book *Powers of Horror,* Kristeva describes this psychic gap as the realm of "abjection."[27] Abjection is a kind of projecting of the body of the mother onto an imaginary outside, and abjection is associated by Kristeva with the ultimate imprint of the death drive, a primordial anguish or fear of a horrifying void. Identity construction, undertaken in and through the process of language, offers some sort of fantasy compensation for the horror of the void or blank that for the unconscious constitutes death. But the split subject, divided between conscious and unconscious desire, is inherently fragile, and the pain of loss reappears whenever a spacing or hiatus of meaning announces itself in the psyche. In this space lie pain, fear, and anguish. In the face of such horror, Lennon responds by screaming; his screams dislocate received social meanings.[28] His screams of pain are at the borders of symbolic representation: he pleads for his parents not to go; he pleads for them to come home.

Lennon's "Mother" ruptures core distinctions between mourning and melancholia, or at least undermines the presumption that mourning for lost love insures against melancholy. For it is Lennon's very ability to grieve here, to publicly mourn his dead mother, that leads to a breakdown in the value of words. It is as if words finally lose all meaning, with destructiveness outstripping the containing functions of language. This is where Lennon finds himself in the latter part of "Mother": drowning in sorrow, screaming in pain. In all of this, Lennon might be said to be playing with the very ambiguity of loss, repeating both the fear of object-loss and the terror of losing oneself.

Are Lennon's screams of pain—the point at which he is placed beyond language—an unleashing of sorrow for his dead mother? Or are his screams an attack upon language for its failure to adequately substitute for loss? There is no sure way of resolving this issue; and surely any attempt to do so reflects a desire to avoid an important question— What are the ways in which we live with loss? Whether we struggle against lost love or struggle against ourselves, whether we acknowledge anger toward the dead or confront the damage done to our own psychic world, these matters touch on the dynamics of mourning and melancholia. We do not have to suffer self-annihilation, however, in acknowledging the pain of mourning. Lennon's problematization of his feelings of loss in "Mother" powerfully suggests that ambivalence is a fundamental part of human experience; Lennon recognizes that an ability to relinquish self-control is essential to reflective self-understanding. The sorrow in John Lennon was declared publicly with "Mother" and the other songs on *Plastic Ono Band*. These were not songs based on a commercial formula; they were songs that came from within.[29]

Lennon's exploration of the links between loss and identity is not, however, simply a private affair. It can also be viewed as intensely political in character. Introducing "Mother" at the One to One Benefit Concert at Madison Square Garden in 1972, Lennon said: "A lot of people thought it was just about my parents, but it's about 99% of the parents alive or half-dead."[30] Lennon's "Mother" challenges dominant cultural conceptions of selfhood by returning to the problem of desire: the passion embedded in the primordial relation to the mother. Culture silences loss, pain, and melancholia in the name of certainty; it underwrites the conviction that we are self-identical with ourselves. Lennon rejects this fantasy. From the lofty ideal of "Beatle" to the complex realm of experience, Lennon declares he is simply a person. *Plastic Ono Band* discovers hope in the unpromising circumstances of sadness, loss, sorrow. "Hold on John / John hold on / It's gonna be all right": contact with emotion provides for a sense of self-continuity that is, paradoxically, discontinuous. As Kristeva says of the intricate connections between loss and autonomy: "For if it is true that those who are slaves to their moods, being drowned in their sorrows, reveal a number of psychic or cognitive frailties, it is equally true that a diversification of moods, variety in sadness, refinement in sorrow or mourning are the imprint of a humankind that is surely not triumphant but subtle, ready to fight, and creative."[31] In loss, Lennon uncovers the private dimension of cultural crisis, an intimate encounter with otherness that he finds necessary, moving, transgressive.

JOHN LENNON REGARDED *Plastic Ono Band* as a continuation of his ongoing concern with relating personal and political life, connecting everyday affairs to society at large.

I think it's the best thing I've ever done. I think it's realistic and it's true to me that has been developing over the years from "In My Life," "I'm a Loser," "Help!" "Strawberry Fields." They're all personal records. I always wrote about me when I could. . . . They were the ones I really wrote from experience and not projecting myself into a situation and writing a nice story about it, which I always found phony.[32]

Note the manner in which Lennon works against the stereotypes of celebrity and entertainment in this passage, pitting the realm of "experience" against "a nice story," the "personal" against the "phony." Yet if Lennon explores identity from the vantage point of personal experience in 1970, the reference to his earlier songs points to a time when he thought about identity in more social terms. Before Lennon began to unravel the private dimensions of cultural crisis (as he did on *Plastic Ono Band*), he explored the ways in which contemporary culture affects private life. Crucially, Lennon undertook his artistic work against the backdrop of the popular-culture explosion of the 1960s.

In the mid-1960s, Beatlemania was reaching its zenith. Having taken the United States by storm in 1964 and racked up four consecutive number-one albums in Britain, The Beatles were a truly monumental force in contemporary music. Their astonishing output of records, tours, and films, while emotionally exhausting and physically draining for the band, was not to slacken. The year 1965 brought further phenomenal achievement. Following fast on the commercial success of and critical praise for *A Hard Day's Night,* The Beatles began filming *Help!,* a movie which sedimented the public image of the Fab Four as brazen but amiable cultural heroes. The album *Help!* was also a smash success, as was The Beatles' summer world tour, which included a concert to the then record-breaking audience of fifty-six thousand people at Shea Stadium in New York. In recognition of their enormous success, the Fab Four appeared on the Queen's Birthday Honours List, having been awarded MBEs. The Beatles had finally realized Lennon's dream: they were, at last, "the toppermost of the poppermost."

Lennon's public image was painfully at odds with his private life, however. He found little freedom and enjoyment arising from his celebrity. The Beatles had certainly brought him wealth and fame, and he acknowledged the material benefits of that fame. But, at a more personal level, he felt himself a prisoner of fame rather than its architect. The pandemonium of life as Beatle John had become burdensome. He could not leave his flat in London without encountering fans and demands for autographs, and neither could his wife, Cynthia. Seeking to avoid such menacing intrusions and to maintain some degree of privacy, Lennon purchased a house in Weybridge, a suburb southwest of London. Although Weybridge offered privacy from the outside world, Lennon felt alienated living in the suburbs and disconnected from his familial life. Peter Brown, an employee of The Beatles at the time, described Lennon in the following way: "It was easy for anyone who knew John well to see how unhappy he was with his lot. He felt duplicitous in his success, hypocritical with his image of the literary but ultimately agreeable, huggable Beatle."[33] The duplicity to which Brown refers concerns the hiatus between his public image and his personal experience: Lennon felt increasingly removed from, and oftentimes bitter about, public perceptions of The Beatles.

Lennon's unhappiness also extended to professional concerns. He had become increasingly weary of touring, feeling that The Beatles were becoming jaded performers. Beatlemania was again to blame: the screaming fans were often louder than The Beatles, the result being that neither audience nor band could hear the music. Touring had also become dangerous. During the 1966 world tour, The Beatles were harassed by protesters and government officials alike. In Japan, a group of militant students strongly objected to The Beatles' performing at the Budokan Hall in Tokyo. The concert represented, the students claimed, a Westernization of Japanese culture. Fearing social unrest, the Japanese government provided round-the-clock security for The Beatles at the Tokyo Hilton. Yet this security came at a substantial cost: the band members were not to leave their hotel rooms. The Beatles had become symbolic prisoners, trapped in collective hysteria. In Manila, there was even greater scandal. The Beatles had already featured prominently in the national press for their sold-out performance to an audience of one hundred thousand people at the Areneta Coliseum. But the coverage of the performance paled in comparison with the coverage of their snubbing of President Ferdinand Marcos and his wife, which occurred when the band members failed to attend a party held in their honor. In the wake of the media frenzy, The Beatles fled the city but were detained at Manila airport, where they were harassed by government officials.[34] By this time, Lennon had decided that The Beatles' touring days were numbered.

Lennon dealt with these personal and professional difficulties by immersing himself in activity; such activity was, from one angle, a strategy of avoidance, a strategy that he had deployed earlier in his life—after the desertion of his parents and the death of his mother. By his own reckoning, this period at the height of the Beatles' fame was a confusing and difficult time, and it seems that it took all of his artistic energy to switch off the turbulence of Beatlemania. Lennon was an especially prolific songwriter at this stage of his career. He was the principal composer of ten of the thirteen songs on *A Hard Day's Night*, including the breathtaking title track, as well as of the majority of songs on *Beatles for Sale* and *Help!* He also wrote the singles "I Feel Fine" and "Ticket to Ride" and led the band into pathbreaking experimentation with "Tomorrow Never Knows" on *Revolver*. In many of these songs, Lennon created a space for critical self-reflection, connecting his own despair to the very social world which had transformed him into a cultural icon.

"I started thinking," said Lennon, "about my own emotions—I don't know when exactly it started like 'I'm a Loser' or 'Hide Your Love Away' or those kinds of things—instead of projecting myself into a situation I would try to express what I felt about myself."[35] Lennon's emerging introspection was well captured in the first of these songs, in which he writes, "I'm a loser / And I'm not what I appear to be." This identity crisis was central to Lennon's songwriting throughout the period, and it was to become more fully developed in compositions such as "You've Got to Hide Your Love Away," "Nowhere Man,"

"Help!," and "In My Life." There can be little doubt, as Lennon himself forcefully acknowledged, that such confessional songwriting allowed for the expression of personal doubts and anxieties. But he was also profoundly aware that his music was scrutinized by the critics and fans. It is thus understandable that he oftentimes sought to conceal the deeper meanings and autobiographical references in his songs, usually by wrapping them up in gobbledygook.

To the extent that Lennon's early Beatles compositions at once reveal and conceal his selfhood, he moved crablike toward an exploration of human subjectivity. His music presents a picture of subjectivity in crisis, of identity perceived as "lost" or "nowhere." In Lennon's poetry and drawings, done mostly while he was on tour, we can detect a similar kind of self-questioning. He published two volumes of prose, *In His Own Write* in 1964 and *A Spaniard in the Works* in 1965. By and large, Lennon's work consisted of political satire, religious parody, punning jokes, and cartoons. A paragraph on the book jacket for *In His Own Write*, entitled "About the Awful," carried the following message from the author: "as far as I'm conceived this correction of short writty is the most wonderfoul larf I've ever ready. God help and breed you all." More of the same is contained within his books. "Father Cradock," he wrote in *Spaniard*, "turns around slowly from the book he is eating and explains it is just a face she is going through." "Harassed Wilsod won the General Erection," writes Lennon in a political satire of British politics, "with a very small majorie over the Torchies. Thus pudding the Laboring Partly back into powell after a very large abcess."[36] Clearly, this was a side of John Lennon different from his public image as a moptop.

These books sedimented Lennon's reputation as the humorist and wit of The Beatles. Both were best-sellers. Indeed, Lennon was honored for *In His Own Write* with a literary luncheon by the London bookstore Foyles on the occasion of Shakespeare's fourth centenary. The *Times Literary Supplement* found in Lennon's prose traces of "Klee, Thurber, the Goons . . . and very noticeably, late Joyce." "Lennon," said *Time* magazine, "has rolled Edward Lear, Lewis Carroll and James Thurber into one great post-Joycean spitball." This was certainly news to Lennon, who claimed never to have read Joyce. Spike Milligan, leader of the Goons, was probably closer to the mark as regards Lennon's comic inspiration; although in time Lennon would come to describe his books as Joycean. Not all the reviews of

Lennon's prose were favorable, however: *A Spaniard in the Works* fared the worst. "The endless half puns," declared *New Statesman,* "are about as funny as a nervous tic." Critic Hilary Corke for *The Listener* wrote, "John Lennon's trademark . . . is the thoroughly childish trick of misspelling common phrases to give them new meanings. Five times out of six he misses." Lennon's forays into writing also provoked much confusion and misunderstanding, especially on the conservative side of the political spectrum. Upon reading *In His Own Write,* one British member of Parliament declared Lennon "in a pathetic state of near illiteracy." Describing him as evidence of the failing state of education, this conservative politician felt that Lennon "had picked up pieces of Tennyson, Browning, and Robert Louis Stevenson while listening with one ear to the football results on the wireless."[37]

The intimations of Joyce which literati on both sides of the Atlantic saw in these stories and poems bracketed, in effect, a more sustained and serious consideration of Lennon's literary contribution. *In His Own Write* and *A Spaniard in the Works* were received, first and foremost, as books by a Beatle. They were art created, so the critics thought, for mass culture. "John Lennon's real test," wrote Tom Wolfe, "will come when he turns loose his wild inventiveness and bitter slant upon a heavier literary form."[38] Eventually, after the pandemonium of Beatlemania had subsided, Lennon did give full rein to his wild inventiveness—although, by then, his focus had switched from literary to social and political issues.

But what did Lennon's literary interest signify? How did it connect to his questioning self? Throughout the years of Beatlemania, there were signs that Lennon was becoming increasingly taxed, personally and professionally. The frenetic schedule was never ending: there were recording sessions, world concert tours, media commitments, songwriting deadlines. Lennon's writing, often done in dressing rooms or hotel rooms, permitted him a space for reflective thinking when the sounds of the screaming fans had died down. In this sense, his literary endeavors transported him to a world beyond The Beatles, to a world of new ideas, to the splendor of language. In another sense, Lennon's compulsive need to create reflected the emotional imprint of his past, his inner relationship to his mother and his denial of lost love. His enthusiasm for endless activity, coupled with his intense fascination with new experience, might be viewed as a last-ditch attempt to maintain a melancholic identification with his dead mother. As he disengaged from The Beatles, Lennon broke from this self-imposed limitation.

THE 1960s WITNESSED immense personal, cultural, and political changes throughout Western society. Against the dull conformity of the 1950s—which saw the rise of technological expertise in mass production, as well as the rise of mass consumerism and mass culture —the 1960s saw the radical democratization of society and everyday cultural life. One way of understanding such restructuring is in terms of the advent of market domination over culture itself. Modernization and the rise of mass consumerism during this period were widely accused of generating cultural conformity, a new sort of resigned, insipid, middlebrow social consensus. These accusations reached their peak in Herbert Marcuse's biting critique of the emergent "one-dimensional man."[39] The market, according to this view, ruled supreme, not only at the economic level but also within cultural affairs. The acceleration of mass consumption brought about a profound respacing of the links between personal life and cultural life, as the sediment of socialization and tradition began to lose its solidity. Shifting personal, aesthetic, and moral boundaries in society at large were of core importance as the world of social hierarchy and tradition gave way to the flux of identity construction and private insecurity.

The Beatles provoked just such a seismic transformation in the cultural consciousness of the world through the medium of popular music. Against the backdrop of vast economic transformations throughout the world, The Beatles evolved into cultural radicals at a time when society was becoming increasingly wrapped around identity conflicts rather than around orthodox boundaries such as tradition, status, and class. The pressure to discover and create an identity went hand in hand with scientific and technological advances—such as television, the pill, and psychedelic drugs—that promised to liberate human potentials and desires. The Beatles were of their time in capturing the exhilaration, yet also the sense of danger, of transgressing cultural boundaries.

Two of Lennon's most celebrated Beatles songs, "Strawberry Fields Forever" and "I Am the Walrus," highlight this crisscrossing of personal and cultural contexts in the fabrication of identity. These songs, in differing ways, explore the personal dimensions of cultural dislocation.

"Strawberry Fields Forever" was one of the first songs John Lennon wrote after The Beatles retired from touring. It was written in the autumn of 1966 in southern Spain while Lennon was at work on Richard Lester's film *How I Won the War.* Lennon said that the song came to him in fits and starts while he was waiting around the film set. Yet the song's images and associations are drawn primarily from his childhood. As Lennon explained:

I took the name as an image. . . . It's a Salvation Army home that was near the house I lived in with my auntie in the suburbs. One was owned by Gladstone, which was a reformatory for boys, which I could see out my window. And Strawberry Fields was just around the corner from that. It was an old Victorian house converted for Salvation Army orphans, and as a kid I used to go to their garden parties with my friends Ivan, Nigel, and Pete. We'd all go up there and hang out and sell lemonade bottles for a penny and we always had fun at Strawberry Fields.[40]

These comments suggest the profound interconnections between selfhood, memory, and the poetic language of music. Reconstructing "Strawberry Fields Forever" in this context, I argue that by turning to pleasurable childhood memories Lennon displaced the acute sense of loss he felt when The Beatles retired from touring.[41] Fantasy compensates for loss: "we always had fun at Strawberry Fields." But things are not so clear-cut. Strawberry Fields was an orphanage, a home run by the Salvation Army. Thus, while Lennon may have had happy memories of parties held at Strawberry Fields, the fact that it was an orphanage must surely have triggered feelings about his own missing parents. In turning to Strawberry Fields for musical inspiration, Lennon created from something at once alluring and unsettling.

Lennon's ambivalence about Strawberry Fields is reflected in the sounds and styles that The Beatles used to create the song. Extending the group's traditional instrumentation of guitars, bass, and drums, Lennon added the lilting sounds of a mellotron (an electronic instrument that produces semiorchestral resonances), cymbals recorded backwards, and orchestral instruments such as trumpets and cellos. The song's introductory mellotron creates a dreamy sense of sorrow, from which Lennon sings the opening words: "Let me take you down / Cause I'm going to Strawberry Fields." In his insightful musical history, *The Beatles,* Allan Kozinn notes that the recording sessions for "Strawberry Fields Forever" stretched over five weeks.[42] When compared to the fast recording of their earlier works, the lengthy recording process for "Strawberry Fields Forever" indicates the importance of the song to Lennon as well as to the rest of the band.

Kozinn traces the song from Lennon's earliest demo tapes recorded in
Spain, on which the only finished line was "That is you can't, you
know, tune in," through to the three different versions of the song that
The Beatles recorded at Abbey Road Studios. These different recordings, ranging from semiacoustic to electric to orchestral, were the result of Lennon's dissatisfaction with the finished sound. Indeed, the
final version of the song was actually a composite of the last two versions, edited together by producer George Martin.[43]

The question of identity is crucial to "Strawberry Fields Forever."
Ian MacDonald calls the song "a study in uncertain identity." Mark
Hertsgaard writes, "Perhaps the most striking aspect . . . of 'Strawberry Fields Forever' is how precise and articulate Lennon is about
his uncertainty and confusion."[44] These comments should not be
taken to imply that Lennon gives priority to inner experience over the
social world. On the contrary, as we shall see, Lennon's "Strawberry
Fields Forever" problematizes the link, or crisscrossing, between our
inner and outer worlds and in so doing reimagines the relations between selfhood, culture, and contemporary political life.

In the opening verse of the song, Lennon tackles head-on the personal and political implications of cultural conformity.

Living is easy with eyes closed
Misunderstanding all you see
It's getting hard to be someone
But it all works out
It doesn't matter much to me.

Lennon's point, it seems, is that to rely on traditional social anchors
for a sense of identity is equivalent to having one's "eyes closed" and
"misunderstanding" that contemporary culture is ideological through
and through. In a constantly moving social world, self-identity becomes fragmented; being someone of substance and integrity becomes increasingly difficult. Perhaps with reference to the popular-
culture explosion of the 1960s, Lennon makes the point that selfhood
is developed through the articulation of personal struggles and interpersonal differences—differences which constitute our human values
and structure our immersion in the broader cultural arena.

More complex, and more troubling, is the issue of self-actualization:
how do we create and live a meaningful life in a culture of dislocation, a culture in which identity problems can be avoided through an

immersion in tradition, ideology, fundamentalism? It is perhaps not too fanciful to speculate that Lennon is casting a look over his shoulder, back to his (scandalous) remark that The Beatles were more popular than Jesus. The comment, made to English journalist Maureen Cleave in 1966, caused a furor in the Bible Belt of the United States, where Lennon was quickly transformed into a hate figure. On the advice of manager Brian Epstein, and in the interests of band harmony for an upcoming American tour, Lennon offered a public apology in an attempt to quell the commotion. Yet residues of this crisis are discernible in "Strawberry Fields Forever." As the line "It's getting hard to be someone" indicates, Lennon finds in the public turmoil provoked by his Jesus remark a powerful counterpressure to the 1960s cultural stress on identity creation. For if the time of cultural modernism seems fantastically speeded up in terms of defining the self anew, much as in a dream or hallucination, then the counterpressure to such modernist consciousness is the desire for conventional social obedience, expressed in the demand for the self to remain fixed, ordered, and unchanging. Alongside the modernist consciousness in which Lennon drifts, then, a traditionalist regulation of identity runs parallel, operationalized in religion and political ideology. The central point, perhaps, is that both worldviews are central features of contemporary culture. In this context, Lennon's "Strawberry Fields Forever" attempts to spell out the nature of the double bind facing identity construction in the late modern age.

In the second verse, Lennon again identifies cultural pressures as spilling over into personal identity. He does so by drawing attention to the manner in which individualization is experienced as dangerous and threatening in cultural life.

No one I think is in my tree
I mean it must be high or low
That is you can't, you know, tune in
But it's all right
That is I think it's not too bad.

Lennon, in his typically idiosyncratic terms, speaks of the price of individuality as isolation ("No one I think is in my tree"). To define oneself as an individual is, it seems, to experience a deficit in social relatedness ("That is you can't, you know, tune in"). It is identity itself that Lennon seeks to bring low here by focusing upon the experience of uncertainty and specifically on the way in which a sense of personal uncertainty clashes with cultural demands for certitude. There is an implication that identity is actually at one with the demands of culture, that identity bridges the socially acceptable or the stereotype across to the personal domain. European sociologist Zygmunt Bauman expresses this link between identity and culture in *Life in Fragments:*

One thinks of identity whenever one is not sure of where one belongs, that is, one is not sure how to place oneself among the evident variety of behavioural styles and patterns, and how to make sure that people around would accept this placement as right and proper, so that both sides would know how to go on in each other's presence. *"Identity" is a name given to the sought escape from that uncertainty.*[45]

In this context, what matters to Lennon is stripping identity of its cultural fictions and reflecting upon the self free from the distorting influence of ideology.

The result is an antagonistic relation to other people, evaluated in terms of a high/low dichotomy. As Lennon reflected on "Strawberry Fields Forever" in 1980, "The second line goes, 'No one I think is in my tree.' Well, what I was trying to say in that line is 'Nobody seems to be as hip as me, therefore I must be crazy or a genius.' It's that same problem I had when I was five: 'There is something wrong with me because I seem to see things other people don't see. Am I crazy, or am I a genius?'"[46] Individuality here is both affliction and blessing, both madness and genius.

Perhaps it is this duality that brings Lennon back in the final verse to ambivalence itself: the ambivalence not only of identity but of naming or identifying one's own uncertainty.

Always, no, sometimes think it's me
But, you know, I know when it's a dream
I think, I know, I mean, er yes
But it's all wrong
That is, I think I disagree.

Again identity is central here, but this time it is a more subjective sense of identity, the general features of which are sharply contrasted to the realm of illusion ("I know when it's a dream"). Lennon's very uncertainty, his narrational startings and stoppings ("I think, I know, I mean"), underscores the dissonant and conflictive configuring of the mind in its striving for conscious awareness. It is as if Lennon is seeking to press thinking beyond the unthinkable, to turn the logics of mind back against itself, relentlessly negotiating with those internal constraints which shape the contours of poetic writing itself. In this verse, Lennon draws out the agonizing dimension of ambivalence and in the process constructs an image of self and world which is constantly on the brink of dismantling itself.

"Strawberry Fields Forever"—in its maneuverings through ambivalence, its linguistic uncertainty, its spectacular musical inventiveness—finds Lennon not only questioning a rigidly rationalistic world of social values but also trading with uncertainty, fear, and melancholy. In this trade, Lennon attempts to press through personal and cultural constraints in the hope of discovering a liberated world of color, vibrancy, and authenticity. But this breakthrough to a utopian world, while drawing inspiration from the generational revolts of the 1960s and the decade's drug culture, has strong affinities with the delights and dangers of childhood. Both "Strawberry Fields Forever" and Paul McCartney's "Penny Lane" were explicitly written as childhood explorations; they recollect people and places in Liverpool. But for all McCartney's carefully calculated optimism, "Penny Lane" is plainly nostalgic and sometimes regressive, hankering as it does after some mythical, golden age in which happiness reigned supreme. In "Strawberry Fields Forever," by contrast, Lennon returns to an object of childhood delight and fascination. Yet the imaginary bond between childhood and happiness has been ruptured in Lennon's reckoning; part of the critical, poetical task is to uncover the repressions and evasions which structure relations between self and society, and which function to idealize childhood. To take such a viewpoint is not to overlook the aesthetic pleasures of childhood. For Lennon, childhood and the aesthetic are intimately interwoven. Indeed much of "Strawberry Fields Forever" is precisely an attempt to grapple with the certainties of traditional logic from the uncertain vantage point of childhood itself. Here, against the path of repressive reason, Lennon draws from childhood experience to imagine a different way of living, or at least to minimize the burdens and oppressions of daily life:

Strawberry Fields
Nothing is real
And nothing to get hung about
Strawberry Fields Forever.

Lennon turns to memory, fantasy, and imagination in order to give the slip to stereotyped cultural forms.

If "Strawberry Fields Forever" turns from the degrading logic of cultural conformism to the possibility of life lived otherwise, then "I Am the Walrus" is a full-blooded interrogation of the fetishism of social norms, an interrogation in which demystification, far from arising from the radical otherness of childhood memories, is seen as interwoven with the dismantling of meaning itself. Usually regarded as a drug-induced rant of gobbledygook, "I Am the Walrus" is instead Lennon's celebration of the reificatory power of repetition in contemporary political life, a celebration that parodies ideology in its colonizing of the mind, pushes a multiplicity of dialects to their limit, and manages somehow along the way to project the character of the walrus into an emancipatory space beyond our present-day irrationalism.

Lennon's "Walrus" was, by his own reckoning, stolen from Lewis Carroll's anticapitalist poem "The Walrus and the Carpenter." (Lennon acknowledged that he had not realized when he wrote the song that the walrus was, in fact, "the bad guy"; and indeed his failure to realize this adds a novel twist to his claim that "the walrus was Paul" in "Glass Onion.") Beginning with the self-contradictory status of identity, Lennon reclaims all that is ruthlessly excluded in the framing of the self, namely, the otherness of other people: "I am he as you are he / As you are me and we are all together." Lennon here, in a gesture reminiscent of Frankfurt School philosopher Theodor Adorno, is out to recover that which is nonidentical in order to transform the monotonous principle of identity itself. As if to underscore our cultural evasion of the ambiguities of the self/other division, Lennon begins "I Am the Walrus" with a repetitive two-chord sequence, the idea for which arose from the siren of a passing police car outside of his Weybridge home.

Against this droning repetition, Lennon targets a range of stereotypes in attacking conventional morality. He does so in an exquisite, bizarre wordplay, exposing the mores of society as illusions or deceptions fueled by unconscious imagination but not recognized as such. Unmasking the unconscious determinants of everyday life, Lennon blasts a set of obsolescent norms, myths, and ideals, ranging from the dulled sensibility caused by organizational life ("Corporation teashirt, stupid bloody Tuesday man you been a naughty boy / You let your face grow long") to the pervasive links between social control and order

("Mr. City policeman sitting pretty little policeman in a row / See how they fly like Lucy in the sky—see how they run"). At this level, Lennon's "Walrus" is an abstruse satire of conventional social life and the genuinely obnoxious aspects of rationality. More pointedly, the song is an often sharp critique of expert knowledge, the clichés of education, and the emptiness of bourgeois culture. The contemporary fascination with "experts" is turned back upon itself with a vengeance by Lennon. He suggests that our cultural attempts at self-mastery might be better regarded as somehow throttling society itself: "Expert texpert choking smokers don't you think the joker laughs at you? Ha ha ha!" He also takes aim at the masculinist double standard, in particular, the masculinist fantasy of a woman thoroughly done over and enjoying it (the pornographic scenario par excellence) on the one hand and the construction of a woman who enjoys sex as fallen or disgraced on the other: "Crabalocker fishwife pornographic priestess / Boy you been a naughty girl, you let your knickers down."

At another level, one perhaps more marked by radical imagination, Lennon attempts to put the skids on signification itself. To say this is to argue that Lennon's "Walrus" forges an ambiguous relationship to meaning: it not only disavows social reality but also attempts to displace our relationship to the sense-making process as well. Influenced by dada and surrealist art, aesthetic currents in which received social meanings are displaced in favor of randomness and chance, Lennon brings an eclectic blend of images to his writing ("Semolina pilchard climbing up the Eiffel Tower"). This kind of eclecticism, which might be described as profoundly meaningful and meaningless at once, outstrips language. The very texture of signification is ruthlessly undone by the movement of metonymy and the simulacrum of representation. "I Am the Walrus" leads from the domain of satire to the flux of difference. The result is a free flowing language which perpetually fails, lapses, expires. The elaborate syntax of "Walrus," which makes different representations and different social locations mutually implicating, ultimately gives way to the rhythms of the signifying process itself:

I am the eggman, they are the eggmen
I am the walrus
GOO GOO GOO JOOB GOO GOO GOO JOOB GOO GOO GOO JOOB
GOOGOOGOOOOOOOOOOOOOOJOOOOOB.

One common explanation for Lennon's prose in "Walrus" was that it was a playful act of revenge upon his former school in Liverpool, Quarry Bank. According to Lennon's close friend Pete Shotton, a student from the school had written to Lennon explaining that a Quarry Bank English teacher was analyzing Beatles' lyrics. Shotton recalls that Lennon, determined to undercut the teacher's instruction in rational interpretation, began experimenting with an old school rhyme: "Yellow matter custard, green slop pie / All mixed together with a dead dog's eye."[47] He incorporated this rhyme into "Walrus" as "Yellow matter custard dripping from a dead dog's eye." Similarly, he drew from some of the more obvious artistic figures of modernism as a means of furthering this linguistic obliqueness and evasion. In the surrealist writings of Edgar Allen Poe, for instance, Lennon finds a limit to what society can accept of itself ("You should have seen them kicking / Edgar Allen POE"). So too, he takes a shot at American poet Allen Ginsberg, who had taken to chanting Hare Krishna mantras at public events: "Elementary penguin singing Hare Krishna."[48]

Irony, paradox, randomness, metonymy: these are the stylistic devices with which Lennon's "Walrus" explores the changing relations between self and society and, ultimately, the limits of signification itself.

LENNON'S DIFFICULTY acknowledging feelings of loss was an underlying driving force in his personal life and artistic endeavors. He was in equal measure emotionally frustrated and challenged by loss. In an artistic sense, Lennon's attempt to come to grips with loss provided the impetus for some of his most creative and reflective work. Certainly, *John Lennon/Plastic Ono Band* represents a major breakthrough for autobiographical work: the album shows, in a powerfully emotional way, that there can be no genuine self-understanding without mourning, no personal growth without grief, no lasting change without the hard work of dealing with ambivalence.

But Lennon's dealings with loss may be read not only in terms of its impact upon his personal life but also in the way his dealings reflect broader cultural problematics concerning the very negotiation of love and loss. His preoccupation with loss and its difficulty, I have suggested, challenges dominant cultural conceptions in which loss is subjugated to self-mastery. That Lennon himself was aware of the extent to which loss and pain permeated his life is evident from such mournful songs as "Mother," "Julia," and "My Mummy's Dead." But I have suggested that Lennon's preoccupation with mourning is also implicit in songs such as "Strawberry Fields Forever" and "I Am the Walrus." Indeed, these songs make the ambivalence of loss central not only to private life but also to culture at large. Private hopes and dreads feed into, and react against, our cultural heritage. The loss of cultural ideals—whether expressed as mourning for the fading of rationality, certitude, or self-transparency—influences (and is influenced by) personal grief. In psychoanalytic terms, this can be described as a sort of short-circuiting of mourning, a fracturing which fuels melancholy. Here the ability to mourn is dislocated by an identification with lost love, an identification which underpins melancholia. Lennon challenges this crossover from mourning to melancholia: he shows, in songs like "Mother" and "Strawberry Fields Forever," that the work of mourning is never complete.

3

Love

The Bonds of Intimacy

Love is wanting to be loved.

John Lennon

Love is the time and space in which "I" assumes the right
to be extraordinary.

Julia Kristeva

Poised on the dividing line between romanticism and realism, John
Lennon's relationship with Yoko Ono was extraordinary by any reckoning. It was extraordinary in part for its intensity and in part for its
longevity. In the early years, in the lead-up to the split of The Beatles,
Lennon and Ono were rarely apart. She shared his artistic tastes and
values, not to mention his sense of humor. She also shared his desire
to shock, to transgress artistic and political boundaries. Lennon had
finally found a woman that he needed and desired, a relationship to
replace the increasingly forced union of the Fab Four. As a couple,
Lennon and Ono chose—for a time—to live a life of professional
celebrity. Yet they were also self-absorbed—as lovers, as artists, as political radicals. More than any other famous couple in this century,
they invite us to consider the ambiguous relation between love and
society, desire and culture.

Lennon and Ono forged a relationship that stands out for its constant inventiveness. A series of well-publicized artistic events—the
acorn events, the bag events, the bed-ins—advanced the couple's
fame and notoriety to levels unheard-of in popular culture. Their
public image was one of togetherness. They lived together, worked together, and attempted to bring artistry to all aspects of their lives. In a
1970 interview with *Rolling Stone,* Lennon was asked about the couple's public image:

Why can't you be alone without Yoko?
I can be, but I don't wish to be. There is no reason on earth why I
should be without her. There is nothing more important than our relationship, nothing. And we dig being together all the time. And
both of us could survive apart, but for what? I'm not going to sacri-
fice love, real love . . . because in the end you're alone at night.[1]

Lennon's response to the interviewer's question is to insist that there
is no ambiguity concerning his private and public commitments: love
has the upper hand. He desires the love of Ono more than he wants
the love of the public. She is central to his life, to his art, indeed to the
life of his art. So why does Lennon see the other side of this love as
raising the specter of survival? Why such an extreme opposition?

   The answer seems to lie, in part, in the intensity of his passion for
Ono. Nowhere is this passion better captured than in Lennon's music.
"I'm in love for the first time / Don't you know it's gonna last," Lennon
sings in "Don't Let Me Down," an early love song to his muse. Performed at the infamous rooftop concert in 1969 that concludes the
film *Let It Be*, the song finds Lennon shifting between joyous elation
("Nobody ever loved me like she does") and concentrated anxiety
("Don't let me down"). Love songs also dominate his early solo work,
such as "Love," "Oh My Love," and "Oh Yoko!" A decade later, in his
spirited "Dear Yoko," Lennon still declares the urgency of his love.
Denied her presence, even for an hour, he claims to "wilt just like a
faded flower." For many critics, the line revealed Lennon as overly
dependent and needy; indeed, some argued that it showed he lacked
the autonomy that mature love demands. Lennon, by contrast, was
not afraid to admit his anxieties about the relationship. "I hope I die
before Yoko," he commented, "because if Yoko died I wouldn't know
how to survive."[2]

   By 1980, the great romance had been transformed into a great
marriage. It became a great marriage, in Lennon's view, because of his
determination to make their love central in spite of numerous setbacks and difficulties. His commitment to their love led him to withdraw from public life for a time in order to forge a new kind of intimacy with his family (see chapter 5). But after five years of public
withdrawal, the importance of his relationship with Ono went deeper
than this. Ono, Lennon told David Sheff in *Playboy*, "saved my life."[3]

Again, the alarming theme of survival. Lennon, it seems, needed
Ono's emotional support in to order to rediscover himself. He explained that they shared a "teacher-pupil relationship. That's what
people don't understand. She's the teacher and I'm the pupil. I'm the
famous one, the one who's supposed to know everything, but she's my
teacher. She taught me everything I fucking know. She was there
when I was nowhere, when I was the *nowhere man*."[4]

Few biographers have shown any desire to understand what Lennon is getting at here, preferring instead to track back over his more
macho, rock 'n' roll image as the ex-Beatle, no doubt because Lennon's description of his relationship with Ono is problematic, to say
the least. Why, for instance, does Lennon declare himself Ono's pupil?
Why does he describe himself as intellectually subordinate to her?
And why does he construct the other side of such self-knowledge as
being "nowhere"? My view is that Lennon, in seeing Ono as his superior, could narrate his life as a *recovery from loss.* The connection between self-knowledge and loss here is crucial: it is above all because
Lennon desires Ono as an ideal that he is able, paradoxically, to know
something about the depth of his emotional struggles and personal insecurities. It is as if in saying she "saved my life," Lennon is able to
make emotional contact with his deeper fears and anxieties—the hurt
of loss, emotional confusion, fear of the future.

There is, however, another sense in which the construction of this
teacher-pupil relationship is essential to the making of John Lennon.
This sense concerns Lennon's exploration of fantasy and sexuality and,
in particular, the fraught terrain of sexual difference. The crucial indication of the importance of these differences comes from Yoko Ono,
in a statement that immediately followed Lennon's reflections on
their teacher-pupil relationship.

Maybe it's that I have strength, a feminine strength. Because women develop it. In a relationship I think women really have the inner wisdom and
they're carrying that, while men have sort of the wisdom to cope with society,
since they created it. Men never developed the inner wisdom; they didn't
have time. So most men do rely on women's inner wisdom, whether they express that or not. I think John is simply expressing that. Even to say it shows
he understands.[5]

Ono strikingly prefigures some important thematics which preoccupy
feminist debate today—specifically, the relationship between identity

and sexual difference. The gender divide is at the root of the construction of identity: men have the "wisdom to cope with society," while women develop an "inner wisdom." Gender cannot be reduced to socialization, though; there is considerable space granted for gender fluidity in Ono's reckoning. The same might be said of her relationship with Lennon. Here as in so many other contexts it is as if Lennon and Ono's relationship contained a space for exploration of their changing consciousness of identity, sexuality, and gender.

ON 9 NOVEMBER 1966, John Lennon met Yoko Ono for the first time, at a preview of her exhibition "Unfinished Paintings and Objects by Yoko Ono" at the Indica Gallery in London. He was then twenty-six and she thirty-three. One of the most mythologized events of Lennon's life, the Indica meeting has been retold countless times as a tale of romanticism, a meeting of minds. To be sure, Lennon spoke of the Indica meeting in dozens of interviews, usually with a practiced sub-Freudian stress on the interplay of desire and imagination. He had been invited to view the exhibition, he said, by John Dunbar (the owner of the gallery) and had arrived at the gallery at about 10:00 P.M. in his chauffeur-driven Mini. He recalled meeting Ono in the following way:

I saw this ladder on a painting leading up to the ceiling where there was a spyglass hanging down. It's what made me stay. I went up the ladder and I got the spyglass and there was tiny little writing there. . . . You're on this ladder—you feel like a fool—you could fall any minute—and you look through and it just said "YES."

Well, all the so-called avant-garde at the time and everything that was supposedly interesting was all negative, this smash-the-piano-with-a-hammer, break-the-sculpture, boring, negative crap. It was all anti-, anti-, anti-. Anti-art, anti-establishment. And just that "YES" made me stay in a gallery full of apples and nails instead of just walking out saying, "I'm not gonna buy any of this crap."

Then I went up to this thing that said, "Hammer a nail in." I said, "Can I hammer a nail in?" and she said no, because the gallery was actually opening the next day. So the owner, Dunbar, says, "Let him hammer a nail in." It was "He's a millionaire. He might buy it," you know. She's more interested in it looking nice and pretty and white for the opening. . . .

So there was this little conference and she finally said, "Okay, you can hammer a nail in for five shillings." So smart-ass here says "Well, I'll give you an imaginary five shillings and hammer an imaginary nail in." And that's when we really *met*. That's when we locked eyes and she got it and I got it and that was it. The rest, as they say in all the interviews we do, is history.[6]

We will see that imagination—the imaginary shaping of memory, the self-construction of remembered events—is at the heart of Lennon's account of the Indica meeting. It is important at this point to note, however, the very different interpretations of what actually took place at the Indica Gallery in the biographical literature on Lennon.

Ray Coleman describes the Indica meeting as a turning point in Lennon's life. According to Coleman, Yoko Ono had "a profound, devastating effect" upon Lennon, partly the result of sexual attraction and partly the consequence of Lennon's looking for a new emotional force in his life.[7] Albert Goldman, by contrast, describes the Indica encounter, rather tediously, as a female trap from which Lennon would never escape. "Yoko," says Goldman, "was laying for him."[8] These interpretations turn on crucially distinct conceptions of the role of human imagination. In Coleman's construction, imagination functions as a kind of aesthetic epiphany; Lennon's encounter with Ono is saturated with playful pleasures and is viewed as escape from the troubles of the outside world. Perhaps this view is why Coleman brings his discussion of the Indica meeting to a close by reminding the reader that Lennon was a married man and Ono a married woman; the outside world is thus cast as "brake" or "limit" to the nourishing space of imagination. In Goldman's construction, imagination functions purely defensively; it filters out the more painful aspects of reality and thereby creates distortions and illusions. Goldman views Lennon's account of the Indica meeting as a radical rewriting of his past, a rewriting that erases the point that the evening in question was when Lennon first came under Ono's hypnotic spell.

Certainly, imagination is at the very heart of constructions of the Indica meeting. If imagination happens to be at loggerheads with a clear-cut, innocuous view of the event, however, this conflict is surely what Lennon is trying to underscore. Consider the sexual metaphors with which Lennon situates himself in relation to Ono. He follows the artist's prompting and climbs the ladder in order to "see," thus at one stroke aligning himself with a phallocentric culture that insists on visual purism and objectivity. Vision, it seems, has a masculinist history. Yet Lennon's climbing of the ladder is disrupted with an aside, "you feel like a fool"; the primacy of vision in Western culture is brought

low by feelings of discomfort. Here it is possible to detect an infer-
ence to the alleged nobility of the eye as a masculinist heritage gone
sour. But for all the escalating anticipation, the answer at the top of
the ladder—"YES"—is in fact another question: can we seek affirmation without doctrine, without some final truth, without revelation?
Ono's "YES" can be said to signal not only an underwriting of unde-
cidability as such but a profound sexualization of time and of space
("just that 'YES' made me stay in a gallery full of apples and nails").

In the final paragraph of Lennon's narration of their meeting, he
describes a shift from anticipation and longing to sexual desire itself;
he thus draws attention to the precariousness of male sexual identity
in the face of feminine defiance—women's reluctance to be put into
that position in which they take up, and act out, men's sexual fantasies.
Indeed, from one angle, this is precisely what Lennon is driving at:
the war of sexual fantasy. As Ono said of their Indica meeting: "It's so
symbolic you see; the virginal board, for a man to hammer a nail in."[9]
The hammering in of a nail is a phallocentric fantasy incarnate, a fantasy which takes femininity as the ultimate object of male sexual pleasure. Thus, when the woman refuses the man's demand, he is returned to the ambiguity of sexual difference; he is left to ponder
desire and its difficulty. All of this carefully narrated sexual drama is,
it seems, a necessary precondition for the self's consciousness of the
power of imagination —an underlining of, and disruption to, the construction of sexual boundaries. The woman, recognizing the phallocentric social contract, agrees to being "nailed" in exchange for financial payment. Lennon, however, is led by the power of his own
imagination to a different scenario: "I'll give you an imaginary five
shillings and hammer an imaginary nail in." This new scenario is still,
of course, structured upon unequal gender relations (the man pays
the woman), but the debt has now been lifted into the realm of imagining, desire, fantasy. Lennon's enthusiasm for this aspect of the story
becomes evident in that he finally introduces intimacy ("That's when
we locked eyes and she got it and I got it").

From this perspective, to criticize Lennon for idealizing or rewriting the Indica meeting is surely to miss the point. If the foundation of
all intimate relationships is fictional or contingent, then it is only in
the creative remembering (read construction) of the past that the
imaginary dimensions of human experience can be acknowledged;
this creative remembering allows more space for imagination and for

change to be made. All of which is to say that Lennon's underwriting of the powers of imagination is a rhetorical strike at conventional distinctions between fact and fiction, between truth and deception. For Lennon, what is involved in the imaginative construction of intimacy, love, and eroticism is a coupling of desire and rationality, passion and law, but always in a fraught, contradictory, and ambivalent coalition. Love sustains and nourishes the self and ushers in the freedom to play and dream. Yet love can also grow defensive; it can be used to keep at bay painful or distressing feelings.

Lennon was to acknowledge the purely creative aspects of dreaming in his magisterial "Imagine" in 1971. Utopia can become reality, according to Lennon, only if we first dream it for ourselves. Like the dream, society or culture is a mixed collection of the present and the past, of internal and external promptings. If Lennon proclaims the healing dimension of imagination, he does so because for him, as for Sigmund Freud and Herbert Marcuse, imagination is implicated in lost loves, unrealized ambitions, and repressed desires. "Imagination," wrote Marcuse, "envisions the reconciliation of the individual with the whole, of desire with realization, of happiness with reason."[10] "Imagine all the people," Lennon wrote in his classic song, "living life in peace."

YOKO ONO ARRIVED IN LONDON in October 1966, a month before meeting Lennon at the Indica Gallery. She had decided on London rather than New York, where she had lived for some years, on the basis of an invitation to participate in an avant-garde symposium, "Destruction in Art."[11] She came with her second husband, artist Tony Cox, and their daughter, Kyoko. Almost penniless, yet hungry for artistic recognition and success, Ono and Cox devoted themselves to their artistic work. At the symposium, Ono performed, among other things, "Cut Piece," a work she had performed at Carnegie Recital Hall in New York. "Cut Piece" required members of the audience to come forth and cut away pieces of Ono's clothing. Some good press reviews followed. A critic for the *Financial Times* wrote: "It was impossible to disentangle the compulsion of the audience to cut and Yoko Ono's compulsion to be cut."[12] Such favorable press landed Ono the opportunity to exhibit at the Indica Gallery. After the Indica exhibition, she and her husband

commenced work on *Bottoms,* a film which showed the naked buttocks of 365 people. *Bottoms* caused something of a scandal when it
was premiered in London in 1967, and it helped to establish Ono's
name in the popular press.[13]

Born on 18 February 1933 and six years older than Lennon, Ono
was the daughter of a prominent Tokyo banking family of great wealth
and power. She was a lonely child, emotionally distant from both her
aristocratic mother and her absent father. The Onos lived for a time in
San Francisco and New York before the Second World War. After the
war began, they returned to Japan. The American bombing of Tokyo
during the war led the family to escape to a farming village south of
Karuizawa, where they lived in poverty—compared to the material
splendors they had known in Tokyo—trading valuable possessions for
food in order to survive. The end of the war brought with it, in time,
a reinstatement of the family's social position; Ono's father joined the
Bank of Tokyo and was subsequently transferred to its New York office. The family thus moved back to the United States. Ono attended
Harvard University's summer school and gained entry into Sarah
Lawrence College, where she studied for three years as a philosophy
major. But she was bored with the routine of college and eventually
dropped out. She had fallen in love with a young musician from Japan,
Toshi Ichiyanagi, a student at the prestigious Julliard conservatory.
Ono's family did not approve of the penniless Ichiyanagi. When Ono
married him, her family effectively disowned her.

Ono found herself drawn to the world of art. Ichiyanagi encouraged her to try her hand at avant-garde music. In the summer of 1958,
they enrolled in a class on the composition of experimental music at
the New School for Social Research in New York, taught by John
Cage—with whom Ono would later perform.[14] At the same time, she
began painting, experimenting with minimalism and concept art; she
also became involved with Fluxus, a group of avant-garde artists.
After Ono and Ichiyanagi separated in 1961, she pressed ahead,
doggedly, with her artistic efforts. In 1964, she published a limited
edition of "instructional poems" entitled *Grapefruit.* The poems contained instructions such as "Stir inside of your brains with a penis until
things are mixed well"; "Smoke everything you can, including your
pubic hair"; and "Kill all the men you have slept with. Put the bones
in a box and send it out into the sea in a box with flowers." (John

Lennon felt ambivalent about Ono's *Grapefruit,* a copy of which she sent him after their Indica meeting. He said that the book annoyed him at first; in time, he found it highly amusing.)

After Indica, Lennon and Ono met again at a Claus Oldenburg exhibition. Yet for two years their relationship remained one of intellectual exchange. They would sometimes talk on the telephone; he agreed to finance her next art exhibition, "The Half Wind Show," made up of objects such as half a cup, half a chair, half a bed. Both were wary, though, of commencing a love affair; Lennon, especially, worried about his family. They soon discovered, however, that their artistic and intellectual discussions camouflaged erotic feelings. Lennon felt more and more drawn to Ono; the feelings engendered raised deep anxieties within him about both his professional and domestic life.

There was always ambivalence between Lennon and his fellow Beatles, however close they might be. He felt, at times, that the band had chained him to a lifestyle which seemed to be keeping him from achieving his personal goals. At the very time he was writing such classics as "A Day in the Life," "Lucy in the Sky with Diamonds," and "Being for the Benefit of Mr. Kite," he was tormented by the repetitiousness of his domestic life. The failure of his marriage to Cynthia Powell was especially painful: he was emotionally withdrawn from her yet still felt unable to break from her. Lennon reflected on his familial situation some years later in *Skywriting by Word of Mouth:* "Although I'd had numerous interesting 'affairs' in my previous incarnation, I'd never met anyone worth breaking up a happily-married state of boredom for."[15] He sought, instead, to find a way out through drugs. Drugs offered an escape to a world of dreaming, allowing him to reach unknown, mysterious regions of the mind. Emotionally, however, he had stalled. Caught between domestic boredom and psychedelic illusion, Lennon was stuck.

"I'd always had a fantasy," he wrote, "about a woman who would be a beautiful, intelligent, dark-haired, high-cheek-boned, free-spirited artist (à la Juliette Greco)." Yoko Ono, to Lennon's mind, fulfilled the fantasy. "Since I was extraordinarily shy," he continued, "my daydreams necessitated that she be aggressive enough to 'save me,' i.e., 'take me away from all this.' Yoko, although shy herself, picked up my spirits enough to give me the courage to get the hell out."[16] She offered him, in short, the opportunity to overcome his sense of personal and intellectual isolation. He could sympathize with her aesthetic philosophy, sensing that they were going in similar directions. Ono did not, however, turn Lennon from an introspective pop star into an avant-garde practitioner. He had always, from his days at the Liverpool Institute, been fascinated with exploring alternative forms of art. Ono did encourage and support the growing range of Lennon's artistic interests. "She gave him," said Paul McCartney, "the freedom to do all that stuff that he really wanted to do."[17]

In November 1968, Lennon and Ono released their first joint album, *Unfinished Music No. 1: Two Virgins.* The album comprised a series of recordings that the couple had made together at his home studio in Weybridge during the first night that they spent together. Lennon said: "It was midnight when we started *Two Virgins,* it was dawn when we finished, and then we made love at dawn. It was very beautiful." The first of several experimental albums, *Two Virgins* was also emphatically self-reflexive and thus, for its time, radical. Lennon insisted, "It was an awakening for me too. This is me with the woman I love."[18] The album cover of *Two Virgins* was regarded as scandalous, indeed offensive, by Lennon's record company and, in time, by many fans and critics also. Lennon and Ono appeared naked before the camera, their arms around each other; the back of the album also showed them naked, looking over their shoulders. EMI flatly refused to distribute it. Lennon and Ono would not consider an alternative cover and were thus forced to look for another distributor. In the United States, the confiscation of thirty thousand copies of *Two Virgins* by the police in New Jersey generated more publicity; and the album sold faster than copies could be pressed. For Lennon and Ono, however, the public reaction was disheartening: *Two Virgins,* sold over the counter in brown paper wrapping, was treated as pornographic.

Lennon responded with further revisions to his sense of identity. In 1969, he officially changed his name from John Winston Lennon to John Ono Lennon. The decision was, in part, motivated by a feminist commitment and sponsored by Ono. Patriarchy, she stressed, is experienced in and through language. Upon marriage, the woman adopts the man's surname in that act of political sovereignty dubbed the "Name of the Father" by French psychoanalyst Jacques Lacan. Ono, like many feminists, was profoundly troubled by such logic; her song, "Mrs. Lennon," was the first of many that grappled with how patriarchy refashions women's psychic reality. Lennon came to share Ono's feminist sentiments and hence decided to break the rules by adopting her name.

If he had good feminist reasons for changing his middle name, the impulse to do so arose, however, from a deeper emotional disposition. He had long disliked the name Winston;[19] he felt that it condensed the spirit of British nationalism after the politics of Churchill as well as that of empire in its peculiar colonizing character. From this angle, Lennon's decision to change his middle name was not simply the result of an abstract feminist commitment but rather the clash of personal experience, sexual ideology, and politics. If there is a transformation in Lennon's attitude toward gender here, it lies in his discovery of the intimate links between identity, sexuality, and politics, his realization that we are always in the process of defining our potentialities in terms of gender and experiencing the sexual world in all of its ambiguity before we come to think about it in more reflective terms.

These and other notions about his personal and artistic identity underpinned Lennon's pronouncements about sexuality and gender through the years, with many ideas from feminism capturing the foreground of his mind. In 1972, he asserted the global nature of sexual inequality in "Woman Is the Nigger of the World." The title, said Lennon, came from Ono—the coauthor of the song. She had made the statement that is the source of the title during an interview with the English fashion magazine *Nova* in 1969. But Lennon and Ono later divulged that the song was drawn from reflection upon their own relationship also. While committed to women's liberation, Lennon said he had come to realize the many ways in which he remained held in thrall to traditional gender roles. The gulf between his first and second marriages was vital to understanding his transformed gender consciousness. "When I met John," Ono commented, "he was a typical male chauvinist. . . . Women were kept in the background, serving tea, keeping out of the men's talk." As an example, Ono noted that her husband always expected to read the newspaper before she did in the mornings. Mocking himself, Lennon said in a strong Northern accent, "You'll not touch papers till Dad's read it."[20] With his typical humor, he was reflecting on the gender politics of their daily life. Some feminists attacked the song for its condescending portrayal of women as passive and weak, and the song was banned in several countries because of its use of the word "nigger." Significantly, though, Lennon was one of the first male rock stars to broach the issue of the oppression of women.[21]

Almost a decade after he wrote "Woman Is the Nigger of the World," the relation between the sexes still loomed large for Lennon. He witnessed the force of the women's movement in its transformation of gender relationships everywhere, from the culture of revolution to the rhetoric of backlash. He kept abreast of debates and deadlocks in feminist thinking; he read books such as Elizabeth Davis's *The First Sex*.[22] Nonetheless, his interest in feminist politics and theory is insufficient to account for his richly articulated range of views on sexuality and gender. Books were one thing, daily life was another. His experience of reversing gender roles, as he looked after his son Sean while Ono attended to their business affairs, transformed his commitment to, and hopes for, the feminist movement. Of being a househusband, he said it's "the wave of the future, and I'm glad to be in on the forefront of that too." The experience also inspired him to write music once again about his love for his wife, as well as about his feelings on woman as a sensual being more generally. In "Woman," Lennon declared his debt to all women—although he said he was thinking especially of his mother, his aunt Mimi, and his wife—for the emotional and spiritual support they offer men. The song also revealed that Lennon's attitudes toward women were part of larger cultural affinities, his commitment to autonomy and peace.

To UNDERSTAND THE RADICAL changes in Lennon's attitudes toward women, it is necessary to go back to his marriage to Cynthia Powell. It is also useful to consider biographical constructions about the assumed emotional dimensions of that marriage. In April 1963, Cynthia Powell gave birth to their son, Julian. Becoming a father, however, was not the only significant development at this point in Lennon's life. Lennon was not present at the birth because he was on tour. The same week, "Please Please Me" reached the number-one position on the British charts. Private and public life thus tangle, with the latter infiltrating and invading the former. Lennon was not to see his wife and child until the following week, after The Beatles had completed their touring commitments. His pleasure in seeing his son for the first time was short-lived: a crowd soon gathered outside the hospital, hoping to catch sight of Beatle John. Powell, in her book *A Twist of Lennon*, recalled her husband's visit to the hospital:

When he eventually plucked up enough courage to pick the little bundle up he was full of pride and emotion. "He's bloody marvellous, Cyn, isn't he absolutely fantastic . . . ? Who's going to be a famous little rocker like his Dad then?" Whilst this beautiful reunion was taking place, grinning faces were pressing themselves against the glass pane of the partition, groups of nurses and patients were gathering in the corridors, eager to gain a glimpse of a Liverpool celebrity. It started to get noisy, claustrophobic and very embarrassing, like being in a goldfish bowl. This incident was my first glimpse of how my life was to change drastically and it really unnerved me. Very quickly John became jumpy and on edge. He was beginning to feel trapped and it was time for him to escape.[23]

Delayed and fragmentary, Lennon's reunion with his family at the hospital was symptomatic of his private life at the time.

Lennon's punishing schedule during the turbulent years of Beatlemania raises the question of how he could find time for any private life with Powell at all. His devotion to work meant that for all practical purposes family life always came second. The exhausting demands of songwriting, recording, touring, interviews, and television and radio appearances, not to mention the books of poetry, consumed his mental energies. Lennon at this time lived his life as a celebrity. When every day is sixteen or eighteen hours of work, time off is for rest and sleep rather than for constructive family enjoyment. When not touring, he woke late in the afternoon and then often rested on his favorite couch for the remainder of the day—usually watching television with the sound off.[24] He saw nothing strange in his behavior, as he wrote in the autobiographical "I'm Only Sleeping." But he would return soon enough to the punishing schedule of Beatlemania, once more becoming busy in order to avoid the intimacy which his family life offered.

Indeed, Lennon's family life presented itself not as a source of emotional gain or support but as cause for anxious concern within the Beatles camp; female fans were besotted with the Liverpool gods, and reality demanded some minor refashioning in order for the Fab Four to appear sexually available, even if only as figures of fantasy. Lennon's marriage was clearly problematic from the marketing point of view; and so manager Brian Epstein worked out a provisional solution to these difficulties. Lennon's wife was to be symbolically erased: Powell was to remain in the background, to keep out of the spotlight. It simply would not do for fans to know that Beatle John was already taken by a pretty blonde art student. This symbolic erasure of Powell did not prevent media attention for long though, and Lennon became known as the married Beatle. He was thus viewed by the media as torn: on the one hand, he had all the intoxicating excitement of life as a Beatle; on the other, he was stuck with the dreary conventionality of marriage. In this view we find an inscription of binary logic—of sexuality and civility, nature and culture—onto the realm of celebrity.

Many commentators have argued that Lennon's first marriage was a relationship of inequality, of subjection, of patriarchy.[25] They assume that Lennon was a man of action, constituting "history," and that Powell was a woman of grim domestic subjection, placed almost outside of historical time. Significantly, anyone who considers Lennon's intimate life must of necessity deal with the issue of this sexual relationship thoroughly skewed in terms of power. How should his relationship with Powell be remembered? What position are we to attribute to Lennon? Romantic lover or domestic tyrant? And how does his subsequent relationship with Yoko Ono affect our understanding of his first marriage?

Consider these two commentaries. The first is from rock critic Robert Christgau, in which he describes the circumstances that brought together, and drove apart, John Lennon and Cynthia Powell:

Who knew that John had only tied the knot because he'd knocked up this very model of the hip young modern mom? And who knew that she was only a transitional symbol, soon to be outflanked by the liberated chick and the hippie earth mother? Needless to say, she also proved transitional for John, who always went with the zeitgeist or vice versa. Nor did this surprise anyone familiar with the facts. John was married to The Beatles; on his wife he fucked around.[26]

The second is from Ray Coleman's biography, *John Lennon:*

Back at home in Weybridge, Surrey, John's wife Cynthia firmly believed her role was to continue as before Beatlemania: as the rock-solid, unquestioning, loving, home-building wife and devoted mother to their three-year-old son Julian. John's absence as a travelling Beatle had forced her to shoulder all the domestic chores. Passive, maternal, and at all times understanding, except on the subject of drugs, Cynthia was still the contented, tasteful, resilient Hoylake girl who had first won John's heart at art college. . . . Their marriage had been "rolling along nicely with no fireworks," [Cynthia] recalls. Although she had suspected that John had been involved with other women, she had shut herself away from the possibility, preoccupied with running a house, bringing up Julian and cosseting John when he returned from work. His extra-marital affairs did not concern her.[27]

These commentaries suggest that sexuality is itself at the heart of our cultural anxiety about love and intimacy. Both commentaries imply that sexuality at once frames and outstrips the institution of marriage.

But if sexuality is at the core of marriage, sexuality is understood in somewhat different ways in these commentaries. In Christgau's case, it is the contradictions between sex, marriage, and intimacy—or rather the unequal negotiating rights of the sexes—that come to the fore. Christgau positions Lennon within the stereotype of the sexually compulsive male, for whom sexual conquest is the principal concern. Hence, Lennon's marriage to Powell is described as no more and no less than the result of an unplanned pregnancy; and with that description, just as with Epstein's scheme, the woman's subjectivity is erased. Cynthia Powell is simply done over; she comes to figure in the story at all only because she got "knocked up." At stake here is an understanding of masculinity as assertive, dominant, compulsive.

The same contradiction between sex and marriage is present in Coleman's comment, but shifted up a gear into a fully normalized and idealized worldview. Coleman makes the same sort of gender moves that Christgau does: he posits masculinity as assertive, femininity as passive. But, unlike Christgau, he makes no punitive judgment about this gendered distribution of roles. On the contrary, he seems to find much to recommend in this sorting of activity and passivity between husband and wife. Coleman describes Powell as a woman with all the necessary feminine virtues—a "rock-solid, unquestioning, loving, home-building wife and devoted mother." Yet these feminine accomplishments actually serve to disguise her feelings of anxiety and despair; this much is implicit in Coleman's interpretation. After all, she "suspected that John had been involved with other women"; yet it seems that his affairs are nothing that a good dose of denial will not fix ("she had shut herself away from the possibility"). Powell might thus be said to have developed the kind of psychic disposition by which she ignored her husband's affairs, and Coleman implies that this too is a good thing. Such denial keeps the sexes in their places; such repression is intrinsic to the gendered tasks demanded by cultural life. Elsewhere, Coleman asserts that the "temptations" offered to Lennon "would have been almost impossible for a full-blooded male to resist."[28] The full-blooded male and sexual compulsiveness, it seems, go hand in hand.

What this construction suggests, once again, is that biographical framings of Lennon fail to incorporate much reflectiveness—especially on the matter of ideological assumptions about gender, sexuality, or identity. It is thus more fruitful to read such a construction of Lennon's identity as at war with itself.

If, as Lennon remarked, Beatlemania prevented him from really becoming John Lennon, we might wonder how Yoko Ono helped to further his personal reflectiveness. Compare the following episode in the life of Lennon and Ono with what we have considered about Lennon's relationship with Powell. In October 1968, six months pregnant with Lennon's child, Ono was rushed to Queen Charlotte Maternity Hospital in Hammersmith, London, because of complications that were endangering the pregnancy. Lennon was not absent from the hospital on this occasion, however. On the contrary, he was at Ono's side throughout and slept in her room despite protestations from the hospital. When the bed he was using was removed to accommodate another patient, he slept on pillows on the floor in Ono's room. (Ono subsequently recorded a song about the experience: "No Bed for Beatle John.") Anxiety, fear, pain, and loss—these were the psychic states that Lennon shared with his lover. When advised that the fetus would die, Lennon arranged to record the final heartbeats of the unborn child—a recording that was later released on his second collaboration with Ono, *Unfinished Music No. 2: Life with the Lions*.[29] The dead baby was old enough to warrant an official death certificate; Lennon and Ono named the child John Ono Lennon II. The loss of the baby was harrowing, devastating for both of them. "That night at the hospital," recalled Beatles insider Peter Brown, "he [Lennon] cried himself to sleep on the floor at her bedside."[30]

This was far from a knee-jerk emotional response. Lennon had become a more reflective, more caring lover: emotionally, he had matured enough to take responsibility for his actions. He remarked that his relationship with Ono had deepened his understanding of life, even though it had created emotional difficulties with respect to his relationship with his first wife and son. "I've never known love like this before," said Lennon, "and it hit me so hard that I had to halt my marriage to Cyn. And I don't think that was a reckless decision, because I felt very deeply about it and all the implications that would be involved."[31] Critics, commentators, and even fellow celebrities began to realize that his relationship with Ono was special. But, we might ask, how did the relationship change him? How did it make him happier? Most women, Lennon said in a radio interview in 1971, were intellectually and emotionally removed in their intimate relationships; women were constrained by men's demand that they represent sex—play the role of sex object. "I had never met any woman with any kind of mind before, they'd all been dummies," he continued. Ono, by contrast, was radically different: "she brought out the best in me—by encouraging me in my artwork, my films, and my writing, which are all things I did almost like a hobby. She woke me up. . . . I learned to have a *friendship* with her."[32]

In time Lennon offered a more detailed account of the emotional transformation that his relationship with Ono inaugurated. She had helped him deal with his past failures: "I was a hitter. I couldn't express myself and I hit."[33] His frankness about his violence probably referred to certain things he had done in his youth; he gained early press coverage, for instance, when he physically attacked Cavern disc jockey Bob Wooler—who had insinuated that Lennon and Brian Epstein were lovers—at Paul McCartney's twenty-first birthday party in Liverpool. Some critics have sought to take Lennon's violence further, suggesting that he actually beat up women, including his first wife.[34] Although Lennon often attributed his violent tendencies to the macho values of his youth, it seems more likely—and this view is supported by the opinions of friends and lovers—that this inner violence was fashioned from fear.

Lennon had always craved both personal autonomy and emotional stability; he achieved both, eventually, through his relationship with Ono. He tended, however, to sometimes overstate the emotional limitations and dislocations of his past; his comment that he'd "never met any woman with any kind of mind before" was condescending and inaccurate. In particular, he remembered his mother, Julia, as a vibrant and strong woman, a personality who at once fascinated and threatened him. Lennon's memory of his mother is relevant in this context because it can shed light on the freeing of his sense of self that Ono helped him achieve. Lennon implied on several occasions that, because his mother had deserted him, she had slipped to the margins of his mind; her loss was so traumatic, it seems, that it was easier for him to invest in a new life with his Aunt Mimi, even though he remained deeply ambivalent about the conventional bourgeois values to which she subscribed. But his love for his mother, and especially his memory of her carefree and liberated personality, never entirely vanished. Traces of his buried love for her, as well as his desire to be like her, surfaced in his artistic work and produced a strong need to explore alternative forms of consciousness and ways of living. Yet in at least one sphere of his life, the domestic, he found it extremely difficult to break from the conventional patterns that had been laid down in his mind from his early years at Mendips with his strict aunt. Addressing this emotional deadlock was a matter of the utmost concern to Lennon.

It is certainly undeniable that Lennon believed that his desire to be macho, and thus to escape the emotional vulnerabilities of his childhood, often hindered his personal reflectiveness throughout his adult life. In 1971, he commented, "I remember that at sixteen I still had myself."[35] What Lennon still had at sixteen, it seems, was a strong sense of emotional self-understanding. Nancy Chodorow, a feminist psychoanalyst, has argued that the masculine sense of self-identity is built on a denial of love and intimacy shared with the mother; such denial prepares men, she says, for an instrumental, abstract attitude toward the world.[36] Lennon's reflections on the difficulties of achieving a sense of maleness powerfully underline Chodorow's hypothesis. "One has oneself in the beginning," Lennon explained, "and there's a constant process of society and parents and family trying to make you lose yourself. Like, 'Don't cry, don't show any emotion,' that kind of jazz."[37]

Lennon's relationship with Ono permitted him to recover from such emotional detachment—to recover both his past and his inner self. His close friend Pete Shotton added further weight to such an interpretation when he suggested that Ono had facilitated a recovery of the ex-Beatle's inner dynamism: "In short, she enabled the child in John to resurface—the child I had known and loved. You might almost say that Yoko brought John back to life."[38] The recovery of the child within was not without its problems and difficulties. Certainly, by late 1972, Lennon and Ono were caught in a web of relationship dilemmas which were driven by, although not reducible to, declining record sales, immigration battles, and artistic inertia. During this time, Lennon had little inclination for reflectiveness; as he had in previous times of crisis, he wanted to move on. The stage was set for Lennon's "lost weekend."

By 1973, Lennon and Ono had been living together for six years. They had defined themselves as absolutes in each other's lives—their love was drawn into, indeed made to work for, their artistic and political collaborations. The critics often found this blending of personal and professional concerns difficult to comprehend; whenever Lennon diverged from what the critics thought the artistic standards of an ex-Beatle should be, he and Ono were invariably censured. In addition, the countless deportation orders against Lennon began to take their toll. "We allowed ourselves," said Lennon, "to be so affected by outside influences and pressures that we just burst. That's what it was. The pressure was too much, so we burst."[39] Their breakup was, in effect, an outcome of internal and external strains.

According to Ono, the internal strains of their relationship had escalated: "He [Lennon] had to open himself up and face me—and I had to see what he was going through. But . . . I thought I had to 'move on' again because I was suffering being with John. I thought I wanted to be free from being Mrs. Lennon."[40] The impulse to move on was, at root, a denial of their need for interpersonal recognition. Jessica Benjamin, a feminist scholar and psychoanalyst, explains the connections between desire and recognition:

The paradox of recognition, the need for acknowledgment that turns us back to dependence on the other, brings about a struggle for control. This struggle can result in the realization that if we fully negate the other, that is, if we assume complete control over him and destroy his identity and will, then we have negated ourselves as well. For then there is no one there to recognize us, no one there for us to desire.[41]

It is not just mutual dependence that becomes too threatening; the knowledge that love is itself fraught with ambiguities and ambivalences can also become overwhelming. Lennon and Ono had, it seems, denied knowledge of their own difficulties and moved away from the trust which is necessary to sustain the paradoxes of loving.

Enter May Pang. She first met Lennon and Ono in 1970, when working as a secretary for ABKCO Industries in New York (the parent company of The Beatles' Apple Records). Soon thereafter, Pang became one of Lennon and Ono's private secretaries. To begin with, she assisted with the production of their films *Up Your Legs Forever* and *Fly* (see chapter 4) and also traveled between the United States and the United Kingdom to assist with Lennon's album *Imagine*. Pang was later promoted to principal recording assistant and worked on Lennon's solo albums up until his semiretirement, as well as on Ono's albums *Fly, Approximately Infinite Universe,* and *Feeling the Space.* She liaised with the Lennons at their suites on the seventeenth floor of the St. Regis Hotel and later at their Bank Street loft in Greenwich Village. When the Lennons moved to the Dakota, a gothic apartment block at the corner of Central Park West and West Seventy-second Street, Pang was assigned to work from there full-time.

When Lennon and Ono decided to separate for a trial period, Pang was at hand to support the ex-Beatle. Some (including Lennon himself) have stressed that the breakup occurred at Ono's insistence, and that Ono saw Pang principally as an assistant or minder for Lennon. But it also seems clear that by mid-1973 Lennon and Pang had already embarked on a relationship of some kind. After finishing production work on *Mind Games* in September 1973, Lennon moved out of the Dakota. He decided to take a break from New York and—above all—from Yoko Ono. He chose to go, accompanied by Pang, to the West Coast.[42]

In October 1973, Lennon began recording his album *Rock 'n' Roll* in Los Angeles with legendary producer Phil Spector. Lennon had worked previously with Spector on *Plastic Ono Band, Imagine,* and *Some Time in New York City.* But for *Rock 'n' Roll,* their working relationship was different: Lennon granted Spector complete control of the album. Lennon did not want to play guitar or piano; nor did he want anything to do with the production process. Instead, he wanted to concentrate on singing. Arriving at A&M recording studios to commence work on the album, Lennon was delighted to meet the session musicians Spector had booked—such as Leon Russell, Jesse Ed Davis, and Steve Cropper.

Lennon's *Rock 'n' Roll* was a return to his roots. He wanted to record his old favorites, to return to the songs that had inspired him to write music in the first place. He covered songs like Gene Vincent's "Be-Bop-A-Lula," the song he had been playing when he first met Paul McCartney; Ben E. King's "Stand by Me"; and Buddy Holly's "Peggy Sue." But the broader aim of the project was to buy him some time out from the pressure of writing hits. By 1973, Lennon was on the slide commercially. In contrast to *Imagine,* which had been a smash success, *Some Time in New York City* had reached only number forty-eight on the charts. His next album, *Mind Games,* had fared somewhat better; the single had peaked at number eighteen, the album at number nine. It was still a poor showing, however, for the ex-Beatle. Lennon's musical fortunes were inevitably compared with those of the other ex-Beatles, against the *Ringo* album, which reached number three, and against Paul McCartney's *Band on the Run,* which was number one for four weeks. Critic Bob Edmands wrote,

Lennon is an austere figure. At a glance, he might be an alienated Marxist in-tellectual, bitter over the number of copies of *Workers Press* he's failing to sell. Alternatively, he could be one of those jaundiced airport lounge lizards—a flashbulb fetishist whose main contribution to entertainment con-sists of stepping on and off jets. The working class hero looks increasingly like a prisoner of his own private war.[43]

Lennon the superstar was in decline.

One of the first tracks recorded during the Spector sessions was the rock classic "Angel Baby." Lennon laid down his vocal track for the song late in the evening; he asked May Pang to join him in the record-ing booth. He intended the song for her. Even though the song was recorded at the beginning of the sessions, there were already sig-nificant tensions between Lennon and Spector. Spector worked ex-tremely slowly in building his renowned "wall of sound"; he recorded the rhythm section, the horn section, and the guitars separately, re-questing that the musicians run through the song time and again as he experimented with sounds and special effects. This pace differed con-siderably from the swiftness with which Lennon worked in the studio. As producer Richard Perry remarked, Lennon "had amazing energy and electricity. He worked at a fast pace."[44] Tired of Spector's pains-taking method of layering sounds, Lennon joined some of the other musicians who were drinking alcohol to kill time. After drinking for some hours, Lennon confronted Spector. He wanted to know when he was going to record his vocal. Spector casually replied that he'd get around to it. Lennon was incredulous; he was being treated as if he were an assistant on his own album. He picked up a headset and smashed it on the mixing console. It was a sign of things to come.

Late that evening, Lennon gave full vent to his rage. Leaving the A&M studios, Lennon and Jesse Ed Davis staged a mock fight in the parking lot. But it quickly turned into something more violent. At-tempting to take control, Spector had his bodyguard put Lennon in his car, while May Pang was left behind to travel in another car. Traveling through the streets of Bel Air, Lennon became inconsolable; he screamed "May," then "Yoko," then "May" again. Arriving at Stone Canyon Road, at a house borrowed from record producer Lou Adler, Spector and Pang got Lennon inside and attempted to calm him. Spector made him some coffee, hoping it would have a sobering effect, but the coffee seemed to make Lennon more agitated; he cursed at and made a lunge for Spector. Fearful, Spector instructed his bodyguard to take Lennon upstairs to the bedroom, where he was physically restrained; his glasses were removed, and his hands were tied to the bedposts with neckties. In spite of Lennon's shouts of protest, Spector and his bodyguard returned downstairs and left soon thereafter.

According to May Pang, the house was then filled with the sound of glass shattering. Lennon had pried himself loose from the bed and had thrown a chair through the plate glass window. In a fit of rage, he then went about destroying the house. Elliot Mintz, who visited Lennon and Pang the following morning, told me about the destruction that he witnessed.[45] In addition to smashing windows, Lennon had pulled a chandelier from the ceiling, broken antique chairs, and smashed many platinum albums that had adorned the walls of Lou Adler's house.

The Stone Canyon Road episode was emblematic of Lennon's persistent disposition to engage in acts of self-destruction during his separation from Ono. Lennon famously described this period, a fifteen-month nightmare during which he was sustained primarily by drink and drugs, as his "lost weekend." "I was just insane," Lennon reflected on his time without Ono. "I've never drunk so much in my life, and I've been drinking since I was fifteen. But I really tried to drown myself in the bottle."[46] This assertion calls forth the theme of suicide, Lennon's desire to obliterate himself psychically. He had always been prone to periods of depression, insecurity, and anxiety; yet friends and family had supported him through such periods. In Los Angeles, things were different. He was coming to realize that his relationship with Ono, along with his hopes for the future, had gone awry. The sense of loss underpinning these bouts of depression and self-doubt was experienced as overwhelming; feeling unable to cope, he turned to alcohol and drugs in an effort to block the pain.[47] He was, according to Mintz, out of control for much of this time—which has been convincingly demonstrated by Pang and others. But what is perhaps more significant is that this loss of control refers to a deeper loss: the abandonment of hope. Lennon, says Mintz of the lost weekend, was suffering from a profound sense of emptiness.

The lost weekend became uglier. Lennon created headlines when ejected from the Troubadour nightclub on two occasions. On the first night, he had come to the club with Pang, drummer Jim Keltner and his wife, and guitarist Jesse Ed Davis and his girlfriend to see singer Ann Peebles perform. Lennon and his friends had dined earlier at Lost on Larabee, a restaurant on Santa Monica Boulevard, where they had consumed much alcohol. At the restaurant, he had returned from the rest room, to uproarious laughter, with an unused Kotex stuck to his forehead, which he continued to wear after he got to the Troubadour. Drunk and obnoxious, Lennon yelled obscenities throughout Peebles's performance. He was asked by the management to leave. The next morning, the Troubadour incident was front-page news. A waitress at the club was reported as having told Lennon, after he had pestered her, that he was merely "an asshole with a Kotex on his head."[48] May Pang, in her book, denies that the waitress ever said this. The damage to Lennon's reputation was done, however.

In March 1974, Lennon again caused an uproar at the Troubadour—at a comeback appearance of the Smothers Brothers. Having spent the evening with Pang and his friend Harry Nilsson, Lennon arrived at the Troubadour for the duo's second performance of the night. His party was escorted to the VIP section, where Lennon mixed with Peter Lawford, Jack Haley Jr., and the producer of *Welcome Back Kotter*, Alan Sacks. Lennon and Nilsson were drinking "milk shakes," double brandy alexanders, and clowning around. The Smothers Brothers began their show to strong applause; however, they were soon interrupted by the constant heckling of Lennon and Nilsson. Lennon recalled the episode some years later:

I was drinking brandy alexanders for the first time—that was Harry's drink; they taste like milkshakes, and I was knocking them back as if they were— and suddenly I was in the fourth dimension. In the fourth dimension I noticed what I'd always secretly thought, that Dickie Smothers was an asshole even though I always liked Tommy. And so that's what I said, but because I was drunk, I said it out loud. I was a born heckler. . . . Maybe I shouldn't have said it out loud. Who cares?[49]

The Troubadour management, as well as the rest of the audience, certainly did care about Lennon's fourth dimension antics; Lennon and

Nilsson soon found themselves being ejected from the club by bouncers onto Santa Monica Boulevard. Photographers were waiting in front of the club; again, Lennon's lost weekend was front-page news.[50]

It is possible, as Lennon biographer Jon Wiener has suggested, to detect in Lennon's heckling of the Smothers Brothers a deeper, symbolic destruction of his past.[51] Tommy Smothers had been present at Lennon and Ono's bed-in at Montreal and had sung on the recording of "Give Peace a Chance." With a cruelty strikingly at odds with his commitment to peace, Lennon was now intent on destroying such personal and professional connections. Indeed, it is hard to miss in Lennon's attack on the Smothers Brothers the anguish of a man seeking to wipe out some terrifying inner specters of his past. Lennon's lost weekend seems an image of chronic anxiety; one can sense, in his furious and flamboyant Los Angeles lifestyle, the escalation of emotional denial, the perverse courting of disaster after disaster. Like his austere "Yer Blues," in which rock 'n' roll is fixed under the sign of suicide, written at a time in which his first marriage was collapsing, Lennon's life seems grim—caught between pain and pathos, depression and destruction. No longer engaged with political issues, Lennon felt adrift as a superstar. He seemed to realize that his self-destructiveness was, in part, a response to the mindlessness of his lifestyle in Los Angeles. But grappling with the depth of his feelings for Ono was more difficult. During the lost weekend Lennon raced toward self-annihilation as though he wanted to realize his worst anxieties and fears, to sever his inner world from the complexities of intimacy.

Public scandal and private depression reinforced each other. Lennon felt unable to account for, or defend himself against, media reports about his drunken excesses. The gossip throughout Hollywood was that the Lennon-Spector sessions were, in effect, wild parties; celebrities such as Joni Mitchell and Jack Nicholson called by the studio to see and, no doubt, be seen. The sessions became increasingly riotous. Spector's behavior grew more and more erratic: Spector routinely fought with Lennon, and he was responsible for getting them thrown out of the A&M recording complex after he fired off a gun in the studio one evening. After a serious car accident in early 1974, Spector went into hiding, taking the tapes with him. Lennon was now without a producer and without a record. He sank farther into depression, the nightlife of Hollywood providing the only escape

from his problems. In April 1974, Lennon and Pang moved into a
house on the beach in Santa Monica with Ringo Starr, Harry Nilsson,
Who drummer Keith Moon, and Klaus Voorman. Lennon enlisted
these musicians to work on a new album he wanted to produce for
Nilsson. On this album, entitled *Pussycats*, Lennon fared little better
as producer than he had as vocalist on *Rock 'n' Roll*.

"I didn't want to see or feel anything," reflected Lennon of his intense denial.[52] However, he slowly began to resolve some of his anxieties and deal with his sense of enforced solitude by writing music
again. Sitting by the swimming pool of his beach house in the after-
noons, he would play guitar; he started work on his first songs since
the commercial and critical disaster *Some Time in New York City*.
"Whatever Gets You thru the Night," "What You Got," "Surprise
Surprise (Sweet Bird of Paradox)," and "#9 Dream" were composed
around this time, as was "Goodnight Vienna," a song he wrote for
Ringo Starr.[53] In July 1974, he and Pang returned to New York City,
where they moved into an apartment near the East River. Soon thereafter, he began work on his new album, *Walls and Bridges*, at Record
Plant Studios with musicians Klaus Voorman, Jim Keltner, and Nicky
Hopkins.

Although Lennon felt that he had little new or original to offer the
public, the songs he wrote for *Walls and Bridges* made him commercially successful once again by invoking the specter of failure. "Nobody Loves You (When You're Down and Out)," "Steel and Glass," and
"Scared," among the most powerful songs Lennon had written in years,
were again rooted in autobiographical confession. Their strength lies
in Lennon's lyrical honesty and simplicity; one does not have to
be suffering the alienation of rock 'n' roll stardom to share the sense
of insecurity and anxiety that Lennon finds within the recesses of
daily life.

I'm scared, I'm scared, I'm scared
Everyday of my life
I just manage to survive
I just want to stay alive.

As was so often the case with Lennon, through creative artistry he
gradually came out of his depression; and this emergence is evident
on *Walls and Bridges* to the extent that he responds to these somber
songs by acknowledging the need for something more uplifting. "What-

ever Gets You thru the Night" offered a concentrated, if contrived, display of Lennon's musical energy; the sublime "#9 Dream" is an enchanting homage to amorous pleasures; and "What You Got" boosts the album into the unexpected terrain of funk rock. *Walls and Bridges* returned Lennon to superstardom, giving him his first number-one single and album since the breakup of The Beatles.

Lennon, however, remained disenchanted with *Walls and Bridges.* "If you listen to *Walls and Bridges*," he said, "you hear somebody that is depressed."[54] He thought he had been in a steep decline since *Imagine*, which had presented certain personal ideas and cultural thematics from *Plastic Ono Band* in a more commercial light. However, as was often the case, Lennon misjudged his own work. *Walls and Bridges* is one of his best solo albums, a triumph in autobiographical disclosure. Lennon's lost weekend of drink and drugs, his tormented wrestling with personal loss, and the breakdown of his very public relationship with Ono might have offered enough excuses for retirement. Instead, Lennon took the opportunity to explore anew the conflictive and ambiguous territory of love, to reflect on his estrangement from Ono and on his emergent dependence on Pang. The result was a crucial transformation in Lennon's understanding of the intertwining of personal unity and dislocation, commitment and abandonment, security and ambivalence.

THE LOST WEEKEND apparently represented nothing but embarrassment to Lennon: "It was such a mess that I can hardly remember what happened. I was away from Yoko and I wanted to come back. When I was drunk, I would just ramble on or scream abuse at her or beg her to come back. I don't know what I was saying or doing half the time."[55] Lennon constructs himself as divided, torn and in denial. This construction raises important questions about what drew him to May Pang. Why did Lennon find it almost impossible to deal emotionally with his separation from Ono? What deep-seated fears and anxieties took hold during this time?

Pang was employed by Lennon and Ono, and in one way, all the tension of the employer-employee relation was present from the outset of Lennon and Pang's intimate relationship. This tension at its best was actualized in their daily business transactions and at its worst was inscribed in their sexual affair. Pang has been variously described as

Lennon's assistant, secretary, caretaker, minder, and lover. But, alongside these roles was her crucial role as a witness to Lennon's pain during the lost weekend. Psychoanalyst Masud Khan has pointed out the
importance of gaining a witness for one's psychic suffering; a witness
allows for the containment of feelings which are too threatening or
overwhelming.[56] Given that Lennon appeared incapable of register-
ing his own grief, or dealing with it, the presence of someone to act as
a "psychic container" for his suffering was crucial. Pang partially fulfilled this psychic need.

Pang has been represented as doubly done over, because of both
her employee status and the demise of her relationship with Lennon
in late 1974. It was not just the media that used this representation as
a rhetorical tactic for understanding Pang in her role as Lennon's mis-
tress. On the contrary, Pang herself stressed the frustrated nature of
her desire, especially the frustration caused by Ono. In a strongly
symbolic sense, Ono and Pang have become situated within a cluster
of binary oppositions in their relation to Lennon: wife/mistress, older
woman/younger woman, dominant/submissive, avant-garde artist/sec-
retary. What gives such oppositions their complexity, as well as their
power to mislead, is ambiguity in the logic of sexual difference itself.
The drama between Pang and Ono lies in this conflict over the intensity of their love for Lennon, a conflict which in one stroke sets
women's relational situation in terms of sexual competition, woman as
torn between subject status and object status.

May Pang's 1983 autobiography, *Loving John* (cowritten with
Henry Edwards), with its cold and devastating portrait of Ono, will
bear some unpacking in order to develop these gender thematics. The
book begins with a disclaimer:

Loving John is the story of the relationship between three people: John
Lennon, Yoko Ono, and May Pang. It is based on the firsthand observations
of May Pang as well as interviews with a number of people who knew both
May and John when they were together. After sifting through the observations and interviews, it is the opinion of the authors that the relationship between May and John was essentially initiated, controlled, and then termi-
nated by Yoko Ono.[57]

Pang thus constructs herself, and her relationship with Lennon, as subordinate to Yoko Ono. Ono is cast as cold and manipulative throughout the book; she is represented as a kind of mastermind lurking in

the shadows, yet ultimately pulling the strings of Lennon and Pang's love affair. Not surprisingly, Lennon is represented as confused, isolated, and dependent. Such personality attributes are clearly necessary, for they are the stuff upon which manipulation thrives; and the reader is, from the beginning, left in little doubt about how the three protagonists are situated in terms of domination and submission.

According to Pang, Ono informed her one morning, in a casual manner, that she should begin a sexual relationship with Lennon, that she should "begin loving John." This pact can be read according to the logic of sexual difference, a pact premised on the special language that women share in their understanding of how to lure, tease, and entice men. Yet it is a pact always threatened by the point of erotic crossover, in which falling in love with a man places women in an antagonistic relation. *Loving John,* then, is marked by a hiatus between directive and desire, law and passion; and Pang excessively labors the point that her love for Lennon was his last hope for maintaining some self-respect in the face of Ono's ruthless manipulation.

Pang's book is mostly set during the period of Lennon's lost weekend. If her relationship with Lennon gave her some special insight into his inner world, however, it is almost impossible to discern it from the myths, fantasies, and unbridled rhetoric that permeate her narrative. Her account of Lennon's distress certainly engages one's sympathies, at least at the beginning. But what quickly emerges is that she offers little analysis of *why* Lennon was struggling for his emotional survival, apart from the tired theme of gender manipulation. There is something both amusing and pathetic in Pang's portrayal of Lennon's enjoyment of his celebrity lifestyle. Parties are attended with the likes of David Bowie and Elizabeth Taylor, and weekends away are spent with Mick and Bianca Jagger; but for all that Lennon appears in a world of privilege that he continually marvels over, as if his time as a Beatle had simply never taken place. As a consequence, Pang is able to exploit Lennon's alleged naiveté to the hilt. When she and Lennon enjoy dinner out at a down-market restaurant, he is thrilled to be back in touch with the simplicities of life; when they spend the day at Disneyland, he acts just like a child.

Reading Pang, you sense she must paradoxically have reduced the complexity and ambiguity of her relationship with Lennon drastically in order to write such a kiss-and-tell book in the first place. Because

Lennon is rhetorically deflated to a hapless child, stripped of any moti-
vational direction, Pang is unable to capture or define what she loves
about her lover, apart from his image of coolness. This paradox, ultimately, undermines any narrative tension that the book might have had.
By the time Lennon tells Pang that Ono has "allowed" him to return to
the Dakota, a point at which the author suddenly discovers herself in a
shattering crisis of identity, we reach a narrative closure which is mani-
festly defensive, if not downright paranoid. Pang alleges that Ono, by
arranging for Lennon to undergo hypnosis to give up smoking, had
Lennon hypnotized into coming back to her. This allegation seems little
more than a full-blown fantasy about the powers of mind control; yet
Pang doggedly maintains the theme of Ono's manipulation of Lennon:

> From the moment eighteen months before when Yoko had suggested that I
> go out with John, I had known that she had the upper hand. But as our rela-
> tionship had progressed, I had allowed myself to think that John had
> changed. He had stopped drinking. He had had the time of his life with Ju-
> lian. He had stopped being a recluse and had learned to have friends once
> again. He was writing. And yet, although I hated to admit it, deep down I be-
> lieved that Yoko would always know how to get John to do what she
> wanted.[58]

Pang concludes her signed and sealed revelation of their "untold
story" by noting: "to me, the man, not the myth, was the important
thing."[59] It is hard, if not impossible, however, to gain a sense of the
love and tragedy that permeated their relationship. Pang's Lennon
suffers from lovelessness and depression, psychic states that seem
more relevant to Pang than to her subject by the time the book uncovers "the real John Lennon." Throughout, she presents his vulnerability via the rhetoric of pop psychology; and she hides her own lack of
understanding of Lennon's situation by sentimentalizing, or avoiding
altogether, the emotional dynamics of his grief during the lost weekend. Lennon's life with Pang looks superficially like that of any celebrity whose career is on the skids.

4

Revolution 9

The Politics of Politics

The underground are just as straight as the overground,
and they don't like change.

John Lennon

We look for politics in the wrong place, with the wrong
terms.

Ulrich Beck

John Lennon disturbs conventional conceptions of political radicalism, drains politics (ordinarily understood) of its content, blurs the
sharp separation of the personal and the political. The concept of the
political has long been bound up primarily with the public sphere;
politics, narrowly defined as the affairs of governments, is a realm set
apart from personal life. But Lennon, as political radical and peace
activist, transmutes this orthodox understanding, transforming the
very meaning of "public engagement." From his artistic contributions
to the peace movement in the 1960s to his time as feminist father in
the late 1970s, Lennon developed a way of thinking personally, poet-
ically, and culturally that points to the uneasy relation of the political
to itself.

In a political culture where the demands of self-preservation increasingly triumph in order to banish experiences of insecurity, emotional impulses and ethical values come under mounting restrictions.
The more political life and cultural life are steadily brought under the
sway of an instrumental rationality, the more passion and desire are
forced underground through repression or denial. But in a world depleted of passion and significance, culture can furnish the possibility
for aesthetic and political redemption—or at least this is the case in
John Lennon's esoteric mediation of the relations between self and
society, if culture supports the imaginative energies of people in their
personal and political engagements. For Lennon, the resurrection of

imagination and desire creates a very renaissance of politics. Politics, in Lennon's view, must be conceived as an index of personal and social happenings, the running together of interests and meanings that keep steering apart, a shared commitment to multifaceted forms of belonging. Such a politics is a reflective cultural politics, one concerned with pleasure, creativity, and autonomy.

My aim in this encounter with Lennon's political aesthetic—that is, his blending of politics and art—is to challenge the conventional view that Lennon's political sensibility simply mirrored the utopian spirit of the 1960s countercultural movement.[1] While Lennon's protests for peace were undeniably of seminal significance to the peace movement, other aspects of his thinking and his work were at odds with the countercultural politics of the time. Indeed, much of Lennon's work directly engages with dominant political antagonisms; and, far from proposing unification of our disparate identities and cultures, he in fact designates conflict, difference, and heterogeneity as central to radical politics. My argument, then, is that Lennon's anti-institutional aesthetic, often marginalized in rememberings of Lennon, is a politics in itself.

ON 30 MAY 1968, The Beatles commenced work at Abbey Road Studios on what was to become known as the "White Album." The song recorded that day was Lennon's "Revolution." (The version recorded on 30 May, subsequently retitled "Revolution 1" once it became apparent that several versions of the song would be released, was the first installment in what I shall call the "Revolution" trilogy, which comprises acoustic, electric, and electronic versions). Written some months earlier, while the band was vacationing at the Maharishi Mahesh Yogi's meditation retreat at Rishikesh in India, "Revolution 1" was considered the possible follow-up single to "Lady Madonna." The song was classic Lennon, concerned as it was with the relationship between personal change and political transformation. "We all want to change the world," sang Lennon in the opening bluesy verse. Universal love and cosmic consciousness, considered of crucial importance by Lennon in the previous summer's "All You Need Is Love," were displaced by a more questioning and critical political stance. The change had arisen from his interest in meditation and Hindu religion. Through experimenting with meditation in India, he had came to ap-

preciate the limitations and dangers of drugs such as LSD. He also recovered much of his artistic direction and personal vitality, and he
penned an astonishing number of songs for the "White Album." Indeed, Lennon subsequently spoke of his time in India as crucial for
reclaiming not only his self-direction and artistic sensibility but also
his broader interest in the political world.

It was in becoming more political that Lennon also became more
critical, and more inventive, about his aesthetic work. The history of
the recording of "Revolution 1" reflects this change. In contrast to the
more upbeat demo that Lennon had recorded at George Harrison's
Esher home-studio after returning from India, the Abbey Road version taped on 30 May was considerably slower and more intuitive. It
was also radically experimental. In this laid-back version, Lennon encouraged the other Beatles to experiment with the song. The recording that ensued ran for more than ten minutes.

Experimentation of this kind was not new to The Beatles; the band
had been deploying novel methods of recording and production since
Rubber Soul. Yet there was something different about the recording
of "Revolution 1." Indeed, there was a kind of revolution occurring
within the band itself: Lennon's welcoming of Yoko Ono, who accompanied Lennon to Abbey Road, into The Beatles' recording session.
Lennon encouraged Ono's participation in the vocal frenzy and instrumental jamming that developed. "The last six minutes were pure
chaos," writes Mark Lewisohn, "with discordant jamming, plenty of
feedback, John Lennon repeatedly screaming 'alright' and then, simply, repeatedly screaming, with lots of on-microphone moaning by
John and . . . Yoko talking and saying such off-the-wall phrases as 'you
become naked.'"[2] (The chaos of which Lewisohn writes was subsequently used on "Revolution 9," an electronic version of the song
which I will discuss in some detail later.) What took place at Abbey
Road on 30 May was indeed a radical departure from the band's previous methods of working, since prior to Ono's involvement no outsiders (except for hired session musicians) had been tolerated. From
this time onward, in effect, Lennon and Ono were inseparable, and
this—to the annoyance of the other Beatles—was nowhere more obvious than in the studio. Lennon was saying to the band, George Martin reflects in the film *Imagine*, "Yoko is now part of me. In other
words, as I have a right and left hand, so I have Yoko, and wherever I
am, she is." While it may be far too simple to blame Ono for the

breakup of The Beatles, her involvement in the band's recording sessions certainly caused considerable friction and disharmony.

There was some contention within The Beatles over the fate of
"Revolution 1." McCartney and Harrison argued against the release
of the 30 May recording on the grounds that the song lacked punch.
Lennon, though annoyed, suggested that they record the song again,
but faster. A speedier, electric version, simply entitled "Revolution,"
was recorded in July. Lennon's determination to release "Revolution"
as a single can be viewed not only as a matter of his songwriting competition with McCartney but also in terms of deeper political currents. He had followed with interest the May 1968 student uprising in
Paris, in which the student movement's brief period of solidarity with
substantial sections of the working class, the professional sector, and
the cultural elite generated major clashes with police and, at one
point, threatened to bring down the de Gaulle government. He was
also attentive to the student revolts which had swept across the
United States in reaction to the Vietnam War (political demonstra-
tions occurred at more than two hundred universities and colleges)
and had spread to universities in the United Kingdom.

Lennon's "Revolution" is intensely political and aesthetic at once. It
assumes that at the center of politics there lies a ruthless, destructive
compulsion for self-preservation and self-aggrandizement. Parodying
the political language of the New Left and counterculture press, it takes
aim at the extremism of politics, its breeding of ideological fundamentalism. Lennon laconically notes that political blueprints are intrinsic to
political domination: "You say you've got a real solution / We'd all love to
see the plan." The radical left's position is weak, according to Lennon,
not because the left continues to dream of instituting a new and different kind of society but because its plan is based on an impoverished understanding of human desires and interpersonal relations. Ideological
puritanism and official solutions are, for Lennon, at the nub of political
violence: thus, his criticism of revolutionaries with "minds that hate." All
too often political blueprints turn, paradoxically, from people to ideology, from relationships to institutionalism. The answer, he intimates, is
not the replacement of one system with another but the deepening and
enrichment of social relationships. "Free your mind instead," he sings.

"Revolution" was released as a Beatles single, but as the B-side of
"Hey Jude." Public and media reactions were mixed, with some critics arguing that "Revolution" was too political and others arguing that

it was not political enough. This latter position was articulated with considerable vehemence by the New Left and counterculture press.[3] Lennon was attacked for betraying the radical aspirations of the youth movement and was accused of offering up an assortment of liberal platitudes that divorced questions of politics from any determining social context. Many strongly objected to the chorus of "Revolution," in which Lennon sang "don't you know it's gonna be all right." Given that the United States was fighting a war in Vietnam that was one of the most destructive history had ever witnessed, it was hard for people to fathom Lennon's political optimism. The song, however, certainly has a satirical edge: the irony of the sugar sweet "shoo-be-doo-wah" backing vocals was perhaps lost on some critics.

The left's greatest point of political consternation concerned the question of violence itself. You can "count me out" was Lennon's response to the left. These lyrics were taken as a clear sign of his apoliticism. Indeed, the London Marxist underground newspaper, *Black Dwarf*, published an attack on him, declaring that "Revolution" finds The Beatles "safeguarding their capitalist investment."[4] Lennon, writing an open letter in a subsequent edition, declared himself unbothered by the left's reaction. "I'll tell you," he wrote, "what's wrong with the world: people—so do you want to destroy them? Until you/we change our heads—there's no chance. Tell me of one successful revolution. Who fucked up communism, christianity, capitalism, buddhism, etc.? Sick heads, and nothing else."[5]

The more politicized fans, who felt a sense of disillusionment with Lennon's refusal to consider the uses of violence, were given grounds to be somewhat more optimistic after the release of the "White Album" (officially titled *The Beatles*). Appearing two months after the "Hey Jude/Revolution" single, the White Album contained "Revolution 1," the original, acoustic, bluesy version of the song. On this version, Lennon presents his doubts and anxieties more plaintively; his delivery, in fact, allows the listener to grasp the ambivalence and uncertainty of his politics. Of signal importance was the following addition: after singing "When you talk about destruction / Don't you know you can count me out," Lennon added "in." He later claimed that although he believed that the ends cannot justify the means in political life, he felt uncertain about political violence. He preferred nonviolence; but he acknowledged that there were circumstances where violence might be morally defensible. Many fans concluded that Lennon had become more militant since the release of the single. However, the situation was actually more complicated. Lennon's out/in equivocation was recorded first, on 30 May, and subsequently dropped, replaced by "count me out" for the single. His ambivalence over whether he wanted to be counted in or out of a revolutionary culture made a dramatic return, however, in a promotional film for "Revolution" that The Beatles recorded semi-live soon thereafter. Lennon's equivocation is, characteristically, less "or" than it is "and"—radically multiple, plural, uncertain.

From our contemporary vantage point, the debate spawned by "Revolution" can be viewed as a product of that blend of radicalism and cynicism, euphoria and disillusionment, which marked the political scene of 1968. When viewed with hindsight influenced by Tiananmen Square and the global crash of Marxism, Lennon's anxieties about political transformation seem more on the mark than the criticisms made by some of his detractors. It might still be said, though, that the commercialization of "Revolution" (the song was licensed for a Nike advertisement in 1988 by its copyright owner, Michael Jackson) justifies the very critique of the existing social order made by the New Left.[6] Certainly, the claims and counterclaims to radicalism and conservatism made by Lennon and his critics cannot be easily judged. For one thing, the connections between individual rights, democracy, and freedom have been analyzed by radical political theorists in recent years as increasingly complex in a world that is globally cosmopolitan.[7] For many analysts, globalization reveals plainly enough the exhaustion of received political ideologies, the terrain of left and right—a terrain on which I might add Lennon's "Revolution" has, for the most part, been debated. Another difficulty here is that Lennon's own political biography fails to serve as the ultimate court of appeal in this matter. Despite his short-lived "Maoist phase" in New York in the early 1970s, he later came to repudiate his adoption of Maoism as a period of radical chic; he believed, in fact, that his art had greatly suffered because of this overzealous attempt at politicization.

The decision as to whether "Revolution" should be periodized as a radical or a reactionary moment is thus highly complex, and it is not one that can easily be pursued without reference to the cultural and political milieux in which Lennon worked. From this broader perspective, it is the weaving together of artistic and political currents, and not Lennon's personal behavior or ideological dispositions, that makes "Revolution" a radical cultural achievement. It is necessary, therefore, to link the different expressive elements of the "Revolution" trilogy in order to adequately comprehend the instabilities and uncertainties that Lennon unearths in the intersections between personal and political life. Let us return to the recording of "Revolution" once more in order to further develop this line of argument.

After recording the first, acoustic version of "Revolution 1" on 30 May, Lennon returned to Abbey Road with Yoko Ono a week later to commence work on a new piece. This recording took as its departure point the instrumental jam at the end of "Revolution 1." The new song, titled "Revolution 9," was an epic avant-garde piece of backward recordings and tape loops that runs for just over eight minutes. Contrary to the conventional view that Lennon and Ono merely assembled random sounds for this song, they in fact worked for two days at Abbey Road preparing material for a recording that ran to five sessions. Indeed, Lennon subsequently commented that "Revolution 9" was the most time-consuming and painstakingly recorded of any Beatles track.[8] The repeating phrase "number nine," taken from a sample tape of the Royal Academy of Music, is the song's key signature. Other material, which Mark Lewisohn has analyzed, includes the orchestral overdub from the "A Day in the Life" sessions; backward mellotron sounds; random comments from Lennon, Ono, Harrison, George Martin, and Apple office manager Alistair Taylor; hysterical laughter; and various symphonies and operas (including a loop of the last chord of Sibelius's Seventh Symphony).[9] The finished result was a recording of breathtaking intensity, a work that was at once exhilarating and frightening. The most unlikely Beatles song ever released, "Revolution 9" was music pitted against itself: no melody, chords, or lyrics; no instruments or vocals; and, to add to all this, no Beatles (or at least no Beatles as ordinarily understood). With a stunning swirl of sound, Lennon had effected a radical assault on the human sensorium.

"Revolution 9" needs to be placed in the wider context of radical European modernism and the revolutionary avant-garde. From dada and surrealism to futurism and situationism, the avant-garde flouted received aesthetic traditions in order to break down seemingly secure distinctions between content and form, production and reception, art

and non-art. In political terms, the avant-garde sought to unleash repressed currents of human energy for the building of new cultural relations. It is the task of a radical aesthetic to overshoot institutionalized consciousness in the hope of coming out somewhere on the other
side—to a revolutionized reality. Lennon's "Revolution 9" inherits this
lineage to the extent that it radically challenges traditional modes of
reality perception, draws the listener into its pluralized aural invoca-
tions, and refuses to give in to dominant ideological demands for aesthetic closure and melodic standardization.

Yet it is not self-evident that this radical aesthetic tradition was uppermost in Lennon's mind during the recording of "Revolution 9."
The influence of conceptual and performance art, especially the
musique concrète experiments of John Cage and Karlheinz Stock-
hausen, also brooked large. The lighting rod for Lennon's experimentation was Yoko Ono. She had performed with Cage during the early
1960s through her involvement with Fluxus, a group of artists who
had pioneered developments in musical minimalism, live-action
painting, and avant-garde film.[10] Cage's maxim, that art can be anything one wishes it to be, sums up well the aesthetic spirit of Fluxus.
This sentiment also appealed to Lennon, whose musical and literary
work had become increasingly experimental since The Beatles had retired from touring in 1966. His developing romantic relationship with
Ono seems to have allowed him the opportunity to upgrade this com-
positional experimentation. Their first avant-garde collaboration, *Unfinished Music No. 1: Two Virgins,* was recorded only weeks before
The Beatles commenced work on the "Revolution" trilogy. From this
perspective, "Revolution 9" might be seen as reflecting Lennon's desire to continue this nonrationalized form of aesthetic production in
the context of his more familiar work environment with The Beatles.

Once we have taken into consideration these cultural and aesthetic
factors, more interesting political questions begin to arise in relation
to the "Revolution" trilogy. How, for example, are we to understand
Lennon's crisscrossing of the mass market and the avant-garde?
Should the acoustic, electric, and electronic versions of "Revolution"
be thought of as politically differentiated? Can they all be appre-
hended within the same political logic or ideology, or does each version force a fracturing of our dominant political rhetoric? All of these
questions are open-ended and fluid and perhaps indicate the novel
power of the "Revolution" trilogy to disturb conventional political

forms of thought. Placing "Revolution" in broader cultural and aesthetic contexts also raises serious questions about the political character of the work, particularly the relationship between aesthetics and
politics. For placing "Revolution" is not simply a matter of attempting
to figure out whether Lennon was for or against political violence;
such an approach, as we have seen, colludes with the either/or logic
that Lennon himself sought to outstrip. Nor is it only a matter of es-
tablishing some critical point of purchase upon political life from the
lofty heights of an art that is divorced from contemporary experiments
with politics, such as identity politics, sexual politics, or lifestyle politics. It is rather that Lennon's "Revolution" trilogy effects, in itself, a
crucial sociopolitical intervention: it is an aesthetic work, deeply significant in the history of pop music, which underwrites the open-endedness and transformability of human desires in politics. Taking the
excluded creativity of interpersonal relations and returning it to a
more central position, Lennon's "Revolution 9" borders on a reinvention of the political itself.

Reinvention of politics might seem a contradiction in terms, but I
use it to underscore the point that "Revolution 9" is Lennon's attempt
to deliver the revolutionary avant-garde up to the mass market. The
revolutionary culture proposed is not one of psychedelic surrealism—
Lennon had already accomplished this with "Strawberry Fields Forever," "Lucy in the Sky with Diamonds," "Baby You're a Rich Man,"
and "I Am the Walrus." Rather, "Revolution 9" seeks to fold politics
back into itself in an attempt to bring low our conventional modes of
sense making and self-understanding. Unlike previous currents of the
revolutionary avant-garde, however, Lennon's work reached a global
exposure which shifted this aesthetic tradition from the periphery to
the center. Millions listened to The Beatles' "White Album" in 1968.
Insofar as "Revolution 9" generated anxiety, fear, annoyance, and no
doubt some degree of boredom in its listeners, Lennon offers an instructive lesson in what might be called a fracturing or dislocation
of aesthetic form to the mass market. "Lennon's sortie into sonic
chance," writes Ian MacDonald, "was packaged for a mainstream audience which had never heard of its progenitors, let alone been confronted by their work."[11] Lennon and The Beatles had again broken
new ground.

The "Revolution" trilogy is also radical in another sense. Although
The Beatles often experimented with different ways of approaching

and recording their songs, they did not usually make these experiments available to the public. This practice changed with the release of "Revolution," "Revolution 1," and "Revolution 9." The trilogy vividly demonstrates Lennon's acute multiform aesthetic and reflects his ongoing concern with change, multiplicity, and uncertainty. It is unusual to find all this experimentation taking place within one song (or, more precisely, three different versions of one song), partly because the disparate elements of Lennon's aesthetic were often split between his official Beatles output on the one hand and his non-Beatles work on the other. This splitting between commercialism and the avant-garde raises important contradictions and ambiguities. Yet it would be foolish to think that these different aesthetic moments can be easily sorted out or divided: it is not always clear where one identity ends and another one begins in the case of Lennon.

The ambiguities of Lennon's aesthetic identity become evident after it is recalled that his work with The Beatles is at once simple and sophisticated, commercial and aesthetic, popular and original. For example, in the studio Lennon and the other Beatles frequently engaged in technological experimentation, from double-tracking to tape loops. Random events were incorporated into songs (a radio broadcast of *King Lear* was mixed into "I Am the Walrus"), and tape speeds were varied and often reversed (the guitar solo in "Tomorrow Never Knows" is actually the solo of "Taxman" run backward). Such experimentation notwithstanding, The Beatles remained committed to (and plainly were identified with) the mass market. It was precisely through his ability to interweave simplicity and sophistication that Lennon transformed the music of The Beatles into great art.

But Lennon often experienced such commercial pressures as artistic constraint. It is surely no accident that his growing dissatisfaction with The Beatles in the late 1960s inspired a thoroughgoing revaluation of his life and art. Nor is it any wonder that in Yoko Ono he found an avant-garde practitioner with whom to explore these other modes of artistic and political expression. He discovered that he could push his interest in experimentation to the nth degree with Ono, and without regard for commercial considerations.[12] *Two Virgins* was the first major indication that Lennon wished to transform his music into a full-blown aestheticism; and he further developed this inclination with *Unfinished Music No. 2: Life with the Lions* and *The Wedding Album*. These musical collaborations are crammed with tape loops and reversed recordings, filtered noises and frequencies, random guitar and piano sounds, and vocal experiments. More than just an assault on traditional aesthetic form, these collaborations fashion an art at odds with itself. This is an art conceptualized in terms of an open-ended articulation of elements ("unfinished music" eludes closure).

But if ambiguity pervades Lennon's aesthetic productions, it is not simply because of some pervasive uncertainty over the kind of music or sort of art to which he wants his name attached. On the contrary, the one thing which Lennon appears sure about is the centrality of uncertainty to the creative process. As Lennon put it in 1975:

> As soon as you've clutched onto something, you think—you're always clutching at straws—*this is what life is all about.* . . . "Oh, *this* is it! *Now* I know what I'm doing! Right? Down this road for the next hundred years" . . . and it ain't never like *that.* Whether it's a religious hat or a political hat or a no-political hat: whatever hat it was, always looking for these straw hats. I think I found out it's a waste of time. There is no hat to wear. Just keep moving around and changing clothes is the best. That's all that goes on: *change.*[13]

Does Lennon claim that all change is merely random, an abandonment of the self to fate? Not at all. Lennon claims rather that the self needs to take into account change and ambiguity in its dealings with the world. Lennon's aesthetic identity hovers between commercialism and the avant-garde because he works to sustain a foot in each camp. The breakup of The Beatles was a necessary, but by no means sufficient, condition for the advancement of Lennon's multiform aesthetic, at once commercial, avant-garde, cultural and intensely political. Contrast *Two Virgins* and *Imagine,* or *The Wedding Album* and *Double Fantasy:* Lennon's aesthetic identity subsists in the twilight zone between two worlds. It is in this sense that constructions of Lennon's music emerge as doubled, not so much *from* pop to avant-garde as *between* pop and avant-garde.

LENNON'S BRIDGING OF ART and music, aesthetics and commercialism— I have suggested—is best comprehended from the vantage point of doubleness and ambiguity. But if Lennon's bridging is best comprehended this way at the level of art, it is also true of his politics. He was appalled at the emptiness of social vision, the lack of moral principle, and the corruption infiltrating governmental practices in the Western body politic. Fascinated by the 1960s antiwar movement, he became increasingly aware of the formidable challenges being posed to established authority in the state, the family, and gender relations; and, indeed, the peace campaign which he developed with Ono was in many ways an attempt to extend the terms of participatory democracy inaugurated by these political currents. But he was also anxious about the negative, or self-destructive, elements within the radical movement, and he remained deeply suspicious of the idea that politics can be meaningfully pursued without reference to broader cultural and aesthetic matters. Politics for Lennon is always doubled, locked between thought and action, reflectiveness and reflex, power and protest. His interventions into the political world relentlessly play with this doubleness, and it is perhaps not surprising therefore that our cultural rememberings of Lennon are also inscribed with this ambivalent logic.

My focus on Lennon's political involvements concerns his interventions in the political-ideological and aesthetic-performative fields. Each of these fields corresponds, roughly, to a different biographical period, although there are overlaps and tensions in this linking of personal and political life. Lennon's political criticism focused attention, above all, upon the damaging consequences of sociocultural polarization. Criticism is an apt term here, since this aspect of Lennon's politics involves mostly contemplation and reflection rather than direct political action. During The Beatles' American tour in the summer of 1966, Lennon spoke out against the Vietnam War. Disobeying manager Brian Epstein's injunction against commenting on political affairs, he denounced the war on both political and moral grounds. He also told reporters that the butcher cover for the new Beatles album *Yesterday and Today*, in which the Fab Four are surrounded by bloody meat and decapitated dolls, was "as relevant as Vietnam."[14] He had adopted the role of celebrity-cum-political-critic. He extended this position by appearing in Richard Lester's film *How I Won the War*. In the film, shot in 1966 after The Beatles had retired from touring, Lennon played the role of one Private Gripweed. *How I Won the War* was primarily a satirical critique of the military and was largely canned by the mainstream media for its antiwar position. In its blending of avant-garde and antiwar currents, the film anticipated many of Lennon's subsequent political interests and did much to advance his reputation in countercultural circles.

In the late 1960s and early 1970s, Lennon became more and more interested in the political left. He granted an interview to the Marxist newspaper *Red Mole* in March 1971, in which issues of socialism, feminism, and racism were discussed; and he became friendly with the paper's editors, Tariq Ali and Robin Blackburn.[15] He explained his commitment to radical politics thus:

> I've always been politically minded, you know, and against the status quo. It's pretty basic when you're brought up, like I was, to hate and fear the police as a natural enemy. . . . I mean, it's just a basic working class thing, though it begins to wear off when you get older, get a family and get swallowed up in the system. In my case I've never not been political, though religion tended to overshadow it in my acid days; that would be around '65 or '66. And that religion was directly the result of all that superstar shit—religion was an outlet for my repression. I thought, "Well, there's something else to life, isn't there? This isn't it, surely?" But I was always political in a way, you know.[16]

If Lennon exaggerates his working-class background here, positioning himself against the status quo and political authority, it is also the case that much of his anger is pitted against a social system that he holds responsible for the death of his mother. That he was brought up to hate and fear the police is an outcome less of his childhood socialization with the protective Aunt Mimi than of the emotional catastrophe suffered upon learning that an off duty policeman had killed his mother in a car accident. The psychic stakes of politics, however, are not discussed at such an intensely personal level in the interview with Ali and Blackburn. Instead, the key focus concerns the connections between the revolutionary avant-garde, political resistance, and the mobilization of the working class. The newspaper's cover photograph, interestingly enough, shows Lennon and Ono wearing *Red Mole* T-shirts. Lennon's Marxist sympathies were further exaggerated when the article was published in the United States, in *Ramparts:* it carried the headline "The Working Class Hero Turns Red." Saying that Lennon had turned Red was exaggeration, since Lennon expressed doubts about the practicalities of workers' control as well as some anxieties about the cult of revolutionary leadership. "In Western-style Communism," he said, "we would have to create an almost imaginary workers' image of *themselves* as the father-figure."[17] Like that other imaginative figurehead of the political left, Herbert Marcuse, Lennon had turned Freud on his head in one stroke.

The activities of the countercultural left became increasingly important to Lennon during this period, and he wrote a number of songs to support the movement. He supported the London underground magazine *OZ*, whose editors were arrested on charges of obscenity. At issue was an edition of *OZ* that carried a drawing of lesbian sex on its cover and, inside, bizarre sexual drawings such as depictions of rats entering vaginas—all contributed by teenagers. The editors were found guilty and sentenced to fifteen months in prison. In response, Lennon wrote two songs for the *OZ* defense committee, "God Save Us" and "Do the Oz." The songs were released by Apple in July 1971 (under the name The Electric Oz Band), but they failed to make the charts and are largely forgotten today.

Lennon's most effective critical assault on social norms, however, lay in composing a number of truly popular political songs. "Give Peace a Chance," "Imagine," "Power to the People," and "Happy Xmas (War Is Over)": these linger on as supreme instances of radical political music. All were released as singles and were worldwide hits. In writing these songs, it is as though Lennon found a means to explore new political possibilities for modern society, but in a manner which made critical thinking attractive to a mass audience. Jon Wiener, in *Come Together*, makes much of this:

Even at this peak of his political commitment, however, John did not try to work outside of the capitalist media. On the contrary, he continued to work through the recording industry and toward the AM radio market, two of the more corrupt and debased institutions of the capitalist marketplace. . . . His effort to make commercial hits out of songs like "Power to the People" was more risky and adventurous than the work of ostensibly political songwriters like Tom Paxton and Phil Ochs. There was a kind of closure around their work and their audience that was absent from John's. Far from expecting radical political songs from him, many of his fans felt betrayed by his new advocacy of socialism and feminism. John wanted to use his celebrity to reach an audience as yet unmoved by radical politics.[18]

This deliberate avoidance of a confrontational or antagonistic politics appears to have been central to Lennon's success as a political songwriter. In time, however, he attempted a more militant political approach.

The emergence of what can best be described as Lennon's ideological interventions into politics coincided with that great ferment of radical activity in the United States in the early 1970s, conceived when a new cultural project was underway, one that sought to fuse music and revolt in order to expose the pretensions and deceptions of routine politics. This ideological moment corresponds roughly with

Lennon and Ono's move to New York in late 1971, where they joined
up with outspoken political radicals Jerry Rubin and Abbie Hoffman.[19] Rubin and Hoffman were two of the Chicago Seven, who had
been charged with disrupting the 1968 Democratic National Convention in Chicago. In addition to Rubin and Hoffman, a number of leading political radicals and intellectuals socialized with Lennon and
Ono—including Kate Millett, Allen Ginsberg, Bobby Seale, and Rennie Davis. In New York, Lennon and Ono moved into an apartment in
the West Village, energetically dedicating themselves to the New Left
and countercultural movements.

For Lennon, the focus of this new ideological commitment was a national rock 'n' roll tour aimed at encouraging the youth of the United
States to vote against President Richard Nixon's reelection. The plan
was to end the tour in August 1972 in San Diego at the Republican National Convention with a massive antiwar concert—a kind of political
Woodstock.[20] Lennon's concert tour never happened. When the Nixon
administration learned what the ex-Beatle was planning, the Federal
Bureau of Investigation began a counteroffensive. In February 1972,
the Senate Internal Security Subcommittee of the Judiciary Committee produced a classified memo advising that the New Left was using
Lennon and Ono to "obtain access to college campuses; to stimulate
eighteen-year-olds to register to vote; to press for legislation legalizing
marijuana; to finance their activities; and to recruit persons to come
to San Diego during the Republican National Convention in August
1972." Clearly, Lennon was perceived as a political danger to the Nixon
administration. "If Lennon's visa is terminated," the committee advised, "it would be a strategic counter-measure."[21] On the instructions
of Attorney General John Mitchell, Lennon's visa was revoked and deportation proceedings commenced. This event set in motion a four-
year battle between the Lennons and the Immigration and Naturalization Service, a battle in which Lennon was finally victorious in 1976. In
1972, however, the immediate consequence of these proceedings was
Lennon's gradual withdrawal from radical political activity.

Before his withdrawal, Lennon and Ono undertook several important political engagements in preparation for the planned national
concert tour. Their New Left credentials were sedimented through
their regular column in the new political magazine *SunDance*. They
wrote articles addressing feminism, the politicization of music, and the
avant-garde.[22] They began composing for a new album, *Some Time in*

New York City. Lennon wrote a batch of "headline" songs for the album, addressing a range of contemporary political issues—from feminism ("Woman Is the Nigger of the World") to the violence in Northern Ireland ("The Luck of the Irish"). By Lennon's standards, nearly all the songs he wrote for *Some Time in New York City* were poor; the simplistic lyrics and clichéd political rhetoric of the songs suggested he had written the material more through a sense of dogged commitment rather than through artistic stimulus. The critics, on the whole, hated it; *Rolling Stone* referred to the album as "yesterday's papers."[23] Meanwhile, Lennon and Ono agreed to act as co-hosts for a week on *The Mike Douglas Show,* a high-rating daytime television program. Blending rock and radical politics, the Lennons presented a lineup of guests never before seen on daytime television—including Jerry Rubin, Bobby Seale, Ralph Nader, and Chuck Berry.

But perhaps the most radical political interventions were two performances that Lennon and Ono gave in December 1971. The first was the "Free John Sinclair" rally at the Chrysler Arena in Ann Arbor, Michigan. Sinclair—a radical activist, leading member of the White Panther Party, and manager of the protopunk band MC5—was serving a ten-year jail sentence for selling two marijuana cigarettes to an undercover agent. The rally to exert political pressure to have Sinclair freed included an array of celebrities, including Stevie Wonder and Phil Ochs, as well as New Left radicals such as Rennie Davis, Jerry Rubin, and Bobby Seale. Lennon was the headlining act of the night, following Stevie Wonder. In his first live appearance in the United States in five years, he took the stage at 3 A.M. with Ono, two acoustic guitarists, and a conga player (Jerry Rubin). They sang four new songs: "Attica State," "Sisters, O Sisters," "The Luck of the Irish," and "John Sinclair"—specifically written for the occasion. Introducing the song, Lennon announced: "We came here not only to help John and to spotlight what's going on but also to show and to say to all of you that apathy isn't it, and that we can do something. So flower didn't work. So what? We start again."[24] With these words, Lennon launched into his new song:

It ain't fair, John Sinclair
In the stir for breathing air
Let him be, set him free
Let him be like you and me

Almost before the audience could adjust to these new protest songs, and no doubt still expecting to hear some Beatles or solo hits, Lennon and Ono were gone. New York's *Village Voice* wrote, "The audience was slightly stunned. John and Yoko had performed for fifteen minutes, urged political activism and support for Sinclair and split."[25] The speed of their departure was matched by the speed of Sinclair's release from prison, three days after the rally, on the grounds that the marijuana statutes were about to be changed in Michigan.

A second performance was given a couple of weeks later at the Apollo Theatre in Harlem to raise funds for the relatives of prisoners shot a few months earlier at Attica, a prison in upstate New York. On 13 September 1971, a bloodbath had occurred at the prison when inmates—the majority of whom were black—took hostages, seeking terms for an amnesty. The police, on orders from state governor Nelson Rockefeller, went into the prison, killing both prisoners and guards. At the benefit on 17 December, Lennon performed the song "Attica State" and also played a haunting version of "Imagine." The mainstream press failed to report the benefit, a failure which was all the more astounding given that it was only his second concert performance in the United States as an ex-Beatle.

What distinguishes these ideological engagements from Lennon's political criticism is that they seek to intervene in, to actively shape political policy or denounce some dominant cultural logic. Politics is no longer just a conceptual affair; it is rather a matter of struggle and antagonism. Lennon had arrived at this position from years of critical thinking, as my discussion of the "Revolution" trilogy highlights, and from active struggle dating back to the Vietnam War period. There is also at work in Lennon, however, a countertrend to this valorization of the political and ideological, a countertrend that constitutes a radically different understanding of politics—an aesthetic-performative dimension of the political. This is a politics which strives to reflect upon its own imaginative underpinnings, a political frame of self-understanding that continually turns back upon itself. There was always a strongly aesthetic dimension to Lennon's work, evident in early Beatles songs such as "Yes It Is" and "If I Fell," as well as in his poetry and books. In biographical terms, this aesthetic-performative dimension of Lennon's politics really took off in his artistic collaborations with Ono in the late 1960s. This is an art concerned with the fashioning of a kind of reality essentially different from practical politics, one that accords the political unconscious a central role in any future social change.

Lennon's aesthetic-performative interventions, as opposed to his other styles of political activism, typically invoke the power of the mass media, the ways in which the media produce messages and outcomes at a stroke. The power of the media to influence public opinion is central to the very dynamism of politics, and for Lennon this power is reason enough to attempt to wrap radical politics up in advertising. "War Is Over! If You Want It. Happy Christmas from John and Yoko": through this "advertisement," Lennon and Ono sought to make the antiwar message of pressing international concern. In December 1969, they arranged for billboards carrying this message to go up in twelve cities around the world; in addition, thousands of posters were distributed globally. The message here, in some wild subjectivist moment, is that it is possible to subvert the existing political order in and through imagination. Imagine peace, so the thinking goes, and you might just help fashion a new political world. If this idea seems too utopian, which in one sense it is plainly meant to be, it is worth holding in mind that Lennon's positive purchase upon political life also incorporates something more negative as well. Shock, disturbance, and dislocation are also central objectives. Lennon and Ono, borrowing from the revolutionary avant-garde, seek to estrange politics from its institutionalized forms, to displace rationalism with art, to replace the call to action with the demand for fresh thinking.

"Bagism," first staged by Lennon and Ono in 1968 at the Royal Albert Hall, is precisely one such concept—or perhaps we should say strategy—that aims to dislodge the power of ideology in political relations through shock.[26] Requiring its participants to remain hidden inside a bag, bagism seeks to foster open communication by downgrading the visible. Lennon and Ono, by wrapping themselves up in a bag, seek to demonstrate that the essential quality of the individual is not found in external appearances and to challenge oppressive power relations, most importantly racism and sexism, sustained in and through the visual. Lennon explained the politics of bagism to BBC interviewer Michael Parkinson in 1971, after Parkinson had climbed into a bag with him and Ono. "Imagine," said Lennon, "if a black guy went for a job at the BBC and he had to wear a bag. They wouldn't know what coloured people were and there'd be no prejudice, for a kick off!"[27] The problem with this view, as the reader might have already gathered, is that it is not so simple to strip politics of its dominant cultural forms. Ideologies of race, gender, and class are pervasive in modern society, and it might therefore be more politically effective to hold these symbolic factors in mind than to wish them away. From this perspective, it is perhaps possible to recast bagism as an attempt by Lennon and Ono to engage in political debate free of the distortions of their own public image, while simultaneously underscoring the power of the mass media in the framing of politics.

What can be discerned from these performances and acts about Lennon's politics? Was he simply a celebrity caught up in a new form of culture, or was he part of the revolutionary avant-garde? In his politics, as in his aesthetic work, there is a kind of doubling at work.[28] Lennon moves in the intermediary space between political, ideological, and aesthetic-performative fields; it is precisely in this wavering between fields that we can detect Lennon's ambivalence about politics as such. His work bridges or links various oppositional discourses and narratives: self and other, desire and reason, individual and history, psychological and social, masculine and feminine, celebrity and politics. To say this is to argue that Lennon as a cultural icon is both aesthetic and political. If he estranges music from itself in suitably postmodernist style, introducing the mass market to the avant-garde in "Revolution 9," he does so because at another level he attempts to unhinge radical political thinking from its traditional forms. If his politics is frustratingly open-ended and ambivalent, this is because his artistic and cultural productions are so exquisitely self-reflexive as to appear ageless and unceasingly new. Lennon, as cultural icon, repairs that split in the political sphere between what Hayden White characterizes as the "historical" and the "unhistorical."[29] The historical for White is determined by institutionally designated realms of political authority and power; whereas the unhistorical involves the happenings of daily life, that is, nonformalized activities, events, and social practices. This division between the historical and the unhistorical is challenged in Lennon's political aesthetic, challenged to the extent that Lennon passionately believes that the aesthetics of daily life are just as important as what a society recognizes as its official, historical moments. Ultimately, Lennon attempts to subvert the given social order through an upgrading of the powers of the aesthetic itself.

No MEGASTAR FLUCTUATES between mainstream and avant-garde cinema more than John Lennon. The early Beatles comedy films, *A Hard
Day's Night* (1964) and *Help!* (1965), both directed by Richard Lester,
were replete with Lennon's wisecracking and sardonic humor. In a
surreal blend of the Goons and the Marx Brothers, *A Hard Day's
Night* and *Help!* capture the imaginative reach of Lennon's wit, his
deadpan delivery, his mocking treatment of others. The first film,
cashing in on Beatlemania, sought to expose the world to the unpre-
tentious manner and outrageous humor of the Fab Four. The film's
narrative follows the lives of The Beatles on tour: performing, appearing on television, living in hotels, and being chased by their adoring fans. *A Hard Day's Night* played a vital role in sedimenting the
personal style of each Beatle for the public: John, the literary wit;
Paul, the boy next door; George, the cheeky, introverted romantic;
and Ringo, the lovable joker. Years later, Lennon complained about
these one-dimensional characterizations, saying he had felt infuriated
by the glibness of it. Yet he also said the movie was fun to make and
was probably his favorite Beatles movie. *A Hard Day's Night* was a
smash hit worldwide and was nominated for two Oscars.[30] Critic Andrew Sarris wrote:

A Hard Day's Night has turned out to be the *Citizen Kane* of jukebox musi-
cals, the brilliant crystallisation of such diverse cultural particles as the pop
movie, rock 'n' roll, *cinéma vérité*, the *nouvelle vague*, free cinema, the af-
fectedly hand-held camera, frenzied cutting, the cult of the sexless sub-
adolescent, the semi-documentary, and studied spontaneity.[31]

While Lennon's early Beatles films were a blend of mainstream
commercialism and concentrated experimentation, the same cannot
be said of the avant-garde films on which Lennon collaborated with
Yoko Ono in the late 1960s and early 1970s. He had long been interested in the aesthetic aspects of film and had experimented with the
format of 8 mm home movies in the mid-1960s. Ono had also had
some exposure to the medium through her association with Fluxus,
which sought, among other things, to apply randomness and chance
selection to film. Ono contributed two films to the 1965 Fluxfilm Program: *Number 1*, a slow-motion shot of a match striking; and *Number
4*, a film comprising close-up shots of twelve naked buttocks. From
the time Lennon and Ono became intimately involved in 1968
through to their move to New York in 1971, they wrote and directed

many films, including *Film No. 5—Smile* (1968), *Two Virgins* (1968), *Rape* (1969), *Self-Portrait* (1969), *Apotheosis* (1970), *Up Your Legs Forever* (1970), *Fly* (1970), *Erection* (1971), *Clock* (1971), and *Imagine* (1972).

Perhaps the one consistent feature of these films is their alienation and dispersal of the spectator-subject; they are films which, in various ways, leave the viewer hovering between identification and distance, pleasure and anxiety. Lennon's *Apotheosis* is a perfect example: the film deals with the connections between nature and culture, and specifically with how the two dislocate each other. The film opens with the view from a hot-air balloon as it begins to float upward over the snowy English countryside. Passing over a town square, and then into the sky, the camera-balloon enters the clouds—with the result that the screen is completely white for several minutes. All serene stuff, as far as it goes. But the absence of any musical accompaniment proves more discomforting; apart from some voices and some dogs barking at the beginning of the film, silence dominates. It is in this silence that the gap between nature and culture comes to prominence: nature seems silent when compared to the noise of culture, a contrast which highlights that what we take to be natural is, in fact, always socially framed. Whatever the ideological implications of *Apotheosis*, however, reviewers unanimously disliked the film. Audiences did not enjoy it either. It was booed at the 1971 Cannes Film Festival, and many people walked out of its New York premiere. "The peace-and-love generation," wrote one critic, "couldn't face the peace of the white screen."[32]

Rape and *Fly* were two of the more popular avant-garde films directed by Lennon and Ono. *Rape* is the story of an Austrian woman (Eva Majlath) pursued for several days through the streets of London. Highly unusual, if somewhat contrived, *Rape* is a kind of antifilm. Eva Majlath is not an actress. She does not know the camera crew filming her; nor does she know why they are filming. She is followed not by any screen character but rather by the camera itself—and, by implication, the viewer. From the outset, the film has a menacing feel: it invades another's world, closes in upon another's personal space. At various points, Majlath speaks directly to the camera, but no response is given, not even when she asks for a match to light her cigarette.

Rape, although centering on Majlath throughout, advances no plot. The woman followed becomes increasingly agitated and frightened as the film progresses; but this can be understood more as referring to a state of mind than as exhibiting a development of narrative. The fear that pervades the film is arrived at by a path which leads from the woman's asking to be left alone to her more-desperate attempts to escape the camera. The state of mind evoked (fear, anxiety, and dread) is intensified by the very title of the film. The camera's omnipotent monitoring of a beautiful woman in distress raises the connection between violence and sexuality, which are sometimes interlocked as sexual violence and sometimes kept apart.

Rape, in keeping with other avant-garde films of the time, shifts uneasily between pleasure and fracturing, identification and disjunction, and these shifts give the film its political edge. The viewer necessarily identifies with the camera as observer, an observer both omnipotent and powerless. Identification with the camera invites the viewer to adopt an omnipotent gaze, a gaze which is symptomatic of the fantasy of control and mastery. It is this illusion of omnipotence which film theorist Christian Metz, drawing on Lacan's Freud, sees all cinema as invoking. With reference to Lacan, Metz argues that the spectator-subject inhabits an imaginary realm; there is an identification of the subject with itself as some "pure act of perception."[33] Such distorted experience is Lacan's concept of the mirror-stage transferred to the cultural domain: the image making of cinema permits the spectator to identify with his or her own gaze, but refracted through the gaze of the other. The other in this case is the frightened and vulnerable Majlath. Viewers of *Rape*, one might say, are located as unified, centered subjects of the Lacanian imaginary to the extent that Majlath is an object of desire, an object for the controlling gaze with which the other sees. Yet it is also at the level of the gaze that this imaginary coherence is unstuck, for Majlath pleads to be left alone and, in doing so, makes a demand that the viewer cannot grant. This is a demand which remains disturbing.

The stylistic framing of *Rape* extends this psychic fracturing. In a profound alienation of the viewer's imaginary control of the image-object, an alienation effect that perhaps qualifies as Brechtian, the camera's surveillance of Majlath constantly chops and changes, starts and stops. This choppiness is necessitated by technical requirements. Every time a film roll ends, the cameraman falls behind Majlath, and so each new sequence begins with the camera catching up with her and frightening her once again. The point-of-view shots are similarly disturbing. In keeping with the theme of invasion (personal, emotional, bodily, sexual), *Rape* is replete with big close-ups of Majlath. We see her, for example, holding her hand across her face in order to maintain some personal distance from the camera; she sometimes tries to block the lens to push the viewer away; and the camera's hand-held close-ups capture the sense of personal oppression and frustration that modernist techniques of surveillance have bred.

The second half of the film is even more disquieting, veering from Majlath's distress at constantly being watched to the terror of complete psychological dislocation. Majlath is followed back to her apartment (her sister provided the camera crew with a key to the flat), where she becomes increasingly anxious and angry. Unable to break from the viewer's scrutiny, she begins yelling in German. She moves quickly around the apartment; she cries and is gripped by fear. Finally, she makes a telephone call and begins talking anxiously. The film ends here, with the credits running over the sound of her emotional distress.

What appears as in-depth coverage of one woman's terror in dealing with the scrutiny of a phallocentric world is, in fact, a radical critique of the conquest of personal space by modern technology. In modern society, individuals are expected to present a self-image more or less in keeping with the conventions of social life—in that sorting out of the appropriate from the inappropriate which sociologist Erving Goffman brilliantly documented in *The Presentation of Self in Everyday Life.*[34] The demand for presentation of self-continuity is present in all modern social organization, but it is radicalized in a society where electronic surveillance is possible. By locating personal life in the framework of constant surveillance, *Rape* dramatizes this dilemma. And by specifically focusing on the surveillance of a woman, Lennon and Ono underscore not only the sexual stakes of societal observation but also the point that femininity is considered intrinsically recalcitrant to the social system. It is Majlath's emotional disaffection, which ranges from anger to hysteria, that represents a threat to conventional norms of self-presentation and so may be interpreted as suggesting the normative power of our own self-drilling in surveillance. Indeed, it is hard not to see the final scene of *Rape* as some intense return of the repressed, an unleashing of female hysteria, not as a pathological symptom but rather as psychic rejection of oppressive social relationships.

It is also striking how this traumatic invasion of personal space by the other mirrors the mass-media scrutiny of Lennon and Ono in the late 1960s. Much of this media interest played upon public outrage that Lennon had divorced his wife to take up with another woman. But the intensity of media concentration on Lennon also revealed something else, something more sinister, something rooted in a fear of otherness. The otherness in this case concerned race. Anti-Japanese sentiment was a defining aspect of postwar British culture. The British media, and the press in particular, displayed a deeply racist attitude toward Ono—especially in reporting on her romance with, and subsequent marriage to, Lennon. The outpourings of fear and hatred in these reports on Ono were torrential. She was oftentimes cast as an "evil Japanese witch" who had stolen Lennon from his wife and child. That she was an avant-garde practitioner and an eloquent feminist only made her more threatening in the eyes of many fans, reporters, and critics. Indeed, media coverage of Lennon's private life at this time was pervaded by an excessively moralizing tone, the most unpleasant aspect of which was the display of glee over Lennon and Ono's drug bust in London in 1968. Not surprisingly, the media were also profoundly fascinated with Lennon's political radicalism, his anti-establishment motive, and his involvement in the peace movement. In some ways, Lennon and Ono played up to the anger and outrage which the media both mobilized and sustained. He remarked on several occasions that Ono was him "in drag," a formulation guaranteed to shock those already uncomfortable with an interracial relationship.

Lennon and Ono found the media's denigration of them, especially the racist slurs, hurtful. Perhaps then it is for this reason that, in much of their artistic work, Lennon and Ono are preoccupied with questions about the ways in which our media-driven culture has enthralled people through the fashioning of sensational, and largely fictitious, scandals. For it is arguable that *Rape* is a look into the distorted mirroring by which the media report to the public on encounters with otherness, thereby reconfirming dominant ideologies. The film examines in microscopic detail the manner in which the media violate the other in the process of confirming what we know about ourselves. The anti-Japanese abuse that Ono and Lennon encountered at this point in their lives is given full metaphoric expression in the frightening gestures and alarming rhythms of *Rape*, thus underscoring the symbolic forms of the coercive conditions of law in modern society. Indeed,

Lennon and Ono's *Rape* continually draws attention to this coercive relation between identity and otherness through its dramatization of the oppressive relationship between observer and observed—and, implicitly, the collaboration between the media and their audience.

If *Rape* questions the political implications of identification in an age of surveillance, the same can be said of *Fly*. Filmed over two days in New York in December 1970, *Fly* examines the fraught relation between nature and culture: specifically, between the experience of the body on the one hand and the cultural and sexual pressures impinging upon it on the other. The entire film consists of close-ups of a seemingly unconscious nude woman being explored by a fly. The fly crawls from the woman's feet up to her genitals, which it examines for some time, and then continues its expedition, touring her breasts, armpit, face, ears, and hair. Lennon and Ono manage to pluck a profound symbolic meaning from the insect's bemusing wanderings. *Fly* is, among other things, a metaphorical statement about masculinist culture, its forms of identification and interrogation, its mapping and colonization of sexuality and the body, its framing and gendering of activity and passivity, as well as its more pathological forms of power and control.

Politically speaking, these themes are pointed up by a contrast between the activity of the fly and the passivity of the woman. The fly busily crawls about its business, and this flaunting activism is underscored by the film's soundtrack, which consists of Ono's bizarre, yet highly effective fly sounds and Lennon's backward guitar loops. The passive presence of the seemingly unconscious woman, by contrast, calls forth not only the sexual stereotype of the "frigid woman" but also the exclusion of women from *his*tory. According to French feminist philosopher Luce Irigaray, who invokes the term "derelection" to designate women's inability to express themselves in the masculinist sociosymbolic order, this exclusion is at once psychical and political.[35] It is perhaps for this reason that the seemingly unconscious nude woman in *Fly* stands as both a backward glance at patriarchy and a reminder of the difficulties that women face in the political present. But the passivity of the female here also comes to stand in for that absence or lack which the fly, in some more properly structural and hence masculine sense, attempts to cover over in its hypermanic wanderings. Indeed, it is precisely in this cross-referencing of identification between insect and body, between masculine insistence and feminine subversion, that Lennon and Ono stage an imaginative engagement

with the politics of sexuality itself. Their strategy for effecting a radical deconstruction of sexuality in *Fly* is to highlight not only the splitting which underpins sexual difference and gender hierarchy but also
our unconscious complicity in the established system of gender identity. To say this is to argue that *Fly* uncovers in identification, intimate
and sexual, a splitting of identity and otherness. In other words, there
is always something left over, some subjective aspect of the self, which
is not incorporated in the moment of identification. "I wondered how
many people," said Ono at the film's premiere, "would look at the fly
or at the body."[36]

Even if it is true that as spectators we always take the camera's gaze
as our own, there are still difficult problems of representation and
pleasure that need to be accounted for. What pleasures might one
possibly take in watching a fly crawl about a woman's body for three-
quarters of an hour? *Fly* was one of Lennon and Ono's most successful films (with both critics and public), and there is likely something
more at stake here than just the artistic imaginings of the avant-garde
and the counterculture. What is important in terms of representation
and pleasure in *Fly* is not only the relationship between sexuality and
culture but the complex question of how we view this relationship itself. One of the most interesting aspects of the cinematography is that
in the microfocus on the fly, the woman's body is seen, at first, only in
parts. The female form is represented in fragments: femininity is revealed not only as resistant to totalization (what is the "complete
woman"?) but as larger than life. In this sense of the incomprehen-
sible, there is a rough analogy with Freud's infamous comment
about femininity as a "dark continent." There is something other
which places femininity beyond the reaches of masculinist reason,
something which Freud thought specific to women's psychology,
that disturbs culturally defensive demands for certitude. A number of
feminists have, of course, argued that Freudianism ideologically underwrites women's "inferiority" at the psychological level. Other feminists have argued instead that Freud's description of sexual and gender difference offers a trenchant critique of patriarchy rather than
simply a conceptual legitimation of it. While there is undoubtedly
some truth on both sides of this feminist divide, my point is that *Fly*
might be said to operate precisely in the space of an ambivalent political logic. For the film at once offers up disturbing images of a frag-

mented female form (and hence infuses masculinist fantasies of the feminine body as little more than sexually gratifying part-objects) and goes beyond stereotypical images of female sexuality as something mysterious, alluring, erotic.

Fly is, however, more political and paradoxical than some Freudian analysis of the splittings and repressions that pervade the realm of gender would indicate, significant though that analysis is. The film deals also with the political constraints and distortions to which sexuality and the body are subjected. For in the fly's incessant roaming, one might argue, a bodily scrutiny is transmuted into a political one. The links between sexuality, the body, and political repression were important issues in radical social thought at the time *Fly* was filmed. The writings of sexual radicals such as Herbert Marcuse and Norman O. Brown, both of whom saw sexual and political repression as interlinked, influenced the counterculture and New Left radicals of the 1960s. There can be little doubt that these ideas affected the work of Lennon and Ono, if not directly then at least indirectly.[37] Viewed from this perspective, *Fly* offers a powerful interpretation of the psychic demands and costs of modernity. For it deconstructs modernity's political mapping of the body, and in doing so, it might be said to uncover the normalizing formulae of domination—the domination typical of, in Michel Foucault's terms, power/knowledge. Knowledge, as Foucault makes clear, presupposes and constitutes power, in that it disciplines its subjects into self-fashionings and self-directives that imitate the codes of the political cultural order. "Each person," writes Foucault, "has the duty to know who he is, that is, to try to know what is happening inside him, to acknowledge faults, to recognize temptations, to locate desires."[38] One might speculate from Foucault's statement that *Fly* interrogates such a cultural urge to know, to fix, sexuality: that is, culture's desperate attempt to fix the connection between sexuality and gender, to deny the contingent and the ambivalent, to transform inherently precarious human experience into codes of knowledge and power. Importantly, Foucault argues that power is not simply a constraining force but also a mobilizing phenomenon. And it is equally true that, while Lennon and Ono locate power as a force of domination in *Fly* and *Rape,* they continue to hold out the hope that power can be marshaled for a more creative politics premised upon love, peace, and creativity.

FROM 25 TO 31 MARCH 1969, Lennon and Ono staged a "Bed-In for Peace" in Amsterdam. They rented the presidential suite at the Hilton Hotel and invited the media to attend. Reactions were mixed. After the bed-in was announced, there was much speculation about what, exactly, would take place. Fearing social unrest, the chief of Amsterdam's vice squad warned that the police would intervene to prevent such a "happening."[39] The media, sensing disruption, knew they were onto a good thing. More than fifty journalists and television interviewers turned up on the first day, no doubt hoping that Lennon and Ono would conjure up something to surpass their sexual exhibitionism on the *Two Virgins* album cover of the previous year. The bed-in, however, was a very different affair. When the press were admitted, Lennon and Ono were sitting in bed, wearing pajamas. The message they offered to the media seemed as baffling as it was simple: they planned to stay in bed for a week and let their hair grow, in order to protest against violence.

The Amsterdam bed-in took place one week after Lennon and Ono married on 20 March, at a registry office in Gibraltar. Its aim, according to Lennon, was to exploit the media's interest in them by turning their honeymoon into a public event. "For reasons only known to themselves," said Lennon, "people do print what I say. And I'm saying peace."[40] If there is a reflective appreciation of the powers of celebrity in Lennon's comment, there is also a desire to underwrite the performative element of politics itself. For the Amsterdam bed-in was, among other things, a sustained political critique of living with violence in an age of industrialized war, as well as a critique of a society sickened at the sight of "otherness" and therefore seemingly resistant to social change. Lennon and Ono, in their protest against violence, were seeking to take political debate beyond conventional boundaries, to include in that debate the notion that peace meant more than merely the absence of war.

From one angle, Lennon and Ono's bed-in was an expression of their shared political idealism. The ideal of political peace, they seemed to be saying, needs to be connected with everyday practice in order to be adequately endowed with cultural significance. To drive the point home, they underscored the harmony that the end of war could bring to human relationships through reference to cultural symbolism. Flowers adorned their suite, and there were handwritten posters calling for peace, love, and liberation: "Bed Peace," "Stay in

Bed," "Hair Peace," "Grow Your Hair," "I Love John," "I Love Yoko."
Lennon and Ono were contrasting a dominative rationality, based on
militarism and industrialized war, to the radical social vision of the
1960s counterculture; and in this sense they were merely making the
point, albeit in strikingly personal terms, that peace was an end in itself. Exactly how peace was to become a political reality in a world
which had deployed violence as a mode of ordering human affairs for
centuries was not so easy to see. As if seeking to avoid these more
practical difficulties, they stuck mostly to generalities. They were not
attempting, they argued, to trade in political specifics. The concrete
political difficulties of the world at large were displaced by the more
utopian significations of peace; indeed, for Lennon the idea of peace
as utopia was an essential starting point because the institutionalized
world of politics had become "too serious and too intellectual."[41]

The bed-in was a bold exercise in political radicalism. By staging it,
Lennon and Ono in effect delivered up a critique of militarized ideology to an unsuspecting audience. They were making the point, much
in the spirit of Gandhi and Martin Luther King, that peaceful protest
was the most effective way to free social life from violence. Peace, in
an age of the industrialization of war, was of utmost political significance; thus Lennon argued it was necessary to influence politics in
quite unconventional ways. Humor was of particular importance in
this respect. He claimed that the political establishment could not
handle humor; indeed, he suggested that humor could be used for re-
ducing the influence of violence in the world at large. "Yoko and I are
quite willing to be the world's clowns," he said, "if by doing so it will
do some good."[42] But Lennon and Ono were doing more than simply
parading as the world's clowns: the political irony here runs a good
deal deeper. For in conducting interviews with the press for ten hours
a day in Amsterdam, Lennon and Ono managed to create an illusion
that the "subject of peace" was something really new, that there were
urgent political developments and fresh information relating to the
peaceful ordering of human affairs. More than that, they managed to
displace the very aesthetic ground upon which the bed-in took
place—namely, its performative dimension. The bed-in, as Wulf Herzogenrath writes, "is misconstrued as a media spectacle, for the reporters are not there to visit a performance, they want facts and stories—and John Lennon and Yoko Ono provide them only to a limited
degree."[43] In displacing this performative dimension, Lennon and

Ono provoked a powerful engagement with peace. It was powerful because the political possibilities which they provided were enough to stimulate further public discussion and debate.

If Lennon and Ono were able to link the avant-garde with radical politics in a manner that limited the trace of the former, this is because in practice they managed to project political categories into the aesthetic and cultural domains. In other words, the only way to out-flank traditional social forms is by redeeming that which politics evades and forgets. The bed-in, when viewed as a performance, casts the personal realm of the bedroom as an alternative site for political activity. The private realm, traditionally cast as outside and other in liberal ideology, is revealed as inherent to politics, and in this sense Lennon and Ono brought subconscious political anxieties to the fore, disclosed the personal stakes of political contestation, and under-scored the peculiar significance of private protest in an era of indus-trialized war. In all of this, radical political thinking is linked to the personal sphere time and again. Throughout the bed-in, Lennon and Ono remained on their bed: the bed itself became a site for dreaming politics anew and also for coping with the overwhelming anxieties provoked by a militarized world.

A major source of difficulty for anyone who, like Lennon and Ono, seeks to invoke the power of radical imagination is that very disabling gap between concrete politics and the desired outcomes of social transformation. Many conservative critics dismissed the bed-in as a self-indulgent fantasy; liberal and left-wing commentators also wor-ried that the exercise might redirect the valuable political energies of youth toward suspect (read idealistic) goals. Lennon was very con-cerned about such criticism and had a response. "The reaction to our action," he said, "was successful."[44] His point, it seems, was that—thanks to this intervention—media across the globe were discussing the bed-in and the question of peace. Judged against media coverage of traditional forms of political protest, such as the march, the media attention which Lennon valued so highly was certainly an indication that alternative political possibilities had been brought to world atten-tion. The only problem was that for much of the public that critique had been pitched at such a high level that not even a dog could hear it.

Some years after the bed-in, Lennon and Ono issued the "Declara-tion of Nutopia."

We announce the birth of a conceptual country, NUTOPIA. Citizenship of the country can be obtained by declaration of your awareness of NUTOPIA. NUTOPIA has no land, no boundaries, no passports, only people. NUTOPIA has no laws other than cosmic. All people of NUTOPIA are ambassadors of the country. As two ambassadors of NUTOPIA, we ask for diplomatic immunity and recognition in the United Nations of our country and its people.[45]

This gesture, made when Lennon was facing a deportation order in the United States, was largely viewed as proof of the romantic or illusory politics to which the couple subscribed. It is possible, however, to argue that Lennon and Ono's contribution to the political dialogue about peace is firmly rooted in certain immanent possibilities of social life. Lennon was a committed utopian, certainly; but the view that his utopianism was primarily romantic, or escapist, is flawed in major respects. Such a view fails to acknowledge the creative dimension that Lennon accords to human imagination. For Lennon, this dimension, in becoming part of social life, may dislocate the very forms of political power to which the imaginary is usually rendered subordinate. Cultural theorist Terry Eagleton captures this political difficulty well by distinguishing between "good utopianism," which locates the desirable in what is actual, and "bad utopianism," which seeks the ideal outside the sphere of existing personal and cultural life. "A degraded present," Eagleton writes of good utopianism, "must be patiently scanned for those tendencies which are at once indissolubly bound up with it, yet which—interpreted in a certain way—may be seen to point beyond it."[46] The bed-in performance works at just such a political knife edge, drawing in the media under the aegis of celebrity and news, while simultaneously marshaling the imaginative energies of the public.

The primacy that Lennon grants to imagination does not mean that the problem of institutionalization at the political level can simply be ignored. The fact that the world is dominated by capitalism and patriarchy remains of key importance for political movements and radical politics everywhere; yet this dominance is surely something that Lennon sought to underscore in his own artistic work, even though a certain neglect of the institutional dimensions of politics may also pervade his work. What has been of lasting political importance, however, is the power of Lennon's social vision. At the heart of this vision is the idea that society must come to terms with the amount of psychic commitment, as well as psychic change, that peace presumes. There is a direct relation for Lennon between imagination and politics, even though that relation may be intensely unstable, fraught, and ambivalent.

At a second bed-in, from 26 May to 2 June 1969 in the Queen Elizabeth Hotel in Montreal, Lennon and Ono wrote and recorded "Give Peace a Chance." For Lennon, the song was an exploration in the possibilities of meaning, the blending of ideal and actuality. It was a plea for a chance, no more and no less. In a dramatic example of how the utopian imagination can influence radical political activity, "Give Peace a Chance" caught the utopian aspirations of a new generation. Not long after its release, the song was sung by hundreds of thousands of demonstrators at the Vietnam Moratorium Day on 1 October 1969. It quickly became established thereafter as an anthem of the peace movement.

5

A Day in the Life

The Mysterious Celebrity

> I used to worry about death when I was a kid, now the fear of it means less and less to me.
>
> John Lennon

> It is indeed impossible to imagine our own death; and whenever we attempt to do so we can perceive that we are in fact still present as spectators.
>
> Sigmund Freud

John Lennon gave his last live performance in June 1975. In front of an audience of socialites and celebrities assembled for the television special "Salute to Sir Lew Grade," Lennon performed two songs from *Rock 'n' Roll*, "Slippin' and Slidin'" and "Stand By Me," as well as his peace anthem "Imagine." It was an unusual venue for Lennon's concert finale: he had for many years been in financial dispute with Grade, who then owned the Lennon/McCartney song catalog through his control of ATV Music. Wearing a red jumpsuit, with his long hair tied back, Lennon looked confident and relaxed. Accompanied by a band wearing face masks on the backs of their heads (a "two-faced" band for the "two-faced" Grade), Lennon relished the opportunity to take some liberties with this high-ranking audience. Altering the lyrics of "Imagine," Lennon sang, "Nothing to kill or die for / No immigration too," thus calling attention to his battles with the Immigration and Naturalization Service. Toward the end of the song, when singing "You may say I'm a dreamer," he shouted off-mike, "He's a dreamer"— as if anticipating the cynical response of his audience. With the set over, Lennon gave a bow, just as he had when a Beatle, and walked off the stage. The dreamer was gone.

Lennon knew that it was time to stop. There was something more important than music to which he wanted to devote himself. But he was still under contract with EMI, and he had obligations to meet.

Unwilling to commence a new album, Lennon sought to bide his time. As a follow-up to the chart-topping *Walls and Bridges*, he released *Rock 'n' Roll.* Having recorded new vocals for the tracks produced by Phil Spector and included a bunch of other songs which Lennon himself had produced in New York, Lennon considered the album as complete as it would ever be. Though he remained ambivalent about *Rock 'n' Roll*, he saw its completion as a personal triumph, feeling secure in the knowledge that it would keep his career on track. A filmed interview and promotional clips for the album appeared on the BBC's *Old Grey Whistle Test.* Lennon also joined David Bowie in the studio for the recording of Bowie's 1975 album *Young Americans.* Bowie recorded a version of "Across the Universe," on which Lennon played. Lennon was happy to have the opportunity to do so. "The Beatles," he said, "didn't make a good record of it."[1] Jamming in the studio with Bowie and guitarist Carlos Alomar, Lennon also cowrote Bowie's first U.S. number-one single, "Fame." Yet he did not have new material to record himself, and in late 1975, he released a compilation of greatest hits, *Shaved Fish.*

More important to Lennon than music was the prospect of becoming a father again. He had long regretted his failure to develop a close relationship with his son Julian and was determined not to let his career dominate family life again. His reunion with Yoko Ono in late 1974 brought to a close his lost weekend. The couple announced that their separation "was not a success"; they declared that they were, and always had been, deeply in love. It was the couple's desperate struggle to have a child, however, that was of uppermost importance. In his 1980 interview with David Sheff for *Playboy*, Lennon commented: "We got back together and we decided that this was our life, that having a baby was important to us and that everything else was subsidiary to that, and therefore everything else had to be abandoned. That abandonment gave us the fulfillment we were looking for and the space to breathe and think and reestablish our dreams."[2] The prospect of having a baby with Ono meant not only the creation of another life but the chance to start over again. That chance came on 9 October 1975 (Lennon's birthday), when Ono gave birth to a baby boy.

Opinions differ as to how well Lennon took to caring for his new son, Sean. According to biographer Albert Goldman, the househusband role was simply a sham; Goldman claims that Lennon was a paranoid, depressed recluse who was profoundly uninterested in the welfare of his family. Biographer Ray Coleman, by contrast, portrays Lennon as a loving, devoted father who rejoiced in bringing up his son. It is, however, unnecessary to choose between such extreme variations. Lennon accepted, it seems, Ono's view that since she had carried the child for nine months, he should assume the major responsibility for a time. His new life, as Lennon summed it up, consisted of "baking bread and looking after the baby."[3] Lennon made it clear that the boy was his pride and joy and that caring for Sean was now his most important task. "Sean may not have come out of my belly," said Lennon, "but, *by God,* I made his bones, because I've attended to every meal, and to how he sleeps."[4] He visited the baby's room morning and night to watch him; he bathed, dressed, and fed him; he learned how to cook and was especially proud of the bread that he baked on a weekly basis. As Lennon's friend Elliot Mintz recalled of a late-night telephone call,

[Lennon] said, "an incredible thing happened to me today, Elliot," . . . and he said it with such reverence that I thought he was going to divulge a really significant spiritual experience. I propped myself up and said, "Yes?"

He said, "I baked my first loaf of bread and you can't believe how perfectly it rose, and I've taken a Polaroid photo of it and I think I can get it out to you by messenger tonight."[5]

Lennon had discovered the ingredients for a different life, a life that heralded a new self.

It had been far from easy for Lennon to maintain emotional contact with his first wife and child during the height of Beatlemania. After touring the world, he would arrive home to encounter a boy that he hardly recognized; Lennon remarked that he had had "no relationship *whatsoever*" with Julian in his early years.[6] Perhaps because of this unpleasant memory, Lennon manifested an almost obsessive concern with his new son's health and well-being. He worried about Sean's diet, forbidding any surplus sugar intake; he fussed about how the staff treated the boy; and he was anxious whenever Sean was ill.

Since Lennon had not officially announced his retirement, confusion abounded. Fans could not understand what he was doing. There had been no visible decline in his fame: *Walls and Bridges* had been phenomenally successful, and *Rock 'n' Roll,* while not truly great, reconfirmed that Lennon could play powerful rock. Colleagues could not comprehend his lack of concern about his career. Whenever record-company executives offered millions of dollars for a new record, Lennon explained that he was not interested; when asked why, he answered that he was devoting his time to raising his new son. The media were incredulous: there was a great deal of skepticism about Lennon's newfound domestic tranquillity, and so stories were concocted about his failing state of mind or his poor health. Against all of this pressure, however, Lennon guarded his private life, retreating further inward. Elliot Mintz believes that Lennon became ensnared in a powerful social contradiction at this point of his life.[7] While it is considered normal for new parents to want to be alone with their child and to spend time together as a family, different rules apply for celebrities, who must at all costs maintain their public profile. According to Mintz, Lennon created public confusion because he realized that he was not obliged to follow these rules. Fatherhood was important to him, and he was therefore happy to break from the rituals of celebrity. Lennon, as Mintz has confirmed, wanted to stay at home with his wife and child in the evening, or maybe have friends over for dinner. To the media, it all seemed somewhat unglamorous.

It would be too simplistic to say that Lennon, once retired, simply abandoned music in favor of his son, trading the piano for the playroom. It would be more accurate to say that Lennon discovered the rewards and responsibilities of being the primary caretaker of his child and in doing so came to reevaluate his relationship to art and music. He needed to distance himself from pop music, with all of its commercial pressures. In particular, he wanted to see what creative inspiration might develop in its place. "I had become a craftsman," said Lennon of his songwriting, "and I could have continued being a craftsman. I respect craftsmen but I am not interested in becoming one."[8] In short, Lennon *wanted* to change. At some point in early 1976, he began recording new demos at home in the Dakota, sometimes on guitar, sometimes on piano. "Cookin' (In the Kitchen of Love)," a song he was writing for Ringo Starr; "Tennessee"; "She Is a Friend of Dorothy's"; and "Sally and Billy" were recorded as demos.[9] Lennon recorded these songs over and over again, and each time he would improvise some new lyric, the fate of which depended upon his reaction during subsequent listening.

That Lennon was busy writing and recording these songs in early 1976 adds a further curious twist to his withdrawal from public life. His contract with EMI/Capitol expired on 26 January 1976, and he indicated plainly that he had no interest in negotiating a new deal. As Lennon said, "The idea of being a rock 'n' roll musician sort of suited my talents and mentality, and the freedom was great. But then I found out I wasn't free. I'd got boxed in. It wasn't just because of my contract, but the contract was the physical manifestation of being in prison."[10] In April 1976, freed from the obligations of his recording contract, Lennon returned, strangely enough, to the studio. Assisting Ringo Starr on his album *Rotogravure*, Lennon recorded "Cookin' (In the Kitchen of Love)." At the same time, Lennon was also fighting a forty-two-million-dollar lawsuit being waged against him by Morris Levy. Levy claimed that Lennon had not honored an alleged agreement to record an album for Levy's Adam VIII label, which specialized in mail order. The album in question was *Rock 'n' Roll,* the tapes of which Levy had used to release an album entitled *Roots.* The case was concluded in July in Lennon's favor, and he was awarded $109,000 in damages for lost royalties on *Rock 'n' Roll* and an additional $35,000 in compensatory damages for the harm done to his professional reputation.

While dealing with the court case and looking after Sean, Lennon continued to write and record demo tracks at home. He also found an additional outlet for his artistic energies in writing a book, *Skywriting by Word of Mouth* (although at the time Lennon decided against publication). Published posthumously in 1986, the book contains the kind of frantic wordplay and subtle parody characteristic of Lennon's earlier books, *In His Own Write* and *A Spaniard in the Works.* Indeed *Skywriting* was, if anything, a bolder venture, with chapters including "Lucy in the Scarf with Diabetics," "Chapter 23 or 27: In Which a Harvard Graduate Faints at the Sight of Enlightenment," and "The Importance of Being Erstwhile." "Taken sentence by sentence," John Robertson argues, "*Skywriting* is a remarkable achievement: few other comic writers could match the sheer wit and imagination that invests Lennon's word-play. . . . But the book is almost impossible to read at a sitting—simply because it isn't a book but a collection of unconnected phrases which work just as well in limbo as in context."[11] While Robertson overstates his argument, he does have a point. By and large, Lennon's writing for the volume was undertaken in fits and starts, sometimes as a form of relaxation after a day with Sean, sometimes as escape from business pressures (such as the legal complexities of the Levy case).

If the combined responsibilities of raising Sean and developing his creative work in more reflective and authentic ways caused Lennon to reinvent himself, some profoundly disturbing events made him anxious and depressed. In January 1976, Mal Evans, the former road manager of The Beatles, was shot dead by the police in his Los Angeles flat during a domestic violence incident.[12] Lennon, who had always been fond of Evans, found the news of this fatality deeply distressing. He was further shaken by the deaths of other friends and relatives: Paul McCartney's father died in March, and Elizabeth Stanley, his favorite aunt, died in May 1976. But it was the death of Lennon's father, Freddie, in April 1976 that disturbed him the most. Lennon had telephoned Freddie, who had been diagnosed with cancer of the stomach, during Freddie's final days at Brighton General Hospital. Although they had never been close, Lennon spoke to his father about his newborn son. His father's death seemed to focus Lennon on his own mortality and probably also reminded him more sharply of the tragic loss of his mother, thus precipitating a long period of depression in late 1976 and early 1977. Needing to escape, Lennon took a four-month vacation in Tokyo with his family and Elliot Mintz, where he attempted to sort out his feelings and sense of impending crisis.

When he returned to New York in October 1977, he did so with a renewed artistic drive, and he wrote and recorded a batch of songs at home. His music at this time was especially melancholic, but again the curative power of songwriting was essential to the lifting of depression's dark heart. Lennon, reflecting on the pain he had been in, wrote some great songs: "Emotional Wreck," "I Don't Want to Face It," "Mirror Mirror on the Wall," "I Watch Your Face," "Real Life," "Free as a Bird," "Whatever Happened To," and "One of the Boys." Some of this material was frivolous, such as the playful "One of the Boys." The bulk of it, however, was powerful and rich. "Free as a Bird" had a majestic air, blending expectation and melancholy; "I Don't Want to Face It" was a painfully direct confrontation with all that Lennon disliked about himself; and "Emotional Wreck" quietly mocked the private dilemmas of his withdrawal from public life. Lennon was content with these new songs, having done the same kind of painstaking rewriting that he had done before for most of his best material. In addition to a few aborted projects, such as a planned Broadway musical entitled *The Ballad of John and Yoko*, Lennon continued to write songs throughout 1978 and 1979. During these years, he composed "Everybody's Talkin', Nobody's Talkin'," "Stranger's Room," "My Life," "Beautiful Boy," "Real Love," and "I'm Crazy." What was so remarkable was that Lennon seemed content composing for himself, on his own terms. The songs, as a result, were more intensely personal and openly autobiographical than any that had come before.

In time, however, Lennon would come to deny this creative output during his time of seclusion. "I didn't touch a guitar for five years," he said, referring to his time as a househusband. No biographer has developed an entirely satisfactory explanation for Lennon's denial. Elliot Mintz offered the following frank interpretation: "John was prone to exaggeration to make a point. The fact is that during the years in question there was always music being played." According to Lennon's version of what happened, he wrote the songs for *Double Fantasy* during a trip that he made to Bermuda with Sean in June 1980. "They were inspired songs," Lennon said, contrasting them with what he felt had been the more crafted songs of *Walls and Bridges*.[13] Again, why Lennon insisted on the inspired nature of these songs is not altogether clear. Perhaps he thought it good copy for the press, or perhaps, alternatively, he felt it was the best way to convince the media of his househusband identity. The problem, however, is that Lennon's reflections about the songs of this period are inaccurate. Many of the songs which appear on *Double Fantasy* and *Milk and Honey* were, in actuality, painstakingly created over several years. For instance, Lennon's 1977 song "Emotional Wreck" formed the basis for "Watching the Wheels"; "Everybody's Talkin', Nobody's Talkin'" became "Nobody Told Me"; and "Stranger's Room" eventually became "I'm Losing You." Clearly, Lennon had redrafted the relation between his private self and his public self for commercial convenience.

He was, however, accurate in stressing the degree to which he had reinvented his life: he had voluntarily withdrawn from pop music; he had, at long last, made peace with himself, both psychologically and spiritually; he had devoted himself to raising his son and caring for his wife; and (although he left this out of the account) he had uncovered the inner depths of his desire to write music, poetry, and short stories on his own terms. Lennon had passed a difficult test, perhaps the most difficult test he had ever set himself. But, as music critic Chet Flippo has argued, this experiment in self-discovery and self-invention also had implications for his fans. As Flippo writes: "After all, rock & roll had been John Lennon's only real mother and father and if R&R wasn't good enough for Lennon, why, then, it might not hold much value for the rest of us."[14] Flippo suggests that, although fans admired Lennon, many were deeply threatened by his rejection of fame and celebrity. Accordingly, it is necessary to consider how Lennon's withdrawal from public life threatened the world of celebrity—a threat that proved disastrous to the psychic stability of his murderer, Mark David Chapman.

TO BE A FAN IS TO BE part of a group of individuals who share similar concerns. Fandom, as sociologist John B. Thompson has argued, involves wrapping up a significant part of one's self-identity in an identification with some distant other (the celebrity) and negotiating the necessary shifts between the world of fandom and the practical contexts of everyday social life.[15] Fandom thus involves drawing symbolic boundaries around the self and the other (or, more precisely, the other at a distance). The symbolic dimensions structuring the relation between fan and celebrity can, however, become blurred. Fandom can become a kind of addiction: the fan becomes compulsively preoccupied with the star, and there is an imaginary, idealized merging of fan and celebrity. Or, the fan comes to blame the celebrity for failing to reflect the fan's dreams and wishes. Etymologically, the term "fan" is related to "fanatic," a word that captures the burden of oppressive self-relating and obsessive thinking. Although fandom can be a routine aspect in the forging of self-identity in contemporary societies, the emotional transmutation from fandom to fanaticism is profoundly frightening and disturbing.

Mark David Chapman had long been a fan of Lennon.[16] Chapman himself claimed that he had been drawn to Lennon ever since he was ten years old. As a teenager, he loved listening to The Beatles. He grew his hair long, just as his hero Lennon did. He learned to play the guitar. He often concluded letters to school friends with quotes from Lennon. Imitating what he imagined was his hero's lifestyle, he even experimented with psychedelic drugs for a time, much to his parents' disapproval. Above all, it seems, Chapman was emotionally drawn to Lennon's commitment to social justice, finding in this identification a connection to goodness, integrity, and truth. The process of becoming a Lennon fan permitted Chapman, like many individuals, to imagine himself as he wanted to be, as an elevated, "ideal self." Eventually, though, his strong identification with Lennon underwent a sudden radical change. Sometime in 1970, Chapman became deeply religious and took to wearing a cross around his neck and carrying the Bible around with him. His new interest in religion considerably strained his earlier identification with Lennon. His growing preoccupations with purity and saintliness conflicted with his admiration for the man who had once declared himself more popular than Christ.

Chapman, perhaps not surprisingly, got rid of his Beatles records. At a Bible study group, he condemned Lennon for his antireligious stand. He became increasingly interested in youth issues and in helping socially disadvantaged groups. It was through an involvement with the YMCA that he found a more practical means to satisfy his own moral impulses. He spent some years working at refugee centers, at home and abroad, during the 1970s. However, he was unable to stick to any one job and came to regard himself as a failure. Depression was a persistent problem for Chapman. After moving to Hawaii in 1977, he attempted to commit suicide. In such moments of utter despair, Chapman later claimed, he felt plagued by Satan's demons. He developed an interest in firearms and guns. He became obsessed with the social ills of the modern world, blaming capitalist exploitation one moment and Scientology the next.

In the late 1970s, Chapman suffered a severe mental breakdown. During the time of his recovery, he reinvested Lennon with an otherworldly significance. Lennon, once again, offered Chapman a way out of the difficulties of internal and external reality. Chapman manifested various forms of dependency on Lennon for a sense of self-identity. Like Lennon, he married a somewhat older Japanese-American woman, Gloria Abe. He began taping "John Lennon" over his own name tag at work. On the day that he resigned from his job as a security guard, he signed himself out as "John Lennon." It is easy enough to posit that Chapman, spending each day at home while his wife worked, imagined himself in Lennon's shoes. Whether he actually did, however, is not my central point. What matters is that Chapman's withdrawal from the social world was a retreat into fanaticism, an idealization of celebrity to the nth degree. Chapman withdrew from the social world into an unbounded world of fantasy, a world sustained by imitation of his hero, John Lennon. Significantly, it was in this depressed, paranoid state of mind that Chapman read an October 1980 article in *Esquire* magazine, "John Lennon, Where Are You?" The article, for which Lennon had refused to be interviewed, portrayed the ex-Beatle as having sold out the dreams of the 1960s and represented him as someone who claimed to speak for peace and a better world but was actually concerned only with material comforts. The article described Lennon as a forty-year-old businessman, worth more than $150 million, whose favorite pastime was watching television. For Chapman, the message was clear: Lennon was a fraud, a fraud that the world would be better off without.

On one level, Chapman's disillusionment with Lennon was the other face of a punishing, supermoral disposition—a moral framework, designated by Freud as the superego, that provides for clear-cut discriminations and places identity and morality into a world that is black and white. That Lennon had turned his back on the prospects for social change and was now interested only in his millions was proof enough for Chapman that even the most altruistic of souls can succumb to the ethical wilderness of contemporary life. The "proof" was in the *Esquire* report ("It's written in the magazine, and so it must be true"); this belief is a powerful indication of that sinking into concrete facts which characterizes paranoid-schizoid thinking and was taken as a key indicator of Chapman's mental illness. As Dr. Daniel Schwartz testified for the defense during Chapman's trial,

[Chapman's] identification with Mr. Lennon, after a while, became quite threatening. . . . He then saw his only chance to survive, psychiatrically, psychologically, as being able to make an abrupt break from Lennon. Whereas he had idolized and adored this man, now he suddenly switched to the opposite direction and began to hate him, and he had no real reason, no justifiable reason for the intensity of his feelings against Lennon. He thought of him as a phony.[17]

Chapman was, in short, caught in an emotional deadlock between narcissistic idealization and abject hatred of Lennon. If Chapman was a Lennon fan of the most fanatical kind, imagining himself as his superstar through wild imaginative flights, he was also Lennon's most violent critic, condemning Lennon as a fraud and passing the death sentence as the only remaining hope for moral salvation. Indeed, this dichotomy enables us to understand how Chapman could stand jubilantly next to Lennon outside the Dakota having a copy of *Double*

Fantasy autographed, while all the time planning to kill the superstar he, by now, dreaded.

Fandom, I have suggested, is a common way of cultivating a sense of intimacy with distant others in contemporary culture. Fandom can enrich the emotional development of the self and may contribute significantly to an individual's sense of the interpersonal world. Thompson writes that fandom "enables individuals to tap into a rich source of symbolic materials which can be used to develop a non-reciprocal relation of intimacy or to cultivate a bond, and which can thereby be incorporated reflexively into a project of self-formation."[18] The cultivation of this bond appears here in a positive light; the process of becoming a fan is a process of self-constitution, of enriching the self. But, as it did for Chapman, fandom can also destroy the self. Fandom can turn fanatical. Such fanaticism is a problem not only because it attacks lived experience and generates compulsion but because it wipes out certain core distinctions between mind and world.

The psychological stakes of fandom can be gleaned by considering the emotional investment that the fan puts into the celebrity. In the process of identifying with a celebrity, the fan unleashes a range of fantasies and desires and, through projective identification, transfers personal hopes and dreams onto the celebrity. In doing so, the fan actually experiences desired qualities of the self as being contained by the other, the celebrity. In psychoanalytic terms, this is a kind of splitting: the good or desired parts of the self are put into the other in order to protect this imagined goodness from bad or destructive parts of the self. There is, then, a curious sort of violence intrinsic to fandom, a violence that forces the other to symbolically fulfill the dreams and desires of the self. The relation of fan and celebrity is troubled because violence is built into it.

The celebrity is, however, generally incapable of sustaining such projections. This inability is not the fault of celebrity; nor is it a design flaw in the entertainment industry. The celebrity cannot sustain these projections because the psychic mechanism of projection enters into a form of antagonism with itself: the fan, having projected desired aspects of the self into the other in order to keep destructive aspects of the self in check, discovers with horror these same human failings within the realm of celebrity itself. That is, what has been denied or disowned through idealization comes back from the outside as a

painful intrusion into the world of the fan, a kind of return of the repressed. At this point, the fan experiences the emotional turmoil that
an absorption in the world of celebrity was meant to protect against.
The fan discovers that the celebrity is unable to transcend the trials
and tribulations of everyday life. Perhaps not surprisingly, the fan
often reacts to the discovery with disbelief and disillusionment: the
fan feels cheated or swindled. Sometimes, the pain of disillusionment
is simply too much. In an ironic twist, the fan may come to despise the
once-loved celebrity and to entertain fantasies of revenge for the humiliating betrayal suffered.

There are many reasons why John Lennon came to be suscep-
tible to this psychology of celebrity. By 1980, he had fully dispensed
with being Beatle John Lennon. He had thrown off the trappings of
image. He was now, thanks to a sustained period of self-reflection,
more content with his life. In a 1980 interview with Dave Sholin, for
RKO Radio, Lennon spoke of how he had discovered who *he* thought
he really was. Speaking openly about his relationship with Sean,
Lennon said:

> I don't buy that bit about, you know, quality over quantity. You know, like an
> hour a week of intense, rolling-in-the-hay together is better than twenty min-
> utes everyday of being bitchy. And just being yourself around him. So I don't
> try to be the God Almighty kind of figure that . . . is always smiling and such
> a wonderful father. I'm not putting out an image of this person who knows all.
> . . . Nobody knows about children, that's the thing. You look in the books and
> there's no real experts, everybody's got a different opinion. You learn by de-
> fault, in a way. I've made a lot of mistakes already. But what can you do? But
> I think it's better for him to see me as I am: if I'm grumpy, I'm grumpy; if I'm
> not, I'm not; if I want to play, I play; if I don't, I don't. I don't kow-tow to him,
> I'm as straight with him as I can be. And, yes, I can afford to take the time.
> But anybody with a working wife might be able to afford to take the time.[19]

The question of image—who controls it and for whom—is central
here. Lennon's statement that he is "not putting out an image" contrasts sharply with many of his reflections about life as a Beatle. He
acknowledges that to live beyond the confines of image is to live with
the difficulty of uncertainty. What seems to be at stake here is a revaluation of feelings: it is better to experience emotion, even negative
emotion, if one is to really know oneself and other people.

If Lennon is able to give the slip to the illusions of image making, it
is only because he was previously caught in its seductive, narcissistic

frame. If image is transparent, the stuff of Hollywood dreams, experience is the most profound conceivable mystery. Lennon powerfully underscores the tantalizingly elusive nature of experience by underlining that "there are no experts"; that one learns from each encounter; that mistakes get made; that human interaction is difficult and often painful but also deeply rewarding and joyful. Such self-understanding might be described as the logic of "identity in reverse," whereby Lennon sifts back through the personifications he has embodied (from "Dr. Winston O'Boogie" back to "The Walrus" and further to "Beatle John") and discovers not only what has been psychologically achieved in each image construction but also how the self is easily duped in the fantasy of star-figure. In the RKO interview, Lennon certainly seemed remarkably well adjusted to his new life. He was loved by his family. He was wealthy. And, thanks to *Double Fantasy*, his music was popular once more. In a tragic irony, however, it was precisely Lennon's decoupling of self-experience from the illusions of celebrity that proved too much to bear for Mark David Chapman. For on the day that Lennon gave the RKO interview, 8 December 1980, Chapman waited outside the Dakota apartments at Seventy-second Street and Central Park West in New York. Later that night, he killed Lennon.

NEWS OF JOHN LENNON's death profoundly shocked fans and critics alike. Seemingly secure distinctions between the real world and the world of illusion, between meaning and nonmeaning, indeed between sanity and madness, began to blur. The world's attachment to Lennon's sense of humor, his warmth and charm, his arrogance, his creativity, his imaginative social vision, rounded back upon itself to produce a disturbing sense of violation, suffocation, and dread. Suddenly, Lennon was no longer; but his death, and in particular our relation to it, remained a difficult problem. A problem that would not go away. For those straining to cope, let alone to understand the reasons for Chapman's murder of Lennon, the world had become unmanageable.

The outpouring of public sorrow over Lennon's death was astonishing. Not since the assassination of President John F. Kennedy in 1963 had such emotional devastation been so openly acknowledged in our general culture. Millions worldwide grieved. Many cried for the man whom they had never met, but who had so influenced their lives. Several fans reportedly committed suicide out of despair over Lennon's murder.[20] There came a surge of tributes: heads of state, politicians, movie stars, rock musicians, writers, poets, and artists publicly reminisced about, and declared their appreciation of, Lennon. Frank Sinatra said, "It was a staggering moment when I heard the news. Lennon was a most talented man and, above all, a gentle soul." "I feel," said Chuck Berry, "as if I lost a little part of myself when John died." Ray Charles noted, "I was spellbound and hurt and upset when [Lennon] died, because he was a brilliant musician, and I respected what the man stood for." Norman Mailer said, simply, "We have lost a genius of the spirit."[21]

Many close to Lennon, however, refused to speak to the press. Ringo Starr, who flew to New York to be with Ono, declined to make any statement. He later went into seclusion, as did Bob Dylan. Sean Lennon's godfather, Elton John, refused to make any public comment at the time, as did Mick Jagger and Eric Clapton. Others tried to say something, however inadequate. Paul McCartney, at his home in Sussex, told reporters, "John was a great man who'll be remembered for his unique contributions to art, music and world peace." When asked later that day about Lennon's murder, McCartney replied, "It's a drag."[22] The comment was viewed as glib and unfeeling, and McCartney came to regret it. A few days after the shooting, Yoko Ono called for a ten-minute vigil and issued this statement:

I told Sean what happened. I showed him the picture of his father on the cover of the paper and explained the situation. I took Sean to the spot where John lay after he was shot. Sean wanted to know why the person shot John if he liked John. I explained that he was probably a confused person. Sean said we should find out if he was confused or if he really meant to kill John. I said that was up to the court. He asked what court—a tennis court or a basketball court. That's how Sean used to talk with his father. They were buddies. John would have been proud of Sean if he had heard this. Sean cried later. He also said, "Now Daddy is part of God. I guess when you die you become much more bigger because you're part of everything."

I don't have much more to add to Sean's statement. The silent vigil will take place December 14th at 2pm for ten minutes.

Our thoughts will be with you.

Love, Yoko & Sean.[23]

On Sunday, 14 December 1980, an estimated crowd of one hundred thousand people joined together in silence in New York's Central Park to remember Lennon. Others around the world did likewise. A gathering of thirty thousand people joined in prayer and sang "Give Peace a Chance" outside St. George's Hall on Lime Street in Liverpool. In cities across America, vigils were held to commemorate the life and work of Lennon. In Toronto, thirty-five thousand people gathered in snow for a candlelight vigil. Tens of thousands stopped to mourn Lennon in Paris, Hamburg, Madrid, Brussels, London, Melbourne, and other major cities. In terms of public grief, nothing like it had ever been seen before.

The mass media, not surprisingly, devoted every possible space to Lennon's death, with recent photographs and interviews fetching extraordinary amounts of money. Lennon's image was sold, resold, and circulated within the media industries. *Newsweek, Time,* and *The Sunday Times,* as well as many other papers and magazines, devoted issues to him. Television and radio networks began producing specials on his life and work. But it was Lennon's own output that was in greatest demand in the months that followed his death. Orders for his last single "Starting Over" and the album *Double Fantasy* took Lennon to the top of the charts throughout the world. Indeed, *Double Fantasy* remained at the number-one position for eight weeks and in the top two hundred for more than eighteen months in the United States. It eventually sold more than seven million copies worldwide, which makes it one of the best-selling records in history. The demand for things Lennon was such that his previous hits, for example "Imagine" and "Give Peace a Chance," also reentered the charts.

"ONE CANNOT BE AWARE of one's mortality," writes Zygmunt Bauman, "without conceiving of the inevitability of death as an affront and an indignity; and without thinking of the ways to repair the wrong."[24] Lennon's death created a profound sense of collective loss; and with that loss went all the difficulties of managing pain, anger, and guilt. The sense of loss provoked by Lennon's death was, however, exacerbated—I want to suggest now—by the repression of death in contemporary culture. A closer look at the public mourning of Lennon's death suggests not only an ongoing dialogue with the pain of loss but also an exorcising of the horror of death itself. In putting Lennon's death blatantly on display and making it into something easily graspable and familiar, mass culture reveals itself desperately in thrall to the memory of Lennon. It is as if to reflect on what has been lost would be overwhelmingly frightening. In our grieving for Lennon we have routinely sought, it seems, to "repair the wrong" of his death.

Modernity, in Philippe Ariés's classic formulation, has brought with it a fundamentally new relationship to death.[25] Consciousness of death is at the heart of all human history: it is *the* "radical otherness" which haunts human existence. Death was "tame" in premodern times, says Ariés, meaning that contact with death was a commonplace feature of everyday experience. In the modern era, by contrast, death has become increasingly hidden away, shrouded in secrecy, concealed. Everything connected to illness and death has become subject to technical, medical control, including the process of dying itself. We seek, in other words, to render death unobtrusive. Yet in spite of this cultural repression, the unpredictable nature of death remains. When contact with death and serious illness does come, it is experienced as devastating when measured against this social denial. Death, writes Michel Vovelle, is a "major scandal of the whole of human adventure."[26] What is scandalous is that death returns to consciousness the horror which was thought to be exiled or banished in the act of social design and technical control. Death is thus a brake or limit to self-mastery, and for this reason, surely, our general psychological reaction to death involves painful guilt, rage, hate, and shame. Death, notes sociologist Geoffrey Gorer, "is treated as inherently shameful and abhorrent, so that it can never be discussed or referred to openly, and experience of it tends to be clandestine and accompanied by feelings of guilt and unworthiness."[27]

Death is symbolically loaded with fear in contemporary culture because it is "detached" from social life. One might say, following Freud's classic *Civilization and Its Discontents,* that culture is a trade-off between the forces of life and death, between narcissism and aggression—a trade-off in which men and women exchange a portion of collective self-knowledge for a share of social security.[28] In a tragic irony, an irony that Freud saw as both psychologically and historically complex, the more culture is constructed in the name of security, the more depleted our inner resources for managing everyday strains and stresses become. When people are brought face to face with the death of a loved one, they are likely to experience a sense of shame and humiliation. Such narcissistic injury not only is a natural consequence of the pain of loss but also is attenuated by the loss of certitude and security that culture is meant to protect against. In sum, then, death discloses the human suffering that the pleasures of security are meant to filter from awareness.

Lennon's death, and the events leading up to it, have been extensively researched, documented, traversed, and rewritten by the mass media. An inventory of the majority of tributes, articles, features, and biographies that have sought to "explain" Lennon's death reveals several common traits: all of them were imbued with the detective spirit; all uncovered some secret in the past of victim or killer which suggested the assassination was fated; all gazed at death and traced it back to the absence of security in childhood; all psychologized away the horror of death by displacing it from its subject; all devalued the public display of grief and mourning, preferring either to nostalgically dwell upon past achievements or idealize the future and prospects for immortality.

Fenton Bresler's book *Who Killed John Lennon?* (1989) is representative of such attempts to rework death under the sign of rationalism. Bresler, an investigative journalist and lawyer, argues that there was a government conspiracy behind the murder of Lennon. Mark Chapman, Bresler writes, "was merely a tool, a human gun used and controlled by others to destroy a uniquely powerful radical figure who was likely to prove a rallying point for mass opposition to the policies soon to be implemented, both at home and abroad, by the new United States government headed by Ronald Reagan." On the basis of this presumption, Bresler boldly claims in the book's introduction that he has uncovered new facts about the CIA's role in the Lennon killing. He writes, in true detective spirit: "So let us do our own investigation, such as we can, with no rights of arrest nor recourse to the courts for writs of subpoena or legally enforceable demands for the production of documents. . . . The 'frightening' story now begins."[29]

Bresler's story involved him in more than eight years of tireless investigative work: he tracked down the organizational connections between the CIA and the YMCA, examined the FBI file on Lennon, and interviewed countless police, detectives, and members of the judiciary. Central to Bresler's argument is his adamant assertion that the CIA programmed Chapman to kill Lennon. This assertion was developed from interviews Bresler conducted with Arthur O'Conner, a lieutenant of the New York Police Department, who dealt with Chapman's case. O'Conner told Bresler, "I saw [Chapman] the night of the murder. I studied him intensely. He looked as if he could have been programmed."[30] Bresler bases many of his key claims on O'Conner's comment, and in his zeal to prove the thesis, he is prepared to go to extraordinary lengths. He demolishes the lines of inquiry pursued by the police, dismisses psychiatric reports on Chapman's personality disorder, and, most grotesquely, reconstructs the arrival of Lennon's body at New York's city mortuary and its preparation for cremation.

Yet for all its questioning and speculation, *Who Killed John Lennon?* fails to deliver anything new. The book is essentially shallow in its hunt for possible ways in which government agencies sought to brainwash Chapman. It is shallow because it denies Chapman any human agency in the killing of Lennon. This denial intensifies throughout the book, partly as a result of the conspiratorial theory which Bresler advances and partly as a result of an investigative search to dig up "the truth." In a final desperate bid, Bresler even writes to Chapman at Attica Prison, telling Chapman that he did not act alone in the murder of Lennon and explaining that he had been programmed to do so. In response, Chapman wrote a letter to Bresler flatly denying that any conspiracy lay behind Lennon's murder. "The reasons for Mr. Lennon's death are very complex," Chapman continued, "and I am still trying to sort them out emotionally myself."[31] Bresler fails to see that Chapman's letter refutes his entire book. Even more sadly, Bresler seems unaware that his letter to Chapman was a dreadful violation of the memory of Lennon—the ultimate invasion of his integrity.

Another variant on the theme of "who killed Lennon" has been the public fascination with the trauma generated by his murder, particularly in social and cultural terms. In Kevin Sim's 1988 film *The Man Who Shot John Lennon*, Chapman states: "I murdered a man. I took a lot more with me than just myself. A whole era ended. It was the last nail in the coffin of the 60s."[32] Lennon's murder spells not just the death of an individual but the death of an era: the era of The Beatles, the era of personal and social experimentation, the era of love, peace, and understanding. What disturbances—personal and political—has the killing of this era heralded? Alert to some of these psychological and political issues, Fred Fogo's *I Read the News Today* (1994) offers an intriguing catalog of the cultural patterns of remembering in and through which people have sought to come to grips with John Lennon's death.[33] Fogo starts with the idea that Lennon's death is equated by many, on a deeply symbolic level, with the demise of the cultural ideals of the 1960s, the demise of political dreams for social integration and consensus. Yet the 1960s, says Fogo, were about more than experimentation with utopianism; the era also generated much social conflict and political division. Confusion and dislocation at the personal and political levels deeply marked the times, during which profound political conflict arose around issues of sexuality, the environment, corporate power, and militarism. Lennon stands as a central cultural symbol of the 1960s, argues Fogo, because he reflected its contradictory, change-orientated nature.

If John Lennon stands as an emblem of a historical era, how can we approach his death on objective grounds? Fogo, as a sociologist, seeks to classify our reactions to Lennon's death in order to explain the process of cultural crisis. He writes, dispassionately, of nostalgia, resignation, and acceptance. Nostalgia might take the form of, say, an absorption in the counterculture ethos of the 1960s, with Lennon a central reference point. A rigid narrative about the past, and the importance of Lennon to that past, is the defining feature of such nostalgia. Resignation, by contrast, suggests a different kind of closure. Fogo writes, "In Lennon's death, the group finally had dissolved, and hope had been lost."[34] Here loss is reacted to as overwhelming and final; it cancels out former identities and times, propelling an engagement with the future, but only by necessity and not by choice. Beyond resignation, Fogo writes of acceptance, whereby loss does not equal defeat; rather, it signals creativity and the open-endedness of the future. Voices of acceptance, writes Fogo, view generational identity in a broader historical context. These voices for incorporation focus on Lennon by underscoring his post-Beatles life, his personal development and artistic progress; and, importantly, they also view the relationship of Lennon and Ono as an example of growth, experimentation, and artistic collaboration.[35] Having sorted out these different responses, Fogo concludes—his sociological work done.

What, exactly, do Bresler and Fogo seek in approaching Lennon's death in such a cold and unreflective manner? What anxieties are they concealing? In different ways, both Bresler's detective narration and Fogo's reductive sociology tone down the horror of death, disconnect it from memory, and in the process smooth over our anxieties about our own mortality. As distraction comes to displace grief, Lennon fades. In a way, of course, Lennon is still present as an object of wonder, fear, or contemplation. But, in rationalistic interpretations such as Bresler's and Fogo's, he is kept at a safe distance. The sense that we really miss him is denied or classified as a social category. That we take great delight in Lennon's music but also feel saddened when thinking that things might have been otherwise is disowned. Instead, Lennon's death becomes rationalized, anonymous, exploited.

Thus the death of Lennon, like the deaths of Elvis Presley and Marilyn Monroe before him, has oftentimes been viewed through converging psychologies of denial and rationalization. The first dictates that death, and specifically the horror of death, be repressed in social practice and cultural remembering. The second transforms death into spectacle, entertainment, banality. Relayed through new communication technologies, death is constructed and circulated as an object of consumption, knowledge, and desire. In this commodified space, "the pornography of death" (in Geoffrey Gorer's memorable phrase) rules supreme.[36] Not only is death increasingly detached from everyday life (as Ariés claims), but its horror comes to be "lifted out" from the cultural context in which it occurs. Such decontextualization is part and parcel of the standardized, repetitious presentation of death in the mass media, the most important consequences of which are a fading of its emotional significance and its reconstruction as something trivial. This trivialization of death lies at the very heart of our cultural difficulty in treating seriously matters such as bereavement and loss and gives rise to a dramatic sense of death as an obscene event.

During the 1980s, the memory of Lennon was exploited in many forms across popular culture. Through books, films, documentaries, records, bootleg recordings, posters, prints, and lapel buttons, his image was endlessly displayed and reinvented. Corporations, both authorized and unauthorized, were quick to capitalize on Lennon's posthumous fame. His publishers reprinted *In His Own Write* and *A Spaniard in the Works,* as well as the *Rolling Stone* interview "Lennon Remembers." The editors of *Rolling Stone,* in conjunction with Yoko Ono, commissioned a collection of essays chronicling Lennon's life and death: *The Ballad of John and Yoko.* Geffen Records supplied the marketplace with a continuous supply of Lennon's material, including the singles "Woman" and "Watching the Wheels" in 1981 and the album *The John Lennon Collection* in 1982. This material was not new, but that was not at issue. It seems that it is the fate of popular culture to compensate people for what reality has deprived them of. Four years after Lennon died, Yoko Ono released the albums *Heart Play* and *Milk and Honey* and a single, "Nobody Told Me," that he had recorded at the time of the *Double Fantasy* sessions. More releases followed in 1986. The One to One Benefit Concert from 1972 was released as *Live in New York City,* and an album of some previously unreleased tracks was issued as *Menlove Avenue.* In addition, the BBC released the interview that Andy Peebles had conducted two days before Lennon's death, titled *John and Yoko: The Interview.* RKO Radio went one better, publicizing *John Lennon: The Last Word* as the ex-Beatle's final interview.

With capitalism's infinite capacity to create product and the insatiable appetite of consumers, the mourning of Lennon's death therefore shifted to manufacturing. Lennon was made into a never ending death spectacle: his life was recounted, reframed, and reinvented by a host of people who claimed "special knowledge," all offering "the truth" about his final years—the retirement, the comeback, the end. In 1981, Playboy Press published the full transcript of David Sheff's interviews with Lennon and Ono as a book, *The Playboy Interviews with John Lennon and Yoko Ono.* The interviews made fascinating reading, partly because they were undertaken shortly before his death and partly because the nature of his relationship with Ono is discussed in detail by Lennon. The commercial gloss on the book, however, reflected the broader ambitions of the editors. *The Playboy Interviews* was, in the words of editor G. Barry Golson, Lennon's "final testament." The book offered the opportunity to share "a few minutes more" with the dead ex-Beatle.[37] These remarks are typical of the ways popular culture tames the horror of death: the remarks bring Lennon back from the land of the dead for a few more minutes so that we can actually know the real man and, hence, dominate him by accessing his last testament.

More books soon followed. The first to offer an insider's account of Lennon came from Peter Brown, an old friend of Lennon's and the former chief operating officer of Apple Corps. Published in 1983,

The Love You Make immediately made the best-seller lists in the United States and claimed to reveal the secrets of The Beatles' lives, concentrating especially on Lennon and his tragic death. Next came May Pang's *Loving John*, excerpts of which appeared in *US* magazine. The media picked up many of her more colorful statements for its daily headlines. "John Kicked the Baby and Beat Up His Wife" went one headline, at once depicting Lennon in a terrible light and displacing public grief over his death. Pang's book was followed by *Dakota Days* by John Green, Ono's tarot reader; and its more sensational excerpts were also published in *Penthouse*. Green's book, built upon the predictable argument that Ono manipulated her husband, claimed that Lennon often visited prostitutes in his final years. That no evidence was offered to support this, or any of the other wild conjectures made by Green, was beside the point: it was as if Lennon's sexual exploits could be fabricated and multiplied endlessly now that he was dead. And, indeed, *The Love You Make, Loving John,* and *Dakota Days* strongly influenced Albert Goldman's *The Lives of John Lennon* (1987) and Frederic Seaman's *The Last Days of John Lennon* (1991), both of which I analyzed in the opening chapter.

Lennon was also the subject of many tributes from contemporary songwriters. Roxy Music released a version of "Jealous Guy" just after his murder. Elton John's "Empty Garden" and Paul Simon's "The Late Great Johnny Ace" were released as elegies to Lennon. George Harrison, joined by Paul McCartney and Ringo Starr, paid his own tribute, "All Those Years Ago." And McCartney's own personal remembrance came in the form of "Here Today" on his 1982 album *Tug of War*.

There is an intimate link between repression of the horror of death and its progressive trivialization, as well as between the denial of mourning and the tendency to commodify grief. I do not want to suggest, however, that all responses to Lennon's death have been caught up in the degraded logic of rationalistic denial or commercial exploitation. On the contrary, Lennon's death created a cultural crisis which, for some, has been deeply disturbing. One of the most important features of the public disturbance caused by Lennon's death has been the attempt to connect social anxiety and private fear, the attempt to examine what Lennon's life might mean in more emotional or personal terms. As Scott Spencer came to reflect about Lennon:

Because he allowed us to know him, to love him, John Lennon gave us the chance to share his death, to resume the preparations for our own. Because we were so used to the way he thought, the habits, the turns, the surprises of his mind, we can enter him as we remember his last moments, to let it be us in the car, pulling up to the curb, opening the door, stepping out, breathing the night. Someone said he was happy that night, and we somehow know what his happiness felt like, and we can imagine ourselves resurgent, electric with energy.[38]

Nostalgic idealization? Perhaps. Yet Spencer's comments do draw attention to the difficult emotional work undertaken in mourning the loss of public figures. According to Spencer, it was Lennon's very public misgivings about himself, his doubts about his artistic contribution, as well as his acknowledged vulnerability, that made him such an important public figure and, ultimately, a figure to be mourned.

It is in relation to the death of Lennon that something like a cultural inversion can also operate, an inversion of the demand for security. From this angle, the sadness of Lennon's death need not be denied; rather, death can also be seen to reindividualize Lennon, to tear his image away from the oppressive dogma of celebrity. Consider, for example, Yoko Ono's album *Season of Glass*, her first recording after Lennon's death. The album cover showed Lennon's blood-covered spectacles, and for this Ono was morally condemned in many sections of the media. Yet the accusation of bad taste might, from another angle, be framed as a more troubling question: who, exactly, is caught up in this tasteless, degrading logic? Ono, for remembering the death of Lennon? Or might this so-called moral indifference to the horrors of Lennon's death reveal something about the self-concealment of our social practice itself? As Ono came to reflect:

People are offended by the glasses and the blood? The glasses are a tiny part of what happened. If people can't stomach the glasses, I'm sorry. There was a dead body. There was blood. His whole body was bloody. There was a load of blood all over the floor. That's the reality. I want people to face up to what happened. He did not commit suicide. He was killed. People are offended by the glasses and the blood? John had to stomach a lot more.[39]

Lennon's death, Ono seems to be saying, cannot be put at a safe distance from the emotional difficulties of daily life. For it is the very cultural pressure to lead life free from the disturbance of death which is

at the heart of social pathology. Lennon's death, according to Ono, has
no neat ending or conclusion; it is a loss to be kept in mind in the creative activity of remembering, in the active construction of memory.
Dealing with the horror of death, of Lennon's death, involves facing
up to one's own mortality, to the cessation of life, to the pain of the
dying body, to that "load of blood all over the floor."

But meaningful consideration of death requires the suspension of
preestablished ways of thinking. Death demands, so to speak, a giving
way to grief, a toleration of mourning, and a recognition of the
painful, disabling effects of shock. These demands, in turn, require
human contact: people need to forge emotional connections with others in order to make death meaningful. And yet it is precisely this immersion in emotion, in interpersonal relations, that is devalued or di-
luted by rationalistic ideologies and practices of contemporary culture.
From this angle, it is possible to see why Ono's selection of Lennon's
blood-covered glasses for the cover of *Season of Glass* generated such
high levels of social anxiety. For the image in question—that pecu-
liarly shocking collision of glasses and blood (which implied the soul
and body of Lennon)—simply brought death too close to home. The
proper objective distance to death had not been maintained. The
trained, contemporary urge to locate death as external reference
("the shooting of a superstar") was thwarted by the *Season of Glass*
photograph. The photograph raised for consideration not simply the
death of a great man but the death of a living presence. In this sense,
the blood on the spectacles "breathed life" into Lennon's death; it
stood for an interior space, a private realm, a realm which had been
violated and destroyed. Does the *Season of Glass* photograph, in transgressing that objective distance proper to death, do violence to the
memory of Lennon? Or does it simply serve as a painful reminder of
the violence of Lennon's death? Or might it be that, in questioning
our reaction to Lennon's murder, Ono has touched on a raw nerve of
cultural repression, a repression which is nothing less than the guilty
pleasure derived from the trivialization of death itself?

"THE UNPRECEDENTED response to Lennon's death," write Jeanie Attie
and Josh Brown, "should not be mistaken for just another well-
orchestrated media event." Lennon's death provided the impetus for
cultural mourning on a worldwide scale—mourning for lost dreams,

ideals, hopes, beliefs. In a way, Lennon's death led to a new encounter with what he meant to us, with what he represented, and, as a result, with the extent to which he would be missed. In acknowledging this loss, we acknowledge that Lennon is missed. Really missed. But the dense, dark void generated by Lennon's absence is, for many of us, too threatening. We are easily seduced, it seems, by the commercial exploitation of his memory. We are complicit in the logic of cultural repression. Denial takes hold of us and transports us to the imagined, furthermost bounds of psychic security. The pain of loss, of death, is canceled in thought.

6

Free as a Bird

Lennon in the Postmodern

Whatever happened to the lives that we once knew.
John Lennon

Like countless others I played The Beatles' records into the
turntable. They measured out my teens. Any Beatles track
instantly transfers me to a specific segment of my past.
Martin Amis

John Lennon remained deeply ambivalent about The Beatles throughout the last decade of his life. In interviews, he was sometimes angry
about living life as an ex-Beatle—most famously in his 1970 "Lennon
Remembers" interview with *Rolling Stone*—and especially about the
long-term impact of Beatlemania upon his private life. At other times
he was more prepared to discuss calmly the significance of the Fab
Four to contemporary culture, although he tended to shy away from
idealizing the past. The time of The Beatles had come and gone, he
seemed to be saying, and it was important to look ahead. Lennon
suggested on several occasions that The Beatles had become a self-
perpetuating force, lodged deeply in people's memories but independent of the actual personal and musical activities of John Lennon,
Paul McCartney, George Harrison, and Ringo Starr.

Against this backdrop, the foremost paradox of the frantic media
search for possible indications of a reunion of The Beatles is that the
search resulted only in more ambivalence and ambiguity, more dis-
sension among fans and critics. Each definitive pronouncement that
The Beatles would never reunite or that the band would surely play
together again met with a cool response from Lennon. In an interview
in 1975, Lennon spoke of his warm relationships with the other ex-
Beatles, and laid to rest (momentarily, at least) rumors of personal
conflict by saying, "There's nothin' going down between us. It's all in

people's heads." Asked what he thought of Harrison's publicly stated refusal to perform again with McCartney, Lennon said:

I could play with all of them. George is entitled to say that, and he'll probably change his mind by Friday. You know, we're all human. We can all change our minds. So I don't take any of my statements or any of their statements as the last word on whether we will. And if we do, the newspapers will learn about it after the fact. If we're gonna play, we're just gonna *play*.[1]

Lennon's enthusiasm for The Beatles in this interview was no doubt inspired by the renewal of his friendship with Paul McCartney during 1974. In May 1974, McCartney joined Lennon in the studio for a late-night jam session for Harry Nilsson's album *Pussy Cats*.[2] McCartney followed this session up by inviting his ex–songwriting partner to visit him during the recording of a new album, *Venus and Mars*.[3]

But Lennon was not always optimistic about either The Beatles or his own career. In *Skywriting by Word of Mouth*, at the height of his withdrawal from public life in 1978, he wrote, "It's irrelevant to me whether I ever record again. I started with rock and roll and ended with pure rock and roll (my *Rock 'N' Roll* album). If the urge ever comes over me and it is irresistible, then I will do it for fun. But otherwise I'd just as soon leave well enough alone."[4]

John Lennon's death in 1980 put to an end speculations about whether The Beatles would ever reunite—or so it seemed. How could The Beatles reunite without John Lennon? Lennon, after all, was the central driving force of the band, and without him The Beatles would not be The Beatles. Yet rumors surfaced in the media, time and again, that the surviving Beatles would reunite. There was even a rumor that Julian Lennon would take his father's place, a story which gained widespread media attention at the time of the Live Aid concert in Britain in 1984, but nothing came of it. In spite of the media hype, there seemed little possibility that the Beatles would regroup. As George Harrison aptly put it in 1989, "As far as I'm concerned, there won't be a Beatles reunion as long as John Lennon remains dead."[5]

Lennon himself, however, often spoke of fate and destiny in such a way that it might be useful to reflect on what exactly is at stake in such discussions about a reunion of The Beatles. Consider Lennon's remarks, in his last *Rolling Stone* interview in 1980, about his retirement from music in 1975:

Sometimes you wonder, I mean really wonder. I know we make our own reality and we always have a choice, but how much is preordained? Is there always a fork in the road and are there two preordained paths that are equally
preordained? There could be hundreds of paths where one could go this way
or that way—there's a choice and it's very strange sometimes.[6]

Earlier in the interview, he mentions the last track of his album *Rock
'n' Roll,* in which he says "This is Dr. Winston O'Boogie, saying goodnight from Record Plant East Studio."[7] He wonders in retrospect
whether he was aware even then of his desire to break from recording. He also reflects on returning to his musical origins: singing "Be-
Bop-A-Lula" at the Record Plant in New York in 1974 just as he had
sung the song in Liverpool in 1956 on the day that he met Paul Mc-
Cartney. Does the beginning implicate the end in some sense? John
Lennon, it seems, was beginning to explore the relationship between
past, present, and future in considerable detail in 1980.

   In the foregoing passage from the *Rolling Stone* interview, Lennon
articulates some crucial questions about our culture's understanding
of identity, time, and memory, questions to which I will frequently return in this final chapter. How much is preordained? Lennon is struggling here with the received wisdom that much of our personal and
social life is culturally determined, with the immense difficulty encountered when we attempt to think things afresh. In daily life, we
prefer pre-scripted ways of acting and making sense: the past is the
past and it should not interfere with the present, let alone affect the
future. Lennon's own answer to such cultural determinism is to invoke the power of imagination, the inventiveness of alternative imaginings, by questioning certitude and mastery: "There could be hundreds of paths where one could go this way or that way—there's a
choice and it's very strange sometimes." Decisions and choices can invoke the strange because they have something intrinsically disorder-
ing about them, something that dislocates self-mastery and self-control, something that reveals that the process of self-discovery can be
just as important as the end result.

Spring 1973

The Beatles were getting back together. The music press excitedly
wrote that John Lennon, George Harrison, and Ringo Starr were al-

ready recording in Los Angeles. There was no sign of Paul McCartney, but no one made too much of that. The rumor was that he would soon join the other Beatles in the studio.

The cause for this speculation was the new solo album Ringo Starr was recording at Sunset Sound Studios in Los Angeles. George Harrison, who had previously collaborated with Starr on his solo recordings, joined session musicians Klaus Voormann, Nicky Hopkins, Vini Poncia, and Jim Keltner to work on the album, titled *Ringo*. Starr, whose previous albums *Sentimental Journey* and *Beaucoup of Blues* had been poorly received, was about to reach his finest commercial moment. The basic tracks for "Photograph" and "You're Sixteen," both of which were to become smash hits, were recorded in the first couple of weeks.

John Lennon arrived at Sunset Sound Studios with a new offering for Starr, the song "I'm the Greatest." He said the line was a steal from boxing champion Muhammad Ali. But, as was the bulk of Lennon's writing, the song was essentially autobiographical. Beginning with when he was a boy in Liverpool, the song finds Lennon's mother telling him that he is great. Fame is the central theme of the song as he travels from childhood to adulthood, with friends and loved ones feeding his rock-star vanity. Indeed, in a demo tape of the song, the final verse contains the words, "Yoko told me I was great." This line was subsequently deleted, and Lennon decided that the only person who might get away with such blatant narcissism was the self-deprecating Starr.

"I'm the Greatest" opens the *Ringo* album, with Starr on lead vocal and drums, Lennon on piano and backing vocals, and Harrison on guitars. It was the first time the three ex-Beatles had played together since 1969. McCartney also contributed a song to the album, "Six O'Clock," but it was recorded at Abbey Road in London. Although *Ringo* was a reunion of sorts, and a major success, it did not realize fans' dreams of a Beatles reunion.[8]

Winter 1995

Twenty-two years later it finally happened: The Beatles reunion. Lennon was brought back from the land of the dead for this get-together. Regarded by some as sheer commercial exploitation and by others as a historic event, the surviving Beatles came together with a virtual Lennon to release two new songs, "Free as a Bird" and "Real Love." Lennon had recorded these songs as demos in the late 1970s in New York and had considered them for his 1980 comeback album, *Double Fantasy.* Ono had considered releasing these tracks with the assistance of studio musicians during the 1980s, but the surviving Beatles, McCartney in particular, appealed to Ono for the tapes with a view to releasing the final recordings. Ono gave the tapes to McCartney in early 1994, after Lennon's posthumous induction into the Rock 'n' Roll Hall of Fame.

The reunion of Paul McCartney, George Harrison, and Ringo Starr came about through a number of activities scheduled by Apple Records for the 1990s. First, there was the production of an authorized history of the Beatles' career, which was premiered as a six-part television series throughout the world in November 1995. The series, which was originally entitled *The Long and Winding Road* but was subsequently changed to *The Beatles Anthology,* began life as early as 1971, when Neil Aspinall (an Apple director) started putting together in chronological order television footage of The Beatles. The project was put on hold for many years, during the legal battles over Apple and royalty payments throughout the 1970s and early 1980s, and was revived as a commercial option only in 1989. At this time, McCartney, Harrison, and Starr agreed to be interviewed for the series. These interviews were interspersed with commentary from John Lennon and performance clips of The Beatles. In the United States, the opening two-hour screening of the series attracted forty-seven million viewers, according to ABC.[9]

Second, in connection with the television series, many old recordings of The Beatles were released in stages. In 1994, Apple released *Live at the BBC,* an album of early radio recordings, which sold a staggering six million copies in its first twelve months alone. Following the success of this project, McCartney, Harrison, and Starr joined with George Martin at Abbey Road Studios to begin the long and arduous task of sifting through EMI's vaults for unreleased songs and alternative takes of already released songs by The Beatles. The materials selected were all remastered, significantly enough, on 1960s equipment rather than state-of-the-art equipment. This, in itself, was a key indication that this 1990s surge in Beatles activity was as much about returning to the past, about systematically reinvesting in the sounds and images of a former golden age but under new conditions, as it was about escaping from the drabness of contemporary musical standardization. The result was the release of three double CDs, *The Beatles Anthology,* featuring rare recordings and outtakes ranging from a 1950s version of "That'll Be the Day" to Lennon's acoustic version of "Strawberry Fields Forever."

Finally, and most dramatically, the surviving Beatles began work in 1994 on two songs that John Lennon had recorded in the late 1970s. "Free as a Bird" and "Real Love" were rerecorded, not at Abbey Road but at The Mill, Paul McCartney's recording studio in Sussex; and accompanying this change in recording site there was also a change in production. The Beatles switched from George Martin, who had produced all of their albums (with the exception of *Let It Be,* which was produced by Phil Spector), to Jeff Lynne, leader of the Electric Light Orchestra and sometime member (along with George Harrison) of the Traveling Wilburys. Lynne was charged with cleaning up the Lennon tapes so that they would be in a suitable condition for additional recording. Once this was done, McCartney, Harrison, and Starr created a new musical accompaniment for the songs, both of which were incomplete in form and structure. After vocal harmonies were added, much in the style of *Abbey Road,* the end result was the production of two new singles by The Beatles.

MUSIC CRITIC PAUL DU NOYER, on the eve of the release of "Free as a Bird," wrote that "the unthinkable has come to pass. The four Beatles have got back together again."[10] There is an interesting ambiguity here over what it is, exactly, that is unthinkable. Is it unthinkable that The Beatles could ever have reunited, even before Lennon's death? Or is it unthinkable only now, in the light of Lennon's death? Without resolving this ambiguity—an ambiguity which may, at any rate, be productive for thinking about the deeper cultural connotations surrounding this profoundly imaginary reunion of The Beatles—let us consider some reflections offered by the surviving Beatles on what it was like to be "working with" Lennon again. Here is McCartney on how the rerecording of Lennon's songs was approached:

I said to Ringo, "Let's pretend that we've nearly finished some recordings and John is going off to Spain on holiday and he's just rung up and said: Look, there's one more song but it's not finished. If you're up for it, take it in the studio, have fun with it, and I'll trust you." So with that scenario in place, Ringo said, "Oh! This could even be joyous!" And it was. It actually was.[11]

Might memories of real events have played a defining role in the framing of McCartney's narrative? I think so. Lennon did, in fact, travel to Spain in 1966 after The Beatles retired from touring, to film *How I Won the War*.[12] McCartney's fantasy plays with this memory; his story enables a slippage or displacement from the present, a recovery of older ways of working, in order to make sense of this technological encounter with a virtual Lennon. Because a specific fantasy was attributed to Lennon's absence ("Let's pretend . . . John is going off to Spain"), an imagined recovery of the band could be achieved. This fantasy, in particular the fantasy of Lennon's trust, was central to the reinvoking of an imaginary ideal of The Beatles.

However, the designation of Lennon as a fantasy ideal also becomes entwined with ambivalence and ambiguity. That is to say, imagining Lennon on vacation permits the recovery of other dimensions of human experience, dimensions which are less traversed by idealization. This recovery can be gleaned from, for instance, McCartney's reflections on some of the difficulties encountered in rerecording "Free as a Bird": "Because we said, 'It's only John who's left us this tape,' we could take the piss. We'd say 'It's out of time! Wouldn't you just know it.' Like if he'd been there, we would have said it. That was our attitude to each other, we were never reverent." Once Lennon was cast outside the recording process, it became possible to apprehend certain limitations and difficulties (such as the tempo of the song). To say this is to argue that fantasies underpinning the relationships between the surviving Beatles helped to shape the new working conditions of the band. The fantasized object of Lennon structured a new kind of space for The Beatles to work together again. As McCartney puts it, "The point is, *we were working with John.* That was the fantastic thing."[13] They were, at any rate, working with Lennon in a manner that necessarily broke down certain distinctions between fantasy and reality, past and present, life and death.

It is important to see that this collective reinvestment in Lennon was problematic, at once allowing the surviving Beatles to work together again while also disturbing their collective sense of the artistic worth of the project. For we are talking about a set of imaginings that posited Lennon as both present and absent, available and missing. This paradox was a vital part of the reunion. At times, the pressure of maintaining this contradictory set of imaginings seems to have become too much. George Harrison, for instance, was uncomfortable with the idea that these recordings were an attempt to reunite the band; and it is perhaps for this reason that he looks tense in the video of "Real Love," in which the three surviving Beatles sing backing vocals to Lennon. The surviving Beatles were forced to come to terms with ambivalence in other forms also. A high degree of ambivalence was attributed to Lennon, specifically in terms of imagining how he would have felt about the recordings. This ambivalence was made especially clear by George Martin at a press conference in London for the release of *Anthology 1*. Asked what he thought Lennon would have made of the reunion and the new singles, Martin replied: "Who's to say? John changed his mind more often than he changed his socks. If you got him in the right mood he would have said 'Yeah, great, fantastic, fab.' In another mood he would have slagged it off."[14] There is certainly a deeply ambiguous impulse at work here, one which accords a central subjective significance to mood or emotion in the transformation of the cultural products of daily life. And, significantly, it is the harnessing of ambiguity to the memory of Lennon.

Lennon was physically absent then from the recordings of 1994–95, but it was his absence that facilitated this radically imaginary reunion of The Beatles. But what happens to the memory of Lennon? Is Lennon embraced or denied at the level of emotion? Does the remembering of Lennon, notwithstanding its generative role in the reunion, also contain particular gaps or breakdowns in personal and cultural experience? Here it might be said that the memory of Lennon generated a profound sense of otherness, as Ringo Starr suggests in the following interview from *Q Magazine*:

Q Magazine: How did you deal with John not being with you for the new records?

     Starr: We had to get over that. We got over it by feeling that he'd gone for lunch, he'd gone for a cup of tea, 'cos all the time we were making records, we were all in the room. All the time. And so we dealt with it, saying that he was just around the corner—but it's a sadness for all of us because you know the three of us got pretty close again there, and still there's that empty hole, that *is* John.[15]

Starr has Lennon closer to him than McCartney's Spanish scenario does; Starr places him "just around the corner." But that imagined proximity is still no defense against ambivalence. On the one hand,

Lennon's absence is something that has to be got over, through the
deployment of particular fantasies (such as his being off at tea), the
central purpose of which is to create some critical distance between
the pull of the past (Lennon as loved other) and the task at hand (the
reunion recording). On the other hand, his absence overwhelms. It is
likened to an empty hole: it is a loss which excites and threatens in
equal measure; it is at once emotional plenitude and depletion and, as
such, constitutes the communicational circuit of self and other, present and past, interior and exterior.

The ambiguity surrounding Lennon's participation in the 1995 reunion of The Beatles is played out, then, in several oppositional
forms: presence and absence, reason and emotion, present and past,
love and loss. As a fantasy object, Lennon cements this simulated,
technologically reconstituted construct of The Beatles. But the central question which arises from all this is the following: what are the
ideological and cultural consequences of such constructions of
Lennon?

THE COMMERCIAL SUCCESS of The Beatles reunion and the *Anthology*
series was phenomenal. Each release went straight to the number-one
position on the *Billboard* charts. After the release of *Anthology 3*, The
Beatles had had three number-one albums in twelve months. "The
last time that ever happened," commented George Martin, "it was
achieved by a group called The Beatles."[16]

The media debate about the reunion of The Beatles was illuminating, though not always in its own terms. Was the reunion output as
good as previous works of The Beatles? Perhaps the more interesting
question is: What does "good" mean in this context? If we like celebrities less for technical reasons than as supports for identity and idealization, then the matter of what was at stake in public discussion over
the cultural value of the reunion moves to prominence. How are we
to judge the artistic worth of these offerings from the Fab Four, especially now that the ex-Beatles are middle-aged and one is no longer
alive? Against the pull of nostalgia, how are we to judge Lennon's
music? And why, above all else, did the reunion matter so much to
people?

Inevitably, discussion focused on whether Lennon would have
wanted to be part of the reunion. This question seems to have helped

people fracture barriers between art and entertainment, pleasure and nostalgia. Critics underscored the wisdom of Lennon's own decision not to record "Free as a Bird" and "Real Love" for *Double Fantasy*. Critics argued that Lennon had decided that these songs were not good enough to release. This argument is debatable given that he was choosing material for a collaborative album and given that he indicated in interviews that he had written songs for future albums.

Critics also drew attention to Lennon's decision not to participate in any Beatles reunion. Those close to Lennon, however, tell a rather different story. Elliot Mintz, Lennon's trusted confidant and friend, suggests that Lennon might well have enjoyed the sort of reunion undertaken by McCartney, Harrison, and Starr for the recordings of "Free as a Bird" and "Real Love."[17] Speaking of the "Eyewitness News" interview that he conducted with Lennon in 1973, Mintz recalled Lennon's positive tone when they talked about The Beatles. Asked whether The Beatles might ever play together again, Lennon responded: "It's quite possible, yes. I don't know why the hell we'd do it—but it's possible." Mintz saw in this comment, as well as in others that Lennon made privately, compelling reminders of Lennon's love for the other Beatles. Yet practicalities, Mintz argued, would have to have been considered. Because all the ex-Beatles were married and deeply involved with their families, a full-scale reunion entailing world tours would never have been seriously entertained. Lennon, in particular, would have been uninterested in a such a proposal. According to Mintz, the idea of recording together might well have appealed to him, however. Clearly, we cannot be sure how Lennon would have responded to the idea, but when considered from this angle, the 1990s Beatles reunion is more likely to have gained Lennon's support than his wrath.

What we can do is reflect on the media discussion of the uses to which Lennon's memory was put for the reunion that did take place. I have noted the existence of a repertoire of vocabularies used to describe Lennon in relation to the reunion: he would have detested it; he would not have been interested in trying to recapture the past; he might have been interested, but not in a full-blown regrouping for tours and the like; he would have loved the idea. There is no final resolution here, but rather an endless process of engagement with a loved but now lost object.

Taken as a whole, our remembering of Lennon is a kind of transformational activity, one bound up with the working through of loss and pain. The debate over Lennon's likely involvement in The Beatles reunion is one, I think, that involves an inventive, though anxious, redemption of our personal investment in his art. To understand the reunion in this way is again to shift the focus away from aesthetic evaluation and toward the psychic compartments of the imagination that underlay our pleasure in passing cultural judgments. The aim here is not so much to map who was for or against the reunion, but instead to consider the multiplicity of points of view that were on offer in the cultural arena about the fate of the project. In this context, an openness to the multiplicity necessarily entails a consideration of the complexity of our feelings about Lennon, specifically a consideration of the ways in which he is remembered in contemporary culture. The other side of the coin is refusing to think about the reunion and why it matters. Such a response involves a dramatic oversimplification—of course Lennon would have participated, or it's clear-cut, Lennon would have hated it.

PERHAPS THE MOST GRIPPING dimension of the 1995 reunion is its deployment of a virtual Lennon. Pushed into the forefront of public attention, Lennon rematerialized on our screens and loudspeakers as a mediated object of fascination and pleasure. His presence—the deployment of his voice and image—on "Free as a Bird" and "Real Love" was spellbinding. This projection of Lennon, in sounds and pictures, marked a new stage in the dissolution of his death. It was also a reframing of our own anxiety over Lennon's absence. These "new" songs, filtered through previously unpublished photographs and clips of his past performances, seemed to create a "new" Lennon. Yet in this very proliferation, juxtaposition, dispersal, and cross-referencing of his music and image, we desperately cling to the memory of Lennon.

To speak of dispersal and cross-referencing is to situate Lennon in the postmodern. In this context Jean Baudrillard's seminal analysis of postmodern culture as a world of simulacra—where images gather up into themselves the complexities and ambiguities of an event and in the process become more real than reality, where everything is a representation, and where the distinction between fact and fiction becomes increasingly unstable—is useful for comprehending mediated aspects of The Beatles reunion, even though I will also suggest that there are serious shortcomings with the arguments associated with postmodernism. For Baudrillard, our image-saturated culture is one in which realities "implode" into their aesthetically spaced representations; images become "hyperreal" through a merging of the copy with the original, the image with the referent. "The real," writes Baudrillard, "becomes that of which it is possible to give an equivalent reproduction—the real is not only what can be reproduced, but that which is always already reproduced, the hyperreal."[18] Baudrillard's hyperworld is one of excess: an overabundance of information, banks of images, multiplex and discontinuous desires. All these things tangle and multiply ad infinitum, so that images represent nothing but themselves.

Culture today for Baudrillard is a kind of deathly surplus in which we witness the death of imagination, the death of meaning, the death of aesthetics. In the absence of anything truly new, postmodern art is an art of recycling, of ransacking the past to create something of interest for today. We are talking, essentially, of a secondhand aesthetics in which cross-referencing and self-referentiality are paramount. Such a standpoint offers a considerable conceptual purchase on contemporary cultural phenomena. What else has contemporary music been in the last few years other than the recycling of past hits, the patching together of former golden sounds with the assistance of new technology, assimilated to the style of rap, hip-hop, or techno? Contemporary art knows no privileged sense of direction; it expands forward and backward simultaneously. Today's aesthetic and cultural production is one of instant obsolescence; the rage of today is destined to be eclipsed before it has sufficient time to force itself into public consciousness.

What gives this media-saturated hyperreality a radical political edge, however, is its drastic alteration of our experience of time, space, and history, such that an indeterminate number of aesthetic configurations may be drawn at any moment. New technological capacities for knowledge production and information transfer, so postmodernists tell us, force a fracturing of the hierarchies of European modernism and unleash other ways of experiencing self and world. The privileging of linearity—linear time, progress, development, the new—becomes especially frayed. It is now easy to undo endings, to

reimagine the past, or to cross to the future in contemporary representation; "with electronic reproduction offering the spectacle of gestures, images, styles and cultures in a perpetual collage of disintegra-
tion and reintegration, the 'new' disappears into a permanent present."[19]
The past is, in effect, no longer secure; or, to put it more accurately,
the past can no longer be consigned to the past in the way that we
once imagined. "What has disappeared," writes Baudrillard, "has every
chance of reappearing. For what dies is annihilated in linear time, but
what disappears passes into the state of constellation. It becomes an
event in a cycle which may bring it back many times."[20]

One might speculate from all this that the 1995 reunion of The
Beatles involves just such a dissolution of the difference between
image and reality, between representation and what is represented.
"Free as a Bird" and "Real Love" are postmodern records of The Beatles as postmodern. They are postmodern to the degree that they sim-
ulate what is not there, what is no more, what is lost. The reunion reveals an image of a collective body, namely, The Beatles, which has
disappeared as substance, identity, or event but is still readily available for aesthetic enjoyment. "Things we live with today," writes Zygmunt Bauman, "are identifiable mostly as vestiges: once parts of a to-
tality which gave them a place and function, but today just pieces
condemned to seek a meaningful design in vain and destined for a
game without end."[21] "Free as a Bird" and "Real Love" are The Beatles as a "game without end." Lennon is drawn back from the dead, rematerialized as image, only to disappear just as quickly again. Indeed,
the video of "Free as a Bird" frames Lennon as an object of hyper-
simulation: a constant flow of images of him dominates. One minute
he is performing at the Cavern in Liverpool, the next he is dancing
with Yoko Ono in the middle of a street (the sequence is taken from
the film *Let It Be*). Lennon travels at a breathtaking pace throughout
the video, shifting forward and backward throughout the career of
Beatle John, appearing in imaginary worlds and places. Lennon, as
televisual image, just *is* this endless play of simulation.

Yet "Free as a Bird" and "Real Love" might also be considered
postmodern in another sense. Simulation, we are told, is no longer
referential matter or substance but rampant desire, hyperimagina-
tion. Simulation invokes images of things that become more real than
reality. Simulation implies fantasy, dream, wish, hallucination. The
framing of Lennon—his images and representations—in these songs

contains an intricate range of imaginings, but perhaps the most powerful reverie is that Lennon's disappearance is reversible. Lennon is
dead, but his disappearance is not absolute or final. Lennon's death
and disappearance are suspended, replaced instead by the endless
repetition of his image. With Lennon recovered, the postmodern
economy of pleasure effected by "Free as a Bird" and "Real Love" re-
sides in the very act of repetition—the repetition of images and representations of Lennon. The distance between the original innovation
and the copied reiteration is effaced. We can detect pleasure, an
economy of enjoyment, in the blurring of innovation and reiteration;
there is a playfulness in drawing from the master plot of The Beatles'
career and giving it novel twists and infinite variations. What, after all,
is the real creativeness of Lennon and The Beatles? The mixing of
various sounds with Lennon's distorted voice as the reprise of "Strawberry Fields Forever" (in which he says "Cranberry Sauce"), or the
copying of this leitmotif as the finale for "Free as a Bird" (in which he
says "turned out nice again")? Which one is more creative, more inventive, more enjoyable?

All of this discussion points to a kind of dissolution of Lennon's past
into the present through a slicing of time into short-lived, reversible
episodes. This slicing of time is such that there can no longer be any
definitive beginning or end to the Fab Four. "Love Me Do" is, of
course, still situated in the early 1960s, and in the same way, the film
Let It Be still signals the impending breakup of the band. But the new,
specifically postmodern moment introduced by the reunion scram-
bles the rule-guided, historical identity of the Fabs as grounded and
thematized. Where, after all, does "Free as a Bird" fit in our collective
consciousness of The Beatles? As the follow-up single to "Help," an
undistinguished filler on *The Magical Mystery Tour,* or as a backfiring
that actually precipitated the breakup of the band? Such questions are
not simply rhetorical. Ringo Starr has said that "Free as a Bird" could
have been made in 1967, whereas George Harrison thinks it sounds
very similar to *Abbey Road,* which shifts the song into 1969. Clearly,
such questions are enough to make one wonder whether "Free as a
Bird" was recorded in the 1990s at all!

SO FAR I HAVE BEEN CONCERNED to retrace the 1995 "reunion" of The
Beatles in terms of broader cultural forces and social logics, and I

have indicated that suggestive links can be made to postmodernist
culture. In this connection, I have focused especially on the dimensions of pleasure, nostalgia, irony, and aesthetic innovation in this reframing of Lennon and The Beatles in the postmodern. However,
there is another dimension of postmodernism which requires consideration at this point, primarily because it draws attention to the ideological nature of postmodernism's celebration of the fragmented, sur-
face-centered character of contemporary cultural production. For
popularized versions and images of the postmodern—typically images
of dislocation and fracturing, loss of personal and cultural identity,
and erosion of communication—also powerfully confirm a postwar
global system that is fundamentally economic. That is to say, it is possible to trace postmodern cultural forms to globally structured relations of economic, political, and symbolic power, and indeed American critic Fredric Jameson has powerfully argued that postmodernism
as an ideology is best grasped as a symptom of deeper structural
changes arising from "multinational capital" or "late capitalism."[22]
Jameson attempts a diagnosis of the postmodern condition in terms of
the rise of global multinational and communicational networks, its
agents and institutions, its restructuring of time and space, its deconstruction of ideological limits, its reification of hi-tech, and its radical
transmutation of the inner textures of human experience. Much of
Jameson's argument can understood in terms of increasing cultural
standardization, as a spiraling to the nth degree of what Herbert Marcuse termed our "one-dimensional" society. Here, it is as if the logic
of commodification has permeated the social and psychic fabric so
thoroughly that critical distance is effaced, that subjecthood is rendered increasingly fragile and fictional, that culture undergoes a
wholesale aestheticization, and that separate political discourses
flicker out.[23]

   Interestingly, the media devoted considerable attention to the economic implications of the reunion of The Beatles. In fact, the media
suggested that the reunion, though dressed up in postmodern garb,
was primarily driven by the economic interests of transnational entertainment corporations. Such a view is articulated with some precision,
for instance, by Bryan Appleyard in "Blame It All on the Beatles." Appleyard argues, in broad terms, that pop music today is thoroughly
permeated by commercial interests which promote consumerism and
individualism in society at large. Music is not only stripped of its aes-

thetic function in late-capitalist society but also governed by the ever expanding logics of globalization. "Pop groups," Appleyard writes,

are, in fact, the shock troops of globalization. Pop seeps across frontiers, softening up the young and paving the way for Levis, Coca-Cola and Microsoft. Pop subverts nationality by imposing a single rock 'n' roll aspiration and, overwhelmingly, that aspiration can only be expressed by American products. Bon Jovi and Michael Jackson are corporate ads for corporate America.[24]

The globalization of commercial music is understood by Appleyard to herald cultural standardization and uniformity (a "single rock 'n' roll aspiration"). For Appleyard, this repressive dimension of the contemporary music scene is itself a fundamental site over which late capitalism works, a site in which simulated desires and needs are suggested by advertising images, from Coca-Cola to Microsoft.

Appleyard argues that we need to take another step back into the history of pop in order to adequately define the links between commercial music on the one hand and its embedding in a global system of commodity production on the other. Pop is not simply an expression of artistic aspirations; it is, rather, a material process in which art is pushed into the service of profit. It is against this conceptual backdrop that Appleyard explains the seemingly contradictory blend of art and commercialization in the music of The Beatles.

Which brings me back to The Beatles. A quarter of a century on, their celebratory resurrection on television and CD has been remarkable—hype maybe, but good hype. Teenagers love them all over again. A new wave of British bands acknowledge them as the true precursors. John, ageless, frail, disembodied, returns from the dead to join his wizened pals in the charts. . . . What this has all made clear, with the wisdom of hindsight, is that The Beatles were the first. This was the Ur-band, the original. They were not, of course, the first pop stars, Elvis and Cliff came along before. But they were the first to define the global role of pop. They took the forms of American music, improvising and softening, and then resold them, first to the British, then to the States and then to the world.

Significantly, while Appleyard identifies pop's dominant ideology as American media culture, he also stresses the increasing internationalization of this corporate cultural domination. "The Beatles," writes Appleyard, "were among the leading precursors of that terrifying, culture-incinerating phenomenon known as globalization."[25]

Appleyard's convincing argument, while only implicitly drawing out the interconnections between commercial music and global capitalism, has the merit of highlighting some of the general characteristics of cultural production in the advanced capitalist countries, emphasizing the ideological dimensions of music as a commodity, and underscoring that music and communication today are fundamentally interwoven with the exercise of economic power. In terms of consumption, for instance, over one million copies of the *Anthology 1* CD/tape package were sold in the United States in its first week of release, four hundred thousand on the first day. One-quarter of a million units of The Beatles' catalog were purchased during the same week. Similar patterns of consumption were documented in other Western countries.[26]

But if Appleyard's viewpoint captures core defining linkages between economic and symbolic power in the contemporary epoch, it serves less well as a diagnosis of cultural forms and reception. First, Appleyard's argument that The Beatles were an ideological incarnation of American media culture is deeply unsatisfactory. It is true, of course, that The Beatles derived much of their musical inspiration from American artists, from Little Richard to Elvis Presley to the Beach Boys. It is also true that the launching of The Beatles as a global pop phenomenon took place after their visit to the United States in 1964, the most important event of which was their appearance on *The Ed Sullivan Show*. But it is surely a mistake to view The Beatles as simply an outgrowth of American entertainment culture. For one thing, this viewpoint not only violently strips The Beatles of their Liverpudlian origins but also seriously downplays the diverse artistic and cultural sources which The Beatles drew upon and redefined. From the classical leanings of "Eleanor Rigby" to the Indian-inspired spirituality of "Within You Without You," from the childlike escapism of "Yellow Submarine" to the comic lunacy of "You Know My Name (Look Up the Number)," The Beatles blended high and low culture, Western and Eastern musical forms, pop and fine art, rock and classical music, vaudeville and comedy, the classical and the contemporary. It is not hard to trace in this blending the opening up of the artistic and cultural experimentations of modernism to a mass audience. And perhaps it is no accident, therefore, that one of the major cultural consequences of the artistically democratic, universal appeal of The Beatles should be a profound ambivalence about their net worth. This kind of ambivalence permits some critics, like Appleyard, to link The Beatles to American cultural imperialism, while others continue to imagine that there is nothing especially political about The Beatles.

More important for our present purposes is a second criticism of Appleyard's argument: namely, that it is economically deterministic as regards the cultural sphere. Appleyard's argument places The Beatles in their time with respect to the rise of mass corporate culture, and indeed much of what he has to say about the reunion focuses on consumerism and cultural standardization. However, this argument provides at best only a partial account of the cultural inputs into the production and reception of The Beatles in the 1990s. It cannot account for the complexity and variety of people's reactions to the reunion, which is hardly surprising given that Appleyard speaks of a "single rock 'n' roll aspiration"—as if cultural reception, from San Francisco to São Paulo, is always uniform. Appleyard's contention that the reunion primarily served the interests of transnational corporations makes much less sense than precisely the opposite possibility: that the surviving Beatles sought to reclaim their own past, as well as to critically examine their own artistic heritage in popular music, *in spite of* the immense commercial pressures that the mass media and recording industry brought to bear. It is surely more plausible to regard the surviving Beatles' work on the reunion and *The Beatles Anthology* as an imaginative amplification of their own past achievements. That the reunion would necessarily entail the distribution and advertising mechanisms of transnational entertainment industries is surely obvious enough.

Rather than engage in such economic pigeonholing, we can better understand the 1990s reunion of The Beatles, I think, as embodying both modernist and postmodernist dimensions of late-twentieth-century culture. These dimensions tangle and cross and contradict one another. *The Beatles Anthology* undeniably reflects a strong modernist desire for linear, fixed cultural forms, categories, and identities. The compilations represent an authoritative, official, historical record of the career of The Beatles from beginning to end—and, to this extent, they are entirely at one with the culture of modernism. The virtual reunion, by contrast, collapses discrete divisions of time and space, dissolving the fixed identities of The Beatles into something more open-ended and fluid. Lennon's "Free as a Bird" and "Real Love" demos are recovered from their consignment to near oblivion;

the genres and fashions of The Beatles are reproduced in an endless variety of cultural forms; and images of Lennon are disseminated into the simulated spaces of the reunion.

Crucially, these modernist and postmodernist cultural forms exist in dynamic relationship to each other. Zygmunt Bauman explains this tension thus: "Postmodernity does not necessarily mean the end, the discreditation or the rejection of modernity. Postmodernity is no more (but no less either) than the modern mind taking a long, attentive and sober look at itself, at its condition and its past works."[27] *The Beatles Anthology* and the reunion offer precisely this creative kind of ambiguity—mixing historical record and fantasy, reality and simulation, certainty and contingency. What matters most is Lennon's location in this technologized landscape: in particular, the ways in which mass-media rememberings of him become inserted into these modernist and postmodernist framings. The reunion constructs Lennon as an identity transacted between the eternal and the evanescent, past and present, memory and image, materiality and metaphor.

PERHAPS NONE OF LENNON's later songs are as personally revealing as "Watching the Wheels." "People say I'm crazy / Doing what I'm doing," Lennon writes of his period as a househusband. Thanks to the advice of worried onlookers who wish to save him from ruin, he documents the strategies presented for getting his career back on track. Surely he wants to return to public life, to the thrills of showbiz? Surely he misses the big time? Lennon answers in the negative; he prefers the love and trust of his family to public adoration. At the same time, he indicates that his relationship to the outside world has changed. He is content now to just watch the wheels of public life spin. Hinting at the psychic price he has paid for fame, he sings, "I just had to let it go." He might have been describing the disillusionment he had undergone in the development of his personal and professional life.

In his early solo work, Lennon invited us to share in the intensity of his emotional life. *John Lennon/Plastic Ono Band* (1970), as discussed in chapter 2, was a brilliant though haunting autobiographical record that reaffirmed the importance of pop music to contemporary culture. Lennon's exploration of his youth, the pain of parental neglect and loss, the burdens of celebrity, and the complexities of human ambivalence resulted in what Wilfrid Mellers called "music both primitive and deeply melancholy."[28] *Imagine* (1971) found Lennon building on this therapeutic catharsis, extending the reach of his autobiographical songwriting from the burdens of the past to his new commitment to Yoko Ono. Rejection of existing social constraints was still a central theme, but with *Imagine* he became more preoccupied with the need to transform self and world: "Imagine all the people / Living for today." No heaven, hell, countries, religion, killing, possessions, greed, or hunger: this was Lennon's utopian vision. One of the most noticeable aspects of *Imagine* was not simply its brilliance but also its surprising originality. Lennon had produced an album that was as powerful as anything recorded by The Beatles and had done so on his own terms, not by trying to rewrite songs like "Strawberry Fields Forever" or "Come Together." *Imagine* was in stark contrast to Paul McCartney's solo albums, like *McCartney* (1970) and *Ram* (1971), which traded on his talent for rewriting Beatles songs. McCartney's early solo work was viewed by many critics as happy, innocent music with unsubtle lyrics. Lennon's early solo albums, by contrast, were seen as stunningly original—sometimes mesmerizing, sometimes perplexing.

"I think we shared our feelings with the world," said Ono.[29] To have achieved such artistic directness suggests an unusual degree of trust on the part of Lennon and Ono: trust in each other, as well as in their audience. Perhaps it is not surprising, therefore, that this sort of trust could not be sustained; indeed, Lennon's collaborative work with Ono, as well as his solo work, suffered from various setbacks after the release of *Imagine*. *Some Time in New York City* (1972) was Lennon and Ono's attempt to place their social awareness in the context of radical politics; and, as I argued in chapter 4, the album represents one of the few occasions where Lennon failed to communicate certain ideas to his audience. *Mind Games* (1973) showed that Lennon had learned from the errors of his political sloganeering. While a much more popular and balanced work—in addition to the hit "Mind Games" it contained such evocative, haunting songs as "Aisumasen (I'm Sorry)" and "You Are Here"—the album was generally perceived as a poor rehash of *Imagine.*

Soon after the release of *Mind Games,* Lennon and Ono split. Living the highs and, mostly, lows of his lost weekend in Los Angeles, Lennon could muster from himself only the inventive, though ultimately flawed, *Rock 'n' Roll* (1973–75) with producer Phil Spector. At this point, he was a man at odds with himself, and nowhere was this more obvious than in his rejection of the way in which the media and the public attempted to place him as a celebrity.

They got mad at me for not saying: "Peace, brother" all the time. I'm human. I wasn't having any peace myself, so I couldn't be going around saying "Peace, brother." Am I supposed to go around like a nun? I can't do it. I couldn't do it in The Beatles and I can't do it by myself. . . . I have to cut through, cut through the mask even if it's self-created.[30]

For Lennon, the mid-1970s were a period of intense personal change. Notwithstanding the media hype surrounding the lost weekend, he in fact broadened his musical range considerably and sought to develop a less doctrinaire attitude about his relationships. By the time of *Walls and Bridges* (1974), he was more personally at ease, or at least more accepting of his ambivalent feelings about himself and his social environment. The album was written and recorded extremely swiftly. Indeed, parallels might be drawn between Lennon's artistic vitality in 1974 and his astonishing creativity at the time of the breakup of his first marriage in 1968. Just as he had composed some of his best songs in India in the late 1960s, so too Lennon reached new creative heights toward the end of 1974. *Walls and Bridges* marked the emergence of a more reflective appreciation of the difficulties of living, expressed as an ongoing search for happiness and trust in a world which does much to shatter such hopes and dreams. Unlike *John Lennon/Plastic Ono Band*, however, *Walls and Bridges* does not present the dismantling of illusions as *the* road to personal fulfillment. On the contrary, the album highlights that there are no neat answers to the difficulties of relationships. Instead, there is only the ambiguous and uncertain terrain of love and loss. It is perhaps for this reason that *Walls and Bridges* waivers uneasily between Lennon's sorrow over breaking up with Ono and his newfound love for May Pang. "Going Down on Love," "Whatever Gets You thru the Night," "Bless You," and "Scared" are all variations on the bafflingly complex terrain of lost love, while "#9 Dream" and "Surprise Surprise (Sweet Bird of Paradox)" capture the thrills of erotic passion. "Lennon knows," Ben Gerson wrote in a review of the album, "that neither dreams nor their puncturing is the answer. . . . When one accepts one's childhood, one's parenthood and the impermanence of what lies between, one can begin to slog along."[31]

Lennon's growing tolerance of the confusion that emotions can generate, coupled with an acceptance of the need to "slog along," allowed him the necessary personal space to develop his music and art in more mature ways. In all of Lennon's post-Beatles output, one finds encounters with utopianism—sometimes cast as distant possibility, sometimes as instant liberation. Lennon's utopianism oscillated considerably between personal dreams and social dramas, and indeed what is arguably the most important legacy of his work consists precisely in this intense worrying away at the intersections between private and public boundaries. On *Walls and Bridges,* Lennon realized, possibly just in time, that the difficult emotional work of sustaining relationships is a challenging and mystifying experience. This realization enlarged the whole notion of utopianism, drawing it into the realm of lived experience, in terms of both connection and suffering, both proximity and distance.

After The Beatles broke up, Lennon forced himself to chronicle the more painful elements of his own history. He did so, most powerfully on *Plastic Ono Band* but on other albums also, by analyzing the psychic price he had paid for failing to adequately mourn the death of his mother, for the suffering that such denial had caused him and others that he loved, and for all the things he had missed out on (such as the love of his first wife Cynthia and son Julian) because of the influence of past pathology. Nevertheless, such painful truths were not always easy to acknowledge, let alone live with, and to avoid this hurt Lennon resorted at various points in the early 1970s to sermons and slogans for his music and art. Lennon's reunion with Yoko Ono at the beginning of 1975 signaled not only a recovery of his estranged emotional past but also an acceptance that his personal history would continue to affect the present, that it could be made tolerable, and indeed that such self-knowledge was essential for authentic living.

Solo albums of breathtaking originality, the breakup of a relationship, career troubles, and a more mature songwriting capability rooted in the discovery of authentic family relationships—all of these took place during the 1970s. Yet what do these developments tell us about Lennon? They are linked in terms of their very incongruity; there was always a significant tension in Lennon's work between the kind of utopianism he imagined and the real psychological conditions of his existence. It is as if in his post-Beatles solo work Lennon was staging some kind of ongoing dialogue with his celebrity as a state of mind and lifestyle. The dialogue was ongoing in the sense that every time a fresh set of pronouncements was made, new developments or anxieties necessitated a reconsideration of his personal circumstances. The excavation of personal repression undertaken on *Plastic Ono Band* and *Imagine* was ultimately displaced by the call to political action on *Some Time in New York City.* Likewise, politics was superseded by the lures of utopian dreaming on *Mind Games.* The switches between utopianism and realism were deconstructed, and perhaps even transfigured, on *Walls and Bridges, Double Fantasy,* and *Milk and Honey.* The point is not so much that one kind of cultural logic came to replace another but rather that the remembering of the past, as well as the anticipation of the future, provided no defense against the unpredictable nature of human experience, the highs and lows of life. It was as if Lennon was saying that he had not expected to discover utopia, the contours of which he evoked on "Imagine," within the inner depths of his mind. Nor had he expected to uncover politics at the heart of his home life. But the truth was that he had. The semiretirement years found Lennon more passionate about both peace and politics, precisely because he embraced them in novel ways.

If we shift to the reunion once more, it is possible to grasp the complex ways in which these emotional dynamics are dramatized. Ironically, Lennon's "Free as a Bird" is preoccupied with the complicity between freedom and limitation. Limitation in this context might arise from The Beatles, celebrity, the past, ideology, or politics. Whatever the source of limitation, Lennon places freedom in an imagined relation to itself:

Free as a bird
It's the next best thing to being
Free as a bird.

To be sure, the song's maudlin chord changes evoke despair, which is compounded once it is remembered that Lennon was declaring his freedom from the oppressive ideology of celebrity and, by implication, The Beatles. In a strange irony, however, he turns nostalgically to the past in the song's chorus. "Whatever happened to / The lives that we once knew," he wrote in lines that Paul McCartney subsequently finished for the reunion recording.

What I am suggesting is that the reunion reconstruction of "Free as a Bird" is a noticeably mournful affair, caught between hope and despair. The song is an intensely ambivalent aesthetic elaboration. It represents a grieving for lost love, as well as for a former way of life, and the intensity of this grief serves as an unacknowledged source of artistic creativity. By and large, music critics reacted negatively to these more mournful or nostalgic elements of The Beatles reunion. Many critics dismissed "Free as a Bird," as well as "Real Love," as dismal attempts to recapture the past, as a kind of hankering for some bygone age. Yet this criticism altogether misses the more creative, redemptive aspects of the nostalgia which permeated the reunion. For it is surely more plausible to see the reunion as an attempt to return to the past for the purposes of better dealing with the present and future. That is to say, the nostalgia encountered here is not simply of the Hollywood variety which packages the past as "product," as one sense of style among others. On the contrary, nostalgia is constructively explored in the reunion, as a means of understanding how we see ourselves today in the light of the past. From this angle, nostalgia has a certain transformative quality, permitting the recovery of lost memories, thoughts, and feelings as a medium for present artistic experience.

But the reunion's rehabilitation of the past for the present raises the thorny question of what it is, exactly, that we are striving to recover, remember, or work through in the case of Lennon. The reunion can best be grasped as an excavation of Lennon, one that seeks to separate the man from his public image. Lennon was forever trying to avoid the repressive logic of dualism: he sought in his personal and artistic life to reconfigure utopianism and realism, politics and aesthetics, celebrity and genuineness. He lived in fear of dogmatism and strove for authenticity, even though this struggle entailed the difficult and, at times, certainly painful recognition that to be human is to be vulnerable.

"The Beatles," writes Philip Norman, "eventually ruled over time itself."[32] Norman underscores the point that the Fab Four not only represented the spirit of an age but also profoundly influenced our perception of historical time itself since the 1960s. This colonization of time, I suggest, is central for understanding the ultimate significance of the 1990s reunion of The Beatles. When people look back on John Lennon's music, and The Beatles', they seem also to be viewing their own private histories, recalling moments of happiness and discontent. Lennon, in this sense, provokes something beyond the seductions of

celebrity; something authentic is discernible in his musical compositions, in his social awareness and politics, in his rejection of the music
business, and in his desire to live life with his family on his own terms.
What we can know about all this is always limited, distorted by rumors,
overdetermined by myths. Yet it is in the disjunction between fiction
and fact that our knowledge of Lennon is perhaps most precious. What
sustains our interest in Lennon is his very vulnerability, his acceptance
of uncertainty and ambivalence. The inner peace he discovered in the
late 1970s differed considerably from that which he had imagined at
the start of the decade.

The reunion forces a further confrontation with these paradoxes of
identity. What was Lennon's vision of the world in his final years?
Where did he place himself in terms of the broader culture? In *Skywriting by Word of Mouth,* Lennon notes: "The lesson for me is clear.
I've already 'lost' one family to produce what? Sgt. Pepper? I am
blessed with a second chance. Being a Beatle nearly cost me my life,
and certainly cost me a great deal of my health. . . . I will not make the
same mistake twice in one lifetime."[33] Lennon wrote this in 1978, between composing "Free as a Bird" and "Real Love." What remained
for Lennon was the chance—a second chance—to live life on his own
terms and to create art free from the disabling pathologies of celebrity. "Free as a Bird" and "Real Love" were part of this imaginative
vision. In the light of his tragic death, these songs—faithfully restored
through the reunion recordings—can be viewed as maps of the territory Lennon was charting.

Notes

Introduction

Epigraphs: Jann Wenner, ed., *Lennon Remembers: The Rolling Stone Interviews by Jann Wenner* (1971; reprint, London: Penguin Books, 1980), 26, 109; Sigmund Freud, "Mourning and Melancholia," in *The Standard Edition of the Complete Psychological Works of Sigmund Freud,* ed. and trans. James Strachey (1966; reprint, London: Hogarth Press, 1986), 14:251.

1. Philip Larkin, "Fighting the Fab," *The Observer,* 9 October 1983, reprinted in *The Lennon Companion: Twenty-five Years of Comment,* ed. Elizabeth Thomson and David Gutman (New York: Schirmer Books, 1987), 248.

2. Kroll's comparison is noted by George Martin in *The Summer of Love* (London: Pan Macmillan, 1994), 155.

3. Quoted in James Sauceda, *The Literary Lennon: A Comedy of Errors* (New York: Pierian Press, 1983), 3.

4. Jann Wenner, "Remembering John Lennon," in *John Lennon: Drawings, Performances, Films,* ed. Wulf Herzogenrath and Dorothee Hansen (London: Thames and Hudson, 1995), 19.

5. Quoted in Paul Du Noyer, *We All Shine On: The Stories behind Every John Lennon Song, 1970–1980* (London: HarperCollins, 1997), 24.

6. Quoted in Wenner, "Remembering John Lennon," 18.

7. Ray Coleman, *John Lennon* (London: Warner Books, 1992), xii.

8. Philip Norman, *Days in the Life: John Lennon Remembered* (London: Century, 1990), 24.

9. Elizabeth Thomson and David Gutman, eds., *The Lennon Companion: Twenty-five Years of Comment* (New York: Schirmer Books, 1987), back jacket.

10. G. Barry Golson, ed., *The Playboy Interviews with John Lennon and Yoko Ono,* conducted by David Sheff (New York: Playboy Press, 1981), 11.

11. Elliot Mintz, telephone interview by author, Los Angeles, Calif., 19 March 1997.

12. Quoted in Ray Coleman, *McCartney: Yesterday and Today* (London: Boxtree, 1995), 97.

13. For an excellent discussion of the parallel Freud makes between mourning, as internal psychological conflict, and the creative dynamics underlying many cultural activities, see Peter Homans, *The Ability to Mourn: Disillusionment and the Social Origins of Psychoanalysis* (Chicago: University of Chicago Press, 1989).

14. The song has not been commercially released; it was aired on the radio series *The Lost Lennon Tapes* as "The News of the Day (Another Bob Dylan Parody)."

15. The conceptual diversity of contemporary psychoanalytic approaches is, of course, immense, and I have written about the relationship between psychoanalysis and contemporary theory at length in previous books. See Anthony Elliott, *Social Theory and Psychoanalysis in Transition: Self and Society from Freud to Kristeva* (Oxford: Blackwell, 1992); *Psychoanalytic Theory: An Introduction* (Oxford: Blackwell, 1994); *Subject to Ourselves: Social Theory, Psychoanalysis, and Postmodernity* (Cambridge: Polity Press, 1996); and *Freud 2000* (Cambridge: Polity Press, 1998); and Anthony Elliott and Stephen Frosh, eds., *Psychoanalysis in Contexts: Paths between Theory and Modern Culture* (London: Routledge, 1995).

16. Sigmund Freud, "An Autobiographical Study," in *The Standard Edition of the Complete Psychological Works of Sigmund Freud,* ed. and trans. James Strachey (1966; reprint, London: Hogarth Press, 1986), 20:7–74. *The Standard Edition* is hereafter cited as SE.

17. *The Making of Sgt. Pepper,* prod. George Martin, dir. Alan Benson, A Really Useful Group, 1992.

18. Lennon's poem is quoted in Peter Brown and Steven Gaines, *The Love You Make: An Insider's Story of the Beatles* (New York: McGraw-Hill, 1983), 438.

Chapter 1: Mind Games

Epigraphs: John Lennon, *Skywriting by Word of Mouth* (New York: HarperPerennial, 1986), 19; Rainer Maria Rilke, quoted in Zygmunt Bauman, *Postmodern Ethics* (Oxford: Blackwell, 1993), 1.

1. George Harrison notes in *The Beatles Anthology* that, during the American tour, "From Me to You," "She Loves You," and "I Want to Hold Your Hand" all occupied in turns the number-one position in New York.

2. Quoted in Miles, comp., *John Lennon in His Own Words* (London: Omnibus Press, 1980), 22.

3. G. Barry Golson, ed., *The Playboy Interviews with John Lennon and Yoko Ono*, conducted by David Sheff (New York: Playboy Press, 1981), 79.

4. Jann Wenner, ed., *Lennon Remembers: The Rolling Stone Interviews by Jann Wenner* (1971; reprint, London: Penguin Books, 1980), 18.

5. Quoted in Philip Norman, *Days in the Life: John Lennon Remembered* (London: Century, 1990), 58.

6. Wulf Herzogenrath, "John Lennon, Artist; Or, Why Was It Impossible for So Long to Acknowledge Him as an Artist?—and Why Do We Still Find It Difficult Today?" in *John Lennon: Drawings, Performances, Films*, ed. Wulf Herzogenrath and Dorothee Hansen (London: Thames and Hudson, 1995), 13.

7. Jonathan Cott, "The Last Rolling Stone Interview," in *The Ballad of John and Yoko*, ed. Jonathan Cott and Christine Doudna (Garden City, N.Y.: Rolling Stone, 1982), 190, 191.

8. Albert Goldman, *The Lives of John Lennon* (New York: Bantam Books, 1988), 3–5.

9. See ibid., 6. Goldman acknowledges that Lennon would sometimes make an exception and permit Sean to sit on his lap. Significantly, Goldman connects Lennon's desire to be "surgically clean" (6) with the star's sexual experiences and notes that Lennon would often walk around the Dakota naked. "Nobody is ever embarrassed by these naked tiffins because John is the emperor who wears no clothes. He can sit naked by the hour with his feet up on the butcher-block table and his dick lying in his lap like a sleeping pet and produce no stir. Sexually speaking, John is off the air" (14). If, however, we take this desexualization of Lennon to be a symptom of the over-sexualization of celebrity in contemporary culture, we can see that obsession and neurosis are indeed frightening (and unthinkable?) realms of experience for Goldman.

10. Goldman, *The Lives of John Lennon*, 6.

11. Ibid., 5, 7.

12. Miles, *John Lennon in His Own Words*, 50.

13. Goldman, *The Lives of John Lennon*, 137.

14. Ibid., 506.

15. Goldman writes, for instance, of Lennon and Ono's addiction to heroin without once considering their own reflections on their heroin use. See Lennon and Ono's comments in Golson, *The Playboy Interviews*, 93–95.

16. Goldman's prime sources of information about Lennon's semiretirement years were Fred Seaman and Marnie Hair. Seaman, who was Lennon's personal assistant, remained employed by Yoko Ono until she terminated his contract in December 1981, after he was discovered taking a bath in her private bathroom. He was subsequently convicted of the theft of Lennon's personal diaries. Neighbor Marnie Hair was also thought by many critics an unreliable source of information on Lennon and Ono; Goldman did not reveal

that Hair had filed a $1.5-million lawsuit against Ono for an injury Hair's child had sustained at Ono's Long Island house. See David Fricke and Jeffrey Ressner, "Imaginary John Lennon: The True Story behind Albert Goldman's Character Assassination of John Lennon," *Rolling Stone,* 20 October 1988, 42–45, 93.

17. Luc Sante, "Beatlephobia," *New York Review of Books,* 22 December 1988, 30–35; Fricke and Ressner, "Imaginary John Lennon," 42–45, 93; and "The Battle over His Memory," *Newsweek,* 17 October 1988, 64–73.

18. Jon Wiener, *Come Together: John Lennon in His Time* (1984; reprint, London: Faber, 1995), xxiv.

19. Golson, *The Playboy Interviews,* 42–43.

20. It is possible that Goldman developed the theme of Lennon's inability to accept his homosexual desires from Lennon's 1980 BBC interview with Andy Peebles. In the interview, Lennon, when discussing his attack on Cavern disc jockey Bob Wooler for suggesting he was having an affair with Epstein, points out that, maybe, he was responding to a fear about homosexuality. If Goldman did develop the theme from this interview, he did so then in his typically undiscerning manner, taking Lennon's reflections literally and according little or no weight to the fact that Lennon had articulated these fears—thus, in one stroke, rendering implausible Goldman's thesis about the ex-Beatle's "repressed" sexuality.

21. For further discussion of Lennon's intimate relations with women, see chapter 3.

22. Goldman, *The Lives of John Lennon,* 683.

23. See Sigmund Freud, "Some Neurotic Symptoms in Jealousy, Paranoia, and Homosexuality," in SE, 13:223–25. See also J. Laplanche and J.-B. Pontalis, *The Language of Psychoanalysis* (London: Hogarth Press, 1985), 349–56.

24. Melanie Klein, "Notes on Some Schizoid Mechanisms," in *Envy and Gratitude and Other Works, 1946–1963* (London: Virago, 1988), chap. 1; see also Anthony Elliott, *Psychoanalytic Theory: An Introduction* (Oxford: Blackwell, 1994), 75–86.

25. Goldman, *The Lives of John Lennon,* 847. Goldman's section on sources suggests that roughly two hundred individuals were interviewed for the book, which leaves the thorny question of how he got twelve hundred interviews. Perhaps there were hundreds of interviews with Fred Seaman and Marnie Hair.

26. Frederic Seaman, *The Last Days of John Lennon: A Personal Memoir* (New York: Birch Lane, 1991), jacket cover.

27. Ibid.

28. Ibid., 40–41.

29. Ibid., jacket cover.

30. Elliot Mintz, "Stand By Me: The Elliot Mintz Interview," *Instant Karma,* no. 52 (December 1991): 6.

31. John Green, *Dakota Days* (London: Comet, 1983), 190.

32. Coleman's book was first published in 1985 by Sidgwick and Jackson Ltd., London, in two volumes: *John Winston Lennon: Volume 1 1940–1966* and *John Ono Lennon: Volume 2 1967–1980*. The edition I refer to throughout is the combined paperback published by Warner Books in 1992.

33. Ray Coleman, *John Lennon* (London: Warner Books, 1992), xii.

34. Ibid., 182, 185.

35. Sigmund Freud, "Leonardo da Vinci and a Memory of His Childhood," in SE, 11:130.

36. Richard Holmes, *Footsteps: Adventures of a Romantic Biographer* (New York: Viking, 1985), 2.

37. E. H. Erikson, "Gandhi's Autobiography: The Leader as a Child," *American Scholar*, 1966, p. 646.

38. Graham McCann, "Biographical Boundaries: Sociology and Marilyn Monroe," *Theory, Culture, and Society* 4 (1987): 619–32, quote on p. 623.

39. Friedrich Nietzsche, *Untimely Mediations*, trans. R. J. Hollingdale (Cambridge: Cambridge University Press, 1983), 97.

40. Roland Barthes, "The Death of the Author," in *Image-Music-Text* (Glasgow: Fontana, 1977); Michel Foucault, "What Is an Author?" in *Language, Counter-Memory, Practice: Selected Essays and Interviews by Michel Foucault,* ed. D. Bouchard (Ithaca: Cornell University Press, 1977), 113–38.

41. Problematizing the notion of self-constitution within the realms of language and intertextuality, poststructuralist critics locate the self within disordered, fragmented, shifting subjectivities as opposed to within the bureaucratized, linear world of the modernist subject-self. A life story is always complicated—indeed, overdetermined—by multiple plots. The notion that biography can ever uncover the "presence" of self or penetrate to the "essence" of identity is itself deconstructed as a cultural fiction. Poststructuralist critics read biographies, by contrast, in terms of their exclusion of difference, denial of otherness, and repression of contingency.

42. Pete Shotton and Nicholas Schaffner, *John Lennon in My Life* (New York: Stein and Day, 1983), 34.

43. Wenner, *Lennon Remembers,* 16.

44. Harrison and McCartney's comments about Lennon's spastic imitations are from *The Beatles Anthology,* no. 4, Apple Corps, 1996, videocassette.

Chapter 2: Mother

Epigraphs: Miles, comp., *John Lennon in His Own Words* (London: Omnibus Press, 1980), 9; Nathalie Sarraute, *Childhood* (London: John Calder, 1983), 221.

1. *John Lennon/Plastic Ono Band* was not the first album Lennon released without the Beatles. He had already released three experimental

albums with Yoko Ono: *Unfinished Music No. 1: Two Virgins* (1968), *Unfinished Music No. 2: Life with the Lions* (1969, the title was a pun on the British TV series *Life with the Lyons*), and *The Wedding Album* (1969). Lennon had also released *The Plastic Ono Band—Live Peace in Toronto 1969*, and he had released two singles before the breakup of The Beatles: "Cold Turkey" and "Give Peace a Chance." *Plastic Ono Band* was, however, the last of the early post-Beatles solo albums to be released. It followed the release of Paul McCartney's *McCartney*, Ringo Starr's *Sentimental Journey*, and George Harrison's *All Things Must Pass*.

2. The bleak personal and social dimensions of *John Lennon/Plastic Ono Band* are powerfully underscored by the sparse musical arrangements of guitar or piano (Lennon), bass (Klaus Voorman), and drums (Ringo Starr).

3. Jann Wenner, ed., *Lennon Remembers: The Rolling Stone Interviews by Jann Wenner* (1971; reprint, London: Penguin Books, 1980), 30.

4. Ibid., 38, 87.

5. Ibid., 158.

6. Ibid., 26.

7. Lennon's exploration of primal therapy is rarely treated in the literature; and, where it is covered, Lennon is usually cast as a victim of therapy. See, for example, Peter Brown and Steven Gaines, *The Love You Make: An Insider's Story of the Beatles* (New York: McGraw-Hill, 1983), 367–71. An exception is Jon Wiener, *Come Together: John Lennon in His Time* (1984; reprint, London: Faber, 1995), 136–38. Lennon's own comments indicate that he remained ambivalent about the benefits of therapy. Indeed he remained skeptical of the overintellectualizing of therapy's role in his work: "They use these expressions like 'primal' for anything that's a scream. . . . Yoko was screaming before Janov was ever heard of. . . . Was Little Richard primaling before each sax solo? That's what I want to know" (Peter Hamill, "Long Night's Journey into Day," in *The Ballad of John and Yoko*, ed. Jonathan Cott and Christine Doudna [Garden City, N.Y.: Rolling Stone, 1982], 148).

8. G. Barry Golson, ed., *The Playboy Interviews with John Lennon and Yoko Ono*, conducted by David Sheff (New York: Playboy Press, 1981), 108.

9. Wenner, *Lennon Remembers*, 140; Ray Coleman, *John Lennon* (London: Warner Books, 1992), 363; Stephen Holden, "Gimme Some Truth: The Songs of John Lennon," in *The Ballad of John and Yoko*, ed. Jonathan Cott and Christine Doudna (Garden City, N.Y.: Rolling Stone, 1982), 280.

10. Mary Smith, John's aunt, recalled the night of Lennon's birth in these terms (quoted in Coleman, *John Lennon*, 24):

I was literally terrified. Transport had stopped because the bombs began always at dusk. There was shrapnel falling and gunfire when there was a little lull I ran into the hospital ward and there was this beautiful little baby. . . . Just as I lifted him up, the warning sirens went off again and visitors were told we could either go down into the cellars or go home but we couldn't stay. John, like the other babies, was put underneath the bed for safety.

11. Golson, *The Playboy Interviews*, 136.

12. Pete Shotton and Nicholas Schaffner, *John Lennon in My Life* (New York: Stein and Day, 1983), 23.

13. Coleman, *John Lennon*, 21. I have followed Coleman's account of the Blackpool episode here, which was drawn from interviews with Mary Smith. Albert Goldman paints a similar picture of the events at Blackpool. As he quotes Freddie Lennon: "Julia went out the door and was about to go up the street when John ran after her. That was the last I saw or heard of him till I was told he'd become a Beatle" (Albert Goldman, *The Lives of John Lennon* [New York: Bantam Books, 1988], 32).

14. In referring to the "family romance" of Blackpool, I wish to underscore that memories of this episode can be understood as a condensation of significant emotional conflicts that troubled the Lennon family. I interpret the transfer of such conflicts onto Blackpool as a shorthand way of reaching some conscious awareness of them. There are resonances here, in analytical terms, with Freud's concept of "screen-memory": memory screens desire, says Freud, because desire is prohibited. As such, screen-memories are disguised images of unconscious desires. So too, the events at "Blackpool" (as Mary Smith and others members of the Lennon extended family have recounted them) denote a means of thinking such emotional dislocation.

15. Golson, *The Playboy Interviews*, 137.

16. Sigmund Freud, *Inhibitions, Symptoms, and Anxiety*, in SE, 20:170. The infant, it seems, relies on the mother in a profoundly imaginary way: through the medium of fantasy, constructions of self and other, sameness and difference become possible. The forging of some preliminary sense of identity, Freud argues, arises through an imagined incorporation of the mother into the self. In effect, Freud argues that what is on the outside (the body of the mother) can be taken inside (psychic space), internalized and devoured. Our primary experiences with the mother become part of the emotional structure of subjectivity.

17. Sigmund Freud, "Mourning and Melancholia," in SE, 14:251. For a discussion of the centrality of mourning to psychoanalysis see Madelon Sprengnether, "Mourning Freud," in *Psychoanalysis in Contexts: Paths between Theory and Modern Culture*, ed. Anthony Elliott and Stephen Frosh (London: Routledge, 1995), 142–65. See also Peter Homans, *The Ability to Mourn: Disillusionment and the Social Origins of Psychoanalysis* (Chicago: University of Chicago Press, 1989).

18. Sigmund Freud, "Mourning and Melancholia," in SE, 14:253.

19. The shift from mourning to melancholia involves acute narcissistic depression. Projective identification and incorporation, as Melanie Klein has shown, give the fantasized dimensions of this idealization and valorization of

self/other merging. Klein describes the object relation as structured by a paranoid, schizoid position. This schizoid splitting underpins the integration of the subject (the division between the "good" and "bad" mother), but it is also linked to a logics of fragmentation in which the subject imagines itself disintegrating. See Klein, "A Contribution to the Psychogenesis of Manic-Depressive States" and "Mourning and Its Relation to Manic-Depressive States." Both essays appear in Melanie Klein, *Love, Guilt, and Reparation and Other Works, 1921–1945* (London: Virago, 1988), 262–89 ("Psychogenesis") and 344–69 ("Mourning").

20. In the psychoanalytic frame of reference, loss lies at the foundation of personal and social life. The Freudian Oedipus complex, as French psychoanalyst Jacques Lacan has emphasized, accounts for the dissolution of the child's narcissistic omnipotence and for his or her insertion into the law-governed world of language and symbols. After Oedipus, the individual lives out a symbolic relationship to loss in and through an object world of introjects and identifications. But the negotiation of loss depends on the ability to mourn, an ability which is profoundly disrupted and disturbed with the advent of melancholia. See Jacques Lacan, "The Agency of the Letter in the Unconscious of Reason since Freud," in *Ecrits* (London: Tavistock, 1977), chap. 5. For a critical appraisal of Lacan's return to Freud, see Anthony Elliott, *Social Theory and Psychoanalysis in Transition: Self and Society from Freud to Kristeva* (Oxford: Blackwell, 1992), chap. 4.

21. Julia Kristeva, *Black Sun: Depression and Melancholia* (New York: Columbia University Press, 1989), 6.

22. David Aberbach, *Surviving Trauma: Loss, Literature, and Psychoanalysis* (New Haven: Yale University Press, 1990).

23. Adam Phillips, *On Flirtation* (London: Faber and Faber, 1994), 85.

24. *John and Yoko: The Interview,* interview by Andy Peebles, recorded 6 December 1980, BBC CD 6002. Lennon also remarked that he had used the sound of bells in "Starting Over" on *Double Fantasy*. The sound of these bells was much lighter, however, and thus suggested the "long trip from 'Mother' to 'Starting Over.'"

25. Kristeva, *Black Sun,* 53.

26. See his comments in Wenner, *Lennon Remembers,* 29. Ray Coleman argues that if Lennon's "Help!" was autobiographical, so too was McCartney's "Yesterday"; in these songs both Lennon and McCartney "were exploring their inner selves" (Ray Coleman, *McCartney: Yesterday and Today* [London: Boxtree, 1995], 50–51).

27. Julia Kristeva, *Powers of Horror* (New York: Columbia University Press, 1982).

28. Note Kristeva: "Aside from the images of the death drive, necessarily displaced on account of being eroticized, the work of death as such, as the zero degree of psychicism, can be spotted precisely in the *dissociation of form* itself, when form is distorted, abstracted, disfigured, hallowed out: ulti-

mate thresholds of inscribable dislocation and jouissance" (Kristeva, *Black Sun,* 27).

29. Interestingly, Lennon referred to Yoko Ono throughout their relationship as "Mother" and "Mother Superior."

30. John Lennon, *Live in New York City,* Capitol CDP 7 46196 2.

31. Kristeva, *Black Sun,* 22.

32. Wenner, *Lennon Remembers,* 29.

33. Brown and Gaines, *The Love You Make,* 165.

34. For a detailed account of the 1966 world tour see ibid., 200–218.

35. Wenner, *Lennon Remembers,* 125–26.

36. John Lennon, *In His Own Write* (published by Jonathan Cape, 1964), back cover ("About the Awful"); *The Penguin John Lennon* (London: Penguin, 1980), 90 ("Father Cradock") and 108 ("the General Erection").

37. "In the two books I wrote," Lennon remarked in a interview in 1971, "even though they were written in a sort of Joycean gobbledygook, there's many knocks at religion and there is a play about a worker and a capitalist" (Geoffrey and Brenda Giuliano, eds., *The Lost Lennon Interviews* [London: Omnibus Press, 1996], 1996, 139). For an information-rich but somewhat pedestrian analysis of Lennon's first two books, see James Sauceda, *The Literary Lennon: A Comedy of Errors* (New York: Pierian Press, 1983); the quotations in the text paragraph appear on pp. 3, 4, 80, 80, and ix.

38. Tom Wolfe, "A Highbrow under All That Hair?" *Book Week,* 3 May 1964, reprinted in *The Lennon Companion: Twenty-five Years of Comment,* ed. Elizabeth Thomson and David Gutman (New York: Schirmer Books, 1987), 47.

39. Herbert Marcuse, *One-Dimensional Man* (Boston: Beacon, 1966).

40. Golson, *The Playboy Interviews,* 131–32.

41. Lennon commented in several interviews about the anxiety he felt after The Beatles retired from touring. Much of this anxiety, it seems, concerned the difficulty of reorienting his personal life to fit with his newly acquired, more leisured public life. But, again, it is interesting to note that The Beatles served as a protection from such anxiety; or, at least, moments of intense anxiety were provoked during changes associated with the band. As Lennon recalls his thoughts at the time of manager Brian Epstein's death in 1967: "I knew that we were in trouble then. I didn't really have any misconceptions about our ability to do anything other than play music and I was scared. I thought, 'we've fuckin' had it'" (Wenner, *Lennon Remembers,* 52).

42. Allan Kozinn, *The Beatles* (London: Phaidon Press, 1995), 148.

43. Until the end of his life, Lennon remained unhappy about the released version of "Strawberry Fields Forever," as he did about many other Beatles songs. In *The Playboy Interviews,* he states that the song was "badly recorded," and he pins some of the blame for this on McCartney (Golson, *The Playboy Interviews,* 162). Lennon's dissatisfaction with the recording fits with my general argument about the sorrow and loss which the song

identifies, the very dynamics of which generate a sense of incompletion. Three versions of the song were released on *The Beatles Anthology 2,* Apple Records 7243 8 34448 2 3.

44. Ian MacDonald, *Revolution in the Head* (London: Pimlico, 1994), 172; Mark Hertsgaard, *A Day in the Life: The Music and Artistry of the Beatles* (London: Macmillan, 1995), 205.

45. Zygmunt Bauman, *Life in Fragments* (Oxford: Blackwell, 1995), 82.

46. Golson, *The Playboy Interviews,* 133.

47. Shotton and Schaffner, *John Lennon in My Life,* 124.

48. See Hertsgaard, *A Day in the Life,* 231.

Chapter 3: Love

Epigraphs: John Lennon, "Love," BMG Music Publ. Ltd. CDP 7952212; Julia Kristeva, *Tales of Love* (New York: Columbia University Press, 1987), 5.

1. Jann Wenner, ed., *Lennon Remembers: The Rolling Stone Interviews by Jann Wenner* (1971; reprint, London: Penguin Books, 1980), 92–94.

2. Miles, comp., *John Lennon in His Own Words* (London: Omnibus Press, 1980), 126.

3. G. Barry Golson, ed., *The Playboy Interviews with John Lennon and Yoko Ono,* conducted by David Sheff (New York: Playboy Press, 1981), 11.

4. Ibid., 85.

5. Ibid.

6. Ibid., 87–88.

7. Ray Coleman, *John Lennon* (London: Warner Books, 1992), 263–64.

8. Albert Goldman, *The Lives of John Lennon* (London: Bantam, 1988), 285.

9. Quoted in Robert Christgau, "Double Fantasy: Portrait of a Relationship," in *The Ballad of John and Yoko,* ed. Jonathan Cott and Christine Doudna (Garden City, N.Y.: Rolling Stone, 1982), 291.

10. Herbert Marcuse, *Eros and Civilization* (London: Ark, 1956), 143.

11. Given the minimalist and utopic thematics of her work, Ono was in many ways well placed to reflect on the concept of violence in art at the symposium—something perhaps lost on critics of her work. My discussion of Ono in the section that follows is drawn largely from Jerry Hopkins, *Yoko Ono: A Biography* (London: Sidgwick and Jackson, 1987); and Peter Brown and Steven Gaines, *The Love You Make: An Insider's Story of the Beatles* (New York: McGraw-Hill, 1983).

12. Quoted in Hopkins, *Yoko Ono,* 60–61.

13. The British Board of Film Censors refused to give *Bottoms,* officially titled *Film No. 4,* a certificate for distribution. When the film finally premiered in the West End, the press hated it. See ibid., 64–65.

14. See ibid., 22.

15. John Lennon, *Skywriting by Word of Mouth* (New York: Harper-Perennial, 1986), 14.

16. Ibid., 13, 14.

17. Quoted in George Martin, *The Summer of Love* (London: Pan Macmillan, 1994), 73.

18. John Lennon/Yoko Ono, *Unfinished Music No. 1: Two Virgins*, RCD 10411, back cover.

19. Pete Shotton confirms that Lennon intensely disliked his middle name from an early age. Shotton's discovery of Lennon's middle name, during a class at school, actually cemented their relationship: he promised Lennon, after physical threats had failed or backfired, that he would not reveal the name to other students. See Pete Shotton and Nicholas Schaffner, *John Lennon in My Life* (New York: Stein and Day, 1983), 20–21.

20. *John and Yoko: The Interview*, interview by Andy Peebles, recorded 6 December 1980, BBC CD 6002.

21. According to Jon Wiener, what makes the song significant is that "it is sung by a man and sung to men" (Wiener, *Come Together: John Lennon in His Time* [1984; reprint, London: Faber, 1995], 215). Lennon, in his 1980 BBC interview, insists that "Woman Is the Nigger of the World" was the first women's liberation song, pointing out that it was released before Helen Reddy's "I Am Woman" (*John and Yoko: The Interview*).

22. See Golson, *The Playboy Interviews*, 36.

23. Cynthia Lennon, *A Twist of Lennon* (London: Star Books, 1978), 87.

24. Lennon's love of watching television with the sound down or off has been recorded in many biographies; see, for example, Shotton and Schaffner, *John Lennon in My Life*, 101 ff.

25. See, for example, Brown and Gaines, *The Love You Make,* chap. 1.

26. Christgau, "Double Fantasy," 292.

27. Coleman, *John Lennon*, 264–66.

28. Ibid., 265.

29. For accounts of Ono's miscarriage, see Hopkins, *Yoko Ono*, 84, 92; and Coleman, *John Lennon*, 292.

30. Brown and Gaines, *The Love You Make*, 320.

31. Miles, *John Lennon in His Own Words*, 68.

32. Quoted in Wiener, *Come Together*, 184–85.

33. Quoted in Paul Du Noyer, *We All Shine On: The Stories behind Every John Lennon Song, 1970–1980* (London: HarperCollins, 1997), 42.

34. Goldman, rather unsurprisingly, makes this claim. For further discussion on this point, see Paul Du Noyer, *We All Shine On*, 42.

35. Wiener, *Come Together*, 184.

36. See Nancy Chodorow, *The Reproduction of Mothering* (Berkeley: University of California Press, 1978). The proposition that masculinist self-identity is, in part, framed upon a negation of love and intimacy is central to

my argument about Lennon's emotional development. It also underlies my
claim that Lennon's relationship with Ono, and his period of self-discovery in
the late 1970s, can be fruitfully narrated as a recovery from loss. Let me
briefly expand on this theoretical backdrop.

In feminist versions of psychoanalysis, the masculinist repudiation of femininity has been theorized along two conceptual axes: the object-relational
school and Lacanian and post-Lacanian perspectives. In the first approach,
developed most notably in the writings of Nancy Chodorow and Jessica Benjamin, the framing of the male sense of self is bound up with a primal loss,
psychic disengagement from the mother. The Oedipal transition provides for
the boy's separation from the mother, but only at the cost of his taking up an
instrumental attitude toward the social world, the masculinist world of unequal sexual relations. Such an abstract, instrumental relation to the self and
others filters out emotional contact with mother love; it is a screening of the
sphere of the feminine, as the expression of care and intimacy.

Lacanian and post-Lacanian feminists, such as Luce Irigaray and Julia
Kristeva, also theorize a defensive repudiation of femininity, but more in
terms of the difficulty of speaking from a feminine position in a phallocentric
symbolic order. For, in Lacanian terms, it is only in relation to the paternal
metaphor, or Name of the Father, that the self acquires language; speaking
always occurs with reference to something outside itself, to Oedipal law. As
refracted through poststructuralist thought, this critique of Freud highlights
the fact that sexuality and sexual identity always operate linguistically, and always as binary opposites: an identification with the masculine is an identification with identity, language, the symbolic; an identification with the feminine is an identification with body, desire, sensuality. In these terms, then,
the masculine subject finds his signifying place only in relation to a femininity cast as outside and other, as some imaginary "whole" that will shore up an
always fragile and divided sense of self.

I discuss in detail the nature of this major division in psychoanalytic feminism in *Psychoanalytic Theory: An Introduction* (Oxford: Blackwell, 1994)
and in *Social Theory and Psychoanalysis in Transition: Self and Society from
Freud to Kristeva* (Oxford: Blackwell, 1992), chap. 5. For a similar, but distinct, interpretation of these theoretical differences, see Jane Flax, *Thinking
Fragments* (Berkeley: University of California Press, 1991). For object-relational accounts of psychosexual development, see Nancy Chodorow, *Feminism and Psychoanalytic Theory* (Cambridge: Polity Press, 1989); and
Jessica Benjamin, *The Bonds of Love* (New York: Pantheon, 1990). For Lacanian and post-Lacanian feminist perspectives, see Julia Kristeva, *Revolution in Poetic Language* (New York: Columbia University Press, 1984); and
Luce Irigaray, *This Sex Which Is Not One* (Ithaca: Cornell University Press,
1985).

37. Wiener, *Come Together*, 184.
38. Shotton and Schaffner, *John Lennon in My Life*, 171.

39. Golson, *The Playboy Interviews,* 26.

40. Ibid., 24.

41. Jessica Benjamin, *The Bonds of Love* (New York: Virago, 1988), 39.

42. The account of Lennon's lost weekend in this section is developed from several sources: Elliot Mintz, interview by author, Los Angeles, Calif., 19 March 1997; May Pang and Henry Edwards, *Loving John: The Untold Story* (New York: Corgi Books, 1983), esp. 107–68; and Wiener, *Come Together,* chap. 23. I draw on Pang's book with a crucial qualification. Mintz explained to me that many of the factual details in Pang's book, such as the events at Stone Canyon Road, are substantially correct. What Pang does not account for, however, is the motivation that underpinned Lennon's self-destructive behavior. Therefore, I draw on Pang only to support specific factual details. Moreover, I subject her analysis of Lennon's personality, and of his relationship with Ono, to critique later in this chapter.

43. Bob Edmands, "Have Pity for the Rich," in *The Beat Goes On: The Rock File Reader,* ed. C. Gillett and S. Frith (London: Pluto Press, 1996), 132–33.

44. Quoted in "An Oral Appreciation," in *The Ballad of John and Yoko,* ed. Jonathan Cott and Christine Doudna (Garden City, N.Y.: Rolling Stone, 1982), 223.

45. Mintz, interview.

46. Golson, *The Playboy Interviews,* 20.

47. The meaning of "lost weekend" thus doubles, unhooking itself from its social context and transcribing itself within the troubled waters of passion, emotion, desire. Indeed here is another aspect to the relation between loss and mourning: is Lennon's lost weekend the loss of another, of Ono, of a way of life, of love and its difficulty? Or is Lennon's lost weekend the fear of losing oneself, the dread of the self being annihilated beyond the boundaries of experience? Perhaps we do not need to choose. For, as we saw in chapter 2, the fear of loss is a fear that criss-crosses between the loss of other people and loss of the self.

48. Pang and Edwards, *Loving John,* 167.

49. Golson, *The Playboy Interviews,* 22–23.

50. The waitress, Brenda Mary Perkins, attempted to take a Polaroid shot of Lennon while he was being ejected from the club. On 27 March 1974, the Los Angeles district attorney dismissed Perkins's claim that Lennon had hit her at the Troubadour. See Coleman, *John Lennon,* 486.

51. See Wiener, *Come Together,* 268.

52. *John and Yoko: The Interview.*

53. For a detailed analysis of Lennon's songwriting during this period, see John Robertson, *The Art and Music of John Lennon* (New York: Omnibus, 1990), chap. 13. Robertson rightly points out that "1974 saw [Lennon] complete two albums, 'Rock 'n' Roll' and 'Walls And Bridges'; produce an album for Harry Nilsson; and collaborate on hit singles for Ringo Starr and Elton

John. Compare that output with 1973 ('Mind Games' and 'I'm The Greatest') or 1975 ('Fame' and 'Across The Universe' with David Bowie) and the weekend doesn't seem so lost after all" (164). In addition, however, I think it is also necessary to stress that much of Lennon's artistic output during the lost weekend had a defensive quality; Lennon described his music of this period as the work of a "semi-sick craftsman" (Miles, *John Lennon in His Own Words,* 105).

54. Golson, *The Playboy Interviews,* 8.

55. Quoted in Robertson, *The Art and Music of John Lennon,* 163.

56. Masud Khan, *Alienation in Perversions* (New York: International Universities Press, 1979).

57. Pang and Edwards, *Loving John,* inside jacket.

58. Ibid., 292.

59. Ibid., 334.

Chapter 4: Revolution 9

Epigraphs: John Lennon, *The Beatle Tapes: From the David Wigg Interviews,* Polydor, UK, 847 185–4; Ulrich Beck, *The Reinvention of Politics* (Cambridge: Polity Press, 1997), 99.

1. Many biographers and commentators have focused on Lennon's political involvements in idealizing or condescending ways: he is either Lennon the great peacemaker of the twentieth century or Lennon the naive, utopian propagandist for peace. In both cases, the critical evaluation of Lennon's politics is unmindfully inserted into the culture of the 1960s. By contrast, Jon Wiener's political biography, *Come Together: John Lennon in His Time* (1984; reprint, London: Faber, 1995), is a detailed and considered assessment of Lennon's radical politics. Wiener places Lennon's politics in the changing context of political culture in the broadest sense, linking Lennon's political dispositions to the New Left throughout.

I depart from Wiener, however, in several ways. Not from his general contention of the radical urgency of Lennon's politics: Wiener makes a strong case concerning Lennon's commitment to linking pop and politics, the personal and the political. But rather than focus on allegiances, identifications, and practices as such, I aim to critically analyze the complex, ambivalent political aesthetic that marks Lennon's cultural interventions, to explore the interiority and exteriority of the political cultural realm as engendered by Lennon, and in cultural rememberings of Lennon.

2. Mark Lewisohn, *The Complete Beatles Recording Sessions* (London: Hamlyn, 1988), 135.

3. For a B-side, "Revolution" created considerable controversy. *Time* magazine devoted an article to the song, declaring that its carping political radicalism was "exhilarating." The political left responded with, among other

things, analyses in *New Left Review* and *Black Dwarf*. For a perceptive review of the left's response to "Revolution" see Wiener, *Come Together*, 58–69, 81–84.

4. "Marx Engels/Mick Jagger," *Black Dwarf*, 27 October 1968, 1.

5. John Lennon, "A Very Open Letter to John Hoyland from John Lennon," *Black Dwarf*, 10 January 1969, n.p.

6. See Jon Wiener, "Beatles Buy-Out: How Nike Bought the Beatles' 'Revolution,'" in *Professors, Politics, and Pop* (New York: Verso, 1991), chap. 34.

7. See, for example, Jürgen Habermas, *Between Facts and Norms: Contributions to a Discourse Theory of Law and Democracy* (Cambridge: Polity Press, 1996); David Held, *Democracy and the Global Order* (Cambridge: Polity Press, 1995); and Axel Honneth, *The Struggle for Recognition* (Cambridge: Polity Press, 1996).

8. "I spent more time on 'Revolution 9,'" said Lennon, "than I did on half the other songs I ever wrote" (G. Barry Golson, ed., *The Playboy Interviews with John Lennon and Yoko Ono*, conducted by David Sheff [New York: Playboy Press, 1981], 159).

9. Mark Lewisohn, *The Complete Beatles Chronicle* (New York: Harmony Books, 1992).

10. See Robert Palmer, "The Other Half of the Sky: The Songs of Yoko Ono," in *The Ballad of John and Yoko*, ed. Jonathan Cott and Christine Doudna (Garden City, N.Y.: Rolling Stone, 1982), 285–90. Cf. Jerry Hopkins, *Yoko Ono: A Biography* (London: Sidgwick and Jackson, 1987), chaps. 4–6. Jon Wiener notes that Lennon and Ono visited John Cage upon moving to New York in 1971 (Wiener, *Come Together*, 175).

11. "Revolution 9," argues MacDonald, aims for no less than a "revolution in the head." MacDonald derived the title for his book from his discussion of "Revolution 9" (*Revolution in the Head* [London: Pimlico, 1994], 231).

12. Many of Lennon's avant-garde recordings and mixings remain unreleased. Some were aired on the radio series *The Lost Lennon Tapes*: "Down in Cuba" and "Chi-Chi's Cafe" are fine examples of his work in this respect.

13. Peter Hamill, "Long Night's Journey into Day," in *The Ballad of John and Yoko*, ed. Jonathan Cott and Christine Doudna (Garden City, N.Y.: Rolling Stone, 1982), 153.

14. Philip Norman, *Shout!: The Beatles in Their Generation* (New York: MJF Books, 1981), 265.

15. At the time, Tariq Ali was a leading force in the British New Left and a member of the Vietnam Solidarity Committee; Robin Blackburn was a student radical at the London School of Economics. For an excellent account of Lennon's involvement with *Red Mole*, see Wiener, *Come Together*, chap. 14.

16. Quoted in "Power to the People: John Lennon and Yoko Ono Talk to Robin Blackburn and Tariq Ali," reprinted in *The Lennon Companion:*

Twenty-five Years of Comment, ed. Elizabeth Thomson and David Gutman (New York: Schirmer Books, 1987), 165.

17. Ibid., 173.

18. Wiener, *Come Together,* 156.

19. Lennon met with Rubin and Hoffman on many occasions, but it was with Rubin that he developed a friendship. For discussions of the lives of Hoffman and Rubin, the New Left, and the political climate in the United States at this time, see David Farber, *Chicago '68* (Chicago: University of Chicago Press, 1988); and Marty Jezer, *Abbie Hoffman: American Rebel* (New Brunswick: Rutgers University Press, 1992).

20. At the time of his *Playboy* interview in 1980, Lennon gave a different version of the proposed tour. He began by noting his own naiveté in going along with Hoffman and Rubin. Later, he suggested that he and Ono had never intended to head the concert in San Diego. "The infamous San Diego meeting," says Lennon,

that got us into all the immigration problems was really a nonexistent situation. There was this so-called meeting with Jerry, Abbie, Allen Ginsberg, John Sinclair, John and Yoko, where they were trying to get us to go to the San Diego Republican Convention. When they described their plans, we just kept looking at each other. It was the poets and the straight politicals divided. Ginsberg was with us. He kept saying, "What are we trying to do, create another Chicago?" That's what they wanted. We said, "We ain't buying this. We're not going to draw children into a situation to create violence—so you can overthrow *what?*—and replace it with *what?*"

See Golson, ed., *The Playboy Interviews with John Lennon and Yoko Ono,* 97.

21. The committee's memo was first covered in the press by Chet Flippo, "Lennon's Lawsuit: Memo from Thurmond," *Rolling Stone,* 31 July 1975, 16.

22. See John Lennon, "It's Never Too Late to Start from the Start," *SunDance,* April–May 1972, 67–69; and John Lennon and Yoko Ono, "Imagine," *SunDance,* August–September 1972, 68.

23. Quoted in Paul Du Noyer, *We All Shine On: The Stories behind Every John Lennon Song, 1970–1980* (London: HarperCollins, 1997), 57.

24. Lennon's introduction appears on *The Lost Lennon Tapes,* vol. 5, Multi Coloured Music, Italy.

25. Quoted in Stuart Werbin, "Some Time in New York City: John & Jerry & David & John & Leni & Yoko," in *The Ballad of John and Yoko,* ed. Jonathan Cott and Christine Doudna (Garden City, N.Y.: Rolling Stone, 1982), 130–31.

26. For further discussion see Dorothee Hansen, "Bagism: A Series of Performances in Which John Lennon and Yoko Ono Wrapped Themselves in a Bag, 1968–1971," in *John Lennon: Drawings, Performances, Film,* ed. Wulf Herzogenrath and Dorothee Hansen (London: Thames and Hudson, 1995), 176–79.

27. Ray Coleman, *John Lennon* (London: Warner Books, 1992), 331.

28. The doubling of which I write is one of psychic intensities and cultural locations. Drawn from Freud's explorations of the fantasization of the self/other divide, I view the doubling of Lennon's political aesthetic as an attempt to recover prior selves, identities, histories, memories. From this angle, Lennon's explorations with Ono of avant-garde music are a form of re-elaboration of that earlier interest in artistic matters which he developed in his youth and in art college in Liverpool.

In terms of understanding the ways in which doubling affects cultural re-memberings of Lennon's identity, I am influenced by Homi K. Bhabha, who writes about "the ambivalence of language itself in the construction of the Janus-faced discourse of the nation." Bhabha sees the nation as a symbolic doubling of authorized and excluded identities: "the ambivalent figure of the nation is a problem of its transitional history, its conceptual indeterminacy, its wavering between vocabularies" (Bhabha, *Nation and Narration* [London: Routledge, 1990], introduction). But if this is true of the nation, it is also true of politics itself, and especially of the fashioning of political identities. The task of this chapter then is to understand doubling in terms of the interplay of interiority and exteriority.

29. Hayden White, *The Content of the Form* (Baltimore: Johns Hopkins University Press, 1987).

30. Mike Kaplan, ed., *Variety: International Showbusiness Reference* (New York: Garland Publishing, 1981), 629–30.

31. Andrew Sarris, "A Hard Day's Night," *Village Voice*, 27 August 1964, reprinted in *The Lennon Companion: Twenty-five Years of Comment*, ed. Elizabeth Thomson and David Gutman (New York: Schirmer Books, 1987), 50.

32. Jonas Mekas quoted in J. Hoberman, "The Films of John and Yoko," in *The Ballad of John and Yoko*, ed. Jonathan Cott and Christine Doudna (Garden City, N.Y.: Rolling Stone, 1982), 267. Lennon took such criticism to heart; in subsequent films he sought to link minimalism to a faster time frame. For instance, the film *Erection* showed the eighteen-month construction of the London International Hotel in North Kensington in the fantastically speeded-up time of eighteen minutes.

33. Christian Metz, *Psychoanalysis and Cinema* (London: Macmillan, 1982), 49. Metz also writes: "And it is true that as he identifies with himself as look, the spectator can do no other than identify with the camera too, which has looked before him at what he is now looking at and whose stationing (= framing) determines the vanishing point" (49). How true this is of Lennon and Ono's *Rape*, notwithstanding whatever criticisms might be made of Metz's theoretical position.

34. See Erving Goffman, *The Presentation of Self in Everyday Life* (Harmondsworth: Penguin, 1969).

35. Luce Irigaray, *Ethique de la différance sexuelle* (Paris: Minuit, 1984), 72.

36. Ono cited in Hoberman, "The Films of John and Yoko," 269.

37. For further discussion see Wiener, *Come Together*, chap. 6. Interestingly, Wiener notes that the *New York Times Magazine* ran a story on revolutionary political action which focused on both Marcuse and Lennon (68–69).

38. Michel Foucault, "Technologies of the Self," in *Technologies of the Self*, ed. L. H. Martin, H. Gutman, and P. H. Hutton (London: Tavistock, 1988), 40.

39. See Wiener, *Come Together*, 88.

40. Lennon quoted in Dorothee Hansen, "Bed-In for Peace: Performance at the Amsterdam Hilton, 1969," in *John Lennon: Drawings, Performances, Film*, ed. Wulf Herzogenrath and Dorothee Hansen (London: Thames and Hudson, 1995), 168.

41. Ibid.

42. John Lennon, *The Beatle Tapes: From the David Wigg Interviews*, Polydor, UK, 847 185–4.

43. Wulf Herzogenrath, "John Lennon, Artist: Or, Why Was It Impossible for So Long to Acknowledge Him as an Artist?—and Why Do We Still Find It Difficult Today?" in *John Lennon: Drawings, Performances, Film*, ed. Wulf Herzogenrath and Dorothee Hansen (London: Thames and Hudson, 1995), 12.

44. Quoted in Wiener, *Come Together*, 90. For a discussion of political reactions to the bed-in performances see ibid., chap. 8.

45. Reprinted on the *Mind Games* record sleeve.

46. Terry Eagleton, *Ideology: An Introduction* (London: Verso, 1991), 131.

Chapter 5: A Day in the Life

Epigraphs: Miles, comp., *John Lennon in His Own Words* (London: Omnibus Press, 1980), 126; Sigmund Freud, "Thoughts for the Times of War and Death," in *The Penguin Freud Library* (Harmondsworth: Penguin, 1991), 12:77.

1. G. Barry Golson, ed., *The Playboy Interviews with John Lennon and Yoko Ono*, conducted by David Sheff (New York: Playboy Press, 1981), 162.

2. Ibid., 14. The reference to abandonment here is telling, and it might indeed be taken as a metaphor for the dreaded nightmares of Lennon's own childhood as well as his adult fears of fame. The "space to breathe" he so desired was one well removed from the media's prying cameras.

3. Ibid., 4.

4. Ibid., 5.

5. Quoted by Chet Flippo, "The Private Years," in *The Ballad of John and Yoko*, ed. Jonathan Cott and Christine Doudna (Garden City, N.Y.: Rolling Stone, 1982), 167.

6. John Lennon, interview by Dave Sholin, Laurie Kaye, Ron Hummel, and Bert Keane, RKO Radio Network, New York, New York, 8 December 1980.

7. Elliot Mintz, interview by author, Los Angeles, Calif., 19 March 1997. Ray Coleman had concluded, from his interview with Mintz some years earlier, that Lennon experienced only devotion in relation to his family, but in an interview with me Mintz indicated that Lennon experienced freedom as well as devotion.

8. Golson, *The Playboy Interviews,* 33.

9. My analysis of Lennon's composing and demo tapes during his period of seclusion is informed by two sources. First, the radio series *The Lost Lennon Tapes,* as well as the Vigotone collection *John Lennon.* Second, I draw extensively from John Robertson's careful documentation in *The Art and Music of John Lennon* (New York: Omnibus Press, 1990), esp. chaps. 14 and 15.

10. Golson, *The Playboy Interviews,* 5.

11. Robertson, *The Art and Music of John Lennon,* 178–79.

12. After a violent argument with his girlfriend (which led to the police being called), Evans had barricaded himself in his bedroom. Smashing the door down, the police were confronted by Evans holding a gun; they opened fire.

13. The Lennon quotes in the text paragraph come from *John and Yoko: The Interview,* interview by Andy Peebles, recorded 6 December 1980, BBC CD 6002. Elliot Mintz is quoted in Jon Wiener, *Come Together: John Lennon in His Time* (1984; reprint, London: Faber, 1995), 287.

14. Flippo, "The Private Years," 158.

15. John B. Thompson, *The Media and Modernity: A Social Theory of the Media* (Cambridge: Polity Press, 1995), 220–25. I have drawn extensively from Thompson's account of fandom here.

16. It may be helpful at this point to add some biographical dates. Chapman was born on 10 May 1955 in Fort Worth, Texas, but was raised in Atlanta, Georgia. After graduating from high school, Chapman worked for the YMCA for some years. In 1977, he moved to Hawaii (where his mother had moved after divorcing his father). He was twenty-five at the time he assassinated Lennon. The account of Chapman I sketch in the following paragraphs is drawn from a number of sources, the most important being Jon Wiener, "Epilogue: The Struggle of Mark David Chapman," in *Come Together,* 307–11; and Peter Brown and Steven Gaines, *The Love You Make: An Insider's Story of the Beatles* (New York: McGraw-Hill, 1983), 432–38.

17. *The People of the State of New York v. Mark David Chapman.* Eight psychologists and psychiatrists assessed Chapman's state of mind. For the prosecution, Dr. A. Louis McGarry, Dr. Emanuel F. Hammer, and Dr. Martin L. Lubin contended that Chapman suffered from a narcissistic personality

disorder. For the defense, Dr. Daniel Schwartz, Dr. Bernard Diamond, Dr. Richard Bloom, Dr. Joseph Gabriel, and Dr. Dorothy Lewis contended that Chapman's personality disorder was chronic and diagnosed him as a paranoid schizophrenic. Dr. Schwartz also argued that, by killing Lennon, Chapman had psychically circumvented his own suicidal fantasies: "I think that [Chapman's] obsession with his preoccupation of killing Mr. Lennon was serving now as a defense against his own unconscious suicidal wishes. . . . I think that what finally happened was this: killing Mr. Lennon was, in his kind of schizophrenic reasoning, a compromise, a way of handling these suicidal wishes, but in a sense, staying alive himself. He killed the person who, to him, now represented evil and hypocrisy."

18. Thompson, *The Media and Modernity*, 224.

19. Lennon, interview, RKO Radio Network.

20. See "Sharing the Grief," in *The Ballad of John and Yoko*, ed. Jonathan Cott and Christine Doudna (Garden City, N.Y.: Rolling Stone, 1982), 206.

21. Quoted in "An Oral Appreciation," in *The Ballad of John and Yoko*, ed. Jonathan Cott and Christine Doudna (Garden City, N.Y.: Rolling Stone, 1982), 214 (Charles), 228 (Sinatra, Berry, Mailer).

22. Quoted in Ross Benson, *Paul McCartney: Behind the Myth* (London: Victor Gollancz, 1992), 253.

23. Quoted by Ray Coleman, *John Lennon* (London: Warner Books, 1992), 456.

24. Zygmunt Bauman, *Postmodernity and Its Discontents* (Cambridge: Polity Press, 1997), 153.

25. Philippe Ariés, *Western Attitudes towards Death* (Baltimore: Johns Hopkins University Press, 1974). See also Norbert Elias, *The Loneliness of the Dying* (Oxford: Blackwell, 1985). Anthony Giddens speaks of "the sequestration of sickness and death" in the late modern age, linking repression of awareness to the institutional dynamics of contemporary societies (see his *Modernity and Self-Identity* [Cambridge: Polity Press, 1991], 161–62). The best recent discussion of death and its repression in contemporary culture is that of Zygmunt Bauman, to which my discussion here is greatly indebted; see Bauman, *Mortality, Immortality, and Other Life Strategies* (Cambridge: Polity Press, 1992), esp. chap. 4; and Bauman, *Postmodernity and Its Discontents*.

26. Michel Vovelle, *La Mort et l'Occident: De 1300 a nos jours* (Paris: Gallimard, 1983), 382.

27. Geoffrey Gorer, *Death, Grief, and Mourning in Contemporary Britain* (London: Cresset Press, 1965), 171.

28. "Civilization is built upon a renunciation of drives," writes Freud (see *Civilization and Its Discontents*, in SE, 21:64–145).

29. Fenton Bresler, *Who Killed John Lennon?* (New York: St. Martin's Press, 1989), 6.

30. Ibid., 17.

31. Ibid., epilogue.

32. Quoted in ibid., 244–45.

33. Fred Fogo, *I Read the News Today: The Social Drama of John Lennon's Death* (Maryland: Rowman and Littlefield, 1994). Fogo analyzes reactions to Lennon's death in the sociological frame of Victor Turner's social-drama perspective. This perspective advances the view that personal and cultural meanings are readjusted as a consequence of social drama, and thus grants some recognition to the role of feelings in social relations. This recognition is limited, however, to the sociocultural reconstruction of a "breach" in the social order. No significant weight is accorded to the emotional complexity of social formations, such as the role of fantasy and the unconscious. Cf. Anthony Elliott, *Psychoanalytic Theory: An Introduction* (Oxford: Blackwell, 1994), chap. 2.

34. Fogo, *I Read the News Today*, 84.

35. Ibid., 92.

36. Gorer writes of this "pornography of death" in *Death, Grief, and Mourning in Contemporary Britain:* "While natural death becomes more and more smudged in prudery, violent death has played an ever-growing part in the fantasies offered to mass audiences" (173).

37. Golson, *The Playboy Interviews,* jacket cover.

38. Scott Spencer, "Hearing the News," in *The Ballad of John and Yoko,* ed. Jonathan Cott and Christine Doudna (Garden City, N.Y.: Rolling Stone, 1982), 209–10.

39. Coleman, *John Lennon*, 458.

Chapter 6: Free as a Bird

Epigraphs: John Lennon, "Free as a Bird," Lenono Music Inc. 7243 8 82587 2 2; Martin Amis, "Lennon—From Beatle to Househusband," in *The Lennon Companion: Twenty-five Years of Comment*, ed. Elizabeth Thomson and David Gutman (New York: Schirmer Books, 1987), 222–23.

1. Peter Hamill, "Long Night's Journey into Day," in *The Ballad of John and Yoko,* ed. Jonathan Cott and Christine Doudna, (Garden City, N.Y.: Rolling Stone, 1982), 144, 145.

2. According to May Pang, McCartney joined Lennon to perform an impromptu "Midnight Special" (see Pang and Henry Edwards, *Loving John* [New York: Corgi Books, 1983], 208–10). See also John Robertson, *The Art and Music of John Lennon* (New York: Omnibus, 1990), 166–67.

3. Lennon did not visit the New Orleans recording sessions for McCartney's *Venus and Mars.* For a discussion of McCartney's invitation to Lennon to visit New Orleans, see Pang and Edwards *Loving John*, 286–87.

4. John Lennon, *Skywriting by Word of Mouth* (New York: Harper-Perennial, 1986), 18–19.

5. "Hello Goodbye," *Record Collector,* November 1995, 28.

6. Jonathan Cott, "The Last *Rolling Stone* Interview," in *The Ballad of John and Yoko,* ed. Jonathan Cott and Christine Doudna (Garden City, N.Y.: Rolling Stone, 1982), 192.

7. The reference to Record Plant East, rather than West (where much of the album had been recorded with Phil Spector), was perhaps Lennon's way of finally assuming responsibility for this trauma-ridden work.

8. The other intriguing story which circulates is that John Lennon considered turning up with another Beatle for a reunion on the American television show *Saturday Night Live* in 1977. Albert Goldman writes that the other Beatle was Paul McCartney. However, Elliot Mintz told me it was George Harrison who visited Lennon on the night in question (Elliot Mintz, interview by author, Los Angeles, Calif., 19 March 1997).

9. Laurie Aloi, "The Beatles," *The Licensing Book,* December 1995, 10.

10. Paul Du Noyer, "But Now They're Really Important," *Q Magazine,* December 1995, 121.

11. Ibid., 123.

12. See Ray Coleman, *John Lennon* (London: Warner Books, 1992), 254–55.

13. Du Noyer, "But Now They're Really Important," 123.

14. D. White, "Where They Once Belonged," *TNT Magazine,* no. 640, 1995, p. 29.

15. Du Noyer, "But Now They're Really Important," 128.

16. Quoted in *Q Magazine,* January 1997, 34.

17. Mintz, interview.

18. Jean Baudrillard, *Simulations* (New York: Semiotext(e), 1983), 146.

19. Iain Chambers, *Popular Culture: The Metropolitan Experience* (London: Methuen, 1986), 190.

20. Jean Baudrillard, *Cool Memories* (London: Verso, 1990), 92.

21. Zygmunt Bauman, *Intimations of Postmodernity* (London: Routledge, 1992), 150.

22. The symptoms of postmodernist culture defined by Jameson are placed under headings such as "The Waning of Affect," "Euphoria and Self-Annihilation," "'Historicism' Effaces History," "The Breakdown of the Signifying Chain," "The Hysterical Sublime," and "The Abolition of Critical Distance": see "Postmodernism, or The Cultural Logic of Late Capitalism," *New Left Review,* no. 146 (July–August 1984): 59–92. This symptomology of postmodernism is treated in more detail in Fredric Jameson, *Postmodernism, or The Cultural Logic of Late Capitalism* (Durham: Duke University Press, 1991).

23. Indeed, Jameson argues that the postmodern, in everything from an increasingly standardized private life to the mass media controlled by multi-

national corporations, represents "a new and historically original penetration and colonization of Nature and the Unconscious" (Jameson, *Postmodernism*, 49). Cultural production is itself structured by the logics of commodification, of uniformity and equivalence, of cultural differences being crushed by the principle of identical economic value. Jameson's thesis that the cultural manifestations of postmodernism are symptomatic of deeper, structural socioeconomic processes has greatly influenced current cultural theory. What I take up in this chapter, however, is less a detailed consideration of the strengths and weaknesses of this specific argument than an examination of how such a viewpoint might apply to The Beatles reunion. In particular, I explore this argument in relation to matters of economic production and cultural reception.

24. Bryan Appleyard, "Blame It All on the Beatles," *The Independent*, 2 January 1996, 11.

25. Ibid.

26. It might be worth recalling, however, that "Free as a Bird" was released on *Anthology 1* before it was released as a single. More needs to be said, however, about the ideological particularities of this regrouping of The Beatles in terms of its promotion of consumerism and, particularly, its fetishization of the past. I am thinking here of that stockpiling of rare and early Beatles recordings, some of which are extremely poor in sound quality (and verge on the unlistenable), as articles of consumption. A kind of colonization of the past can be seen to be at work with the inclusion of songs such as "Hallelujah, I Love Her So," "You'll Be Mine," and "Cayenne" on *Anthology 1*, all of which were recorded in rehearsal at Paul McCartney's home in Liverpool in 1960. I do not mean to say that the inclusion of these songs diminishes the unique status of The Beatles (on the contrary, it adds to it); I mean instead to highlight the momentum of commercialization itself in the contemporary epoch and of the accumulation of things (tape, sound, speech) for cultural standardization. Here, it is quite right to see the cultural legacy of The Beatles being reshaped for commercial convenience; old rehearsal recordings, now fully coded into a global communication system, have been fetishized and, with appropriate commercial gloss, can be represented as new product, complete with an ISBN number.

27. Zygmunt Bauman, *Modernity and Ambivalence* (Cambridge: Polity Press, 1990), 272.

28. Wilfred Mellers, "Imagine," reprinted in *The Lennon Companion: Twenty-five Years of Comment*, ed. Elizabeth Thomson and David Gutman (New York: Schirmer Books, 1996), 181.

29. Quoted in A. Solt and S. Egan, *Imagine: John Lennon* (New York: Macmillan, 1988), 125.

30. Miles, comp., *John Lennon in His Own Words* (London: Omnibus Press, 1980), 94.

31. Ben Gerson, "Together Again: Walls and Bridges," reprinted in *The Lennon Companion: Twenty-five Years of Comment,* ed. Elizabeth Thomson and David Gutman (New York: Schirmer Books, 1987), 211.

32. Philip Norman, *Shout!: The Beatles in Their Generation* (New York: MJF Books, 1981), 14.

33. Lennon, *Skywriting by Word of Mouth,* 36.

Discography

This discography offers a general guide to Lennon's solo albums, his albums recorded in collaboration with Yoko Ono, and his albums with The Beatles. It does not cover singles and other songwriting credits.

John Lennon

Unfinished Music No. 1: Two Virgins: Two Virgins No. 1; Together; Two Virgins No. 2; Two Virgins No. 3; Two Virgins No. 4; Two Virgins No. 5; Two Virgins No. 6; Hushabye Hushabye; Two Virgins No. 7; Two Virgins No. 8; Two Virgins No. 9; Two Virgins No. 10.
(Apple, 1968)

Unfinished Music No. 2: Life with the Lions: Cambridge 1969; No Bed for Beatle John; Baby's Heartbeat; Two Minutes Silence; Radio Play.
(Zapple, 1969)

The Wedding Album: John and Yoko; Amsterdam.
(Apple, 1969)

The Plastic Ono Band—Live Peace in Toronto 1969: Blue Suede Shoes; Money (That's What I Want); Dizzy Miss Lizzy; Yer Blues; Cold Turkey; Give Peace a Chance; Don't Worry Kyoko (Mummy's Only Looking for a Hand in the Snow); John, John (Let's Hope for Peace).
(Apple, 1969)

John Lennon/Plastic Ono Band: Mother; Hold On John; I Found Out; Working Class Hero; Isolation; Remember; Love; Well Well Well; Look at Me; God; My Mummy's Dead.
(Apple, 1970)

Imagine: Imagine; Crippled Inside; Jealous Guy; It's So Hard; I Don't Want to Be a Soldier; Give Me Some Truth; Oh My Love; How Do You Sleep?; How?; Oh Yoko!
(Apple, 1971)

Some Time in New York City: Woman Is the Nigger of the World; Sisters, o Sisters; Attica State; Born in a Prison; New York City; Sunday Bloody Sunday; The Luck of the Irish; John Sinclair; Angela; We're All Water; Cold Turkey; Don't Worry Kyoko; Well (Baby Please Don't Go); Jamrag; Scumbag; Au.
(Apple, 1972)

Mind Games: Mind Games; Tight As; Aisumasen (I'm Sorry); One Day (At a Time); Bring On the Lucie (Freeda People); Nutopian International Anthem; Intuition; Out the Blue; Only People; I Know (I Know); You Are Here; Meat City.
(Apple, 1973)

Walls and Bridges: Going Down on Love; Whatever Gets You thru the Night; Old Dirt Road; What You Got; Bless You; Scared; #9 Dream; Surprise Surprise (Sweet Bird of Paradox); Steel and Glass; Beef Jerky; Nobody Loves You (When You're Down and Out); Ya Ya.
(Apple, 1974)

Rock 'n' Roll: Be-Bop-a-Lula; Stand by Me; Medley: Ready Teddy/Rip It Up; You Can't Catch Me; Ain't That a Shame; Do You Want to Dance; Sweet Little Sixteen; Slippin' and Slidin'; Peggy Sue; Medley: Bring It on Home to Me/Send Me Some Lovin'; Bony Moronie; Ya Ya; Just Because.
(Apple, 1975)

Shaved Fish: Give Peace a Chance; Cold Turkey; Instant Karma!; Power to the People; Mother; Woman Is the Nigger of the World; Imagine; Whatever Gets You thru the Night; Mind Games; #9 Dream; Happy Xmas (War Is Over); Reprise: Give Peace a Chance.
(Apple, 1975)

Double Fantasy: (Just Like) Starting Over; Kiss Kiss Kiss; Give Me Something; I'm Losing You; I'm Moving On; Beautiful Boy (Darling Boy); Watching the Wheels; I'm Your Angel; Woman; Beautiful Boys; Dear Yoko; Every Man Has a Woman Who Loves Him; Hard Times Are Over.
(Geffen, 1980)

The John Lennon Collection: Give Peace a Chance; Instant Karma!; Power to the People; Whatever Gets You thru the Night; #9 Dream; Mind Games;

Love; Imagine; Jealous Guy; (Just Like) Starting Over; Woman; I'm Losing
You; Beautiful Boy (Darling Boy); Dear Yoko; Watching the Wheels; Cold
Turkey; Move Over Ms. L; Happy Xmas (War Is Over); Stand By Me.
(Geffen, 1982; EMI/Capitol, 1990)

Milk and Honey: I'm Stepping Out; Sleepless Night; I Don't Want to Face It;
Don't Be Scared; Nobody Told Me; O'Sanity; Borrowed Time; Your Hands;
(Forgive Me) My Little Flower Princess; Let Me Count the Ways; Grow Old
with Me; You're the One.
(Polydor, 1984)

John Lennon Live in New York City: New York City; It's So Hard; Woman Is
the Nigger of the World; Well Well Well; Instant Karma!; Mother; Come Together; Imagine; Cold Turkey; Hound Dog; Give Peace a Chance.
(EMI/Capitol, 1986)

John Lennon—Menlove Avenue: Here We Go Again; Rock 'n' Roll People;
Angel Baby; Since My Baby Left Me; To Know Her Is to Love Her; Steel and
Glass; Scared; Old Dirt Road; Nobody Loves You When You're Down and
Out; Bless You.
(Capitol, 1986)

Imagine: John Lennon: Real Love (demo version); Imagine (studio and demo
versions); Give Peace a Chance; How?; God; Mother (live version); Stand by
Me; Jealous Guy; Woman; Beautiful Boy (Darling Boy); (Just Like) Starting
Over; Twist and Shout; Help!; In My Life; Strawberry Fields Forever; A Day
in the Life; Revolution 1; The Ballad of John and Yoko; Julia; Don't Let Me
Down.
(Parlophone/Capitol, 1988)

Lennon: Give Peace a Chance; Blue Suede Shoes; Money (That's What I
Want); Dizzy Miss Lizzy; Yer Blues; Cold Turkey; Instant Karma!; Mother;
Hold On; I Found Out; Working Class Hero; Isolation; Remember; Love;
Well Well Well; Look at Me; God; My Mummy's Dead; Power to the People;
Well (Baby Please Don't Go); Imagine; Crippled Inside; Jealous Guy; It's So
Hard; Give Me Some Truth; Oh My Love; How Do You Sleep?; How?; Oh
Yoko!; Happy Xmas (War Is Over); Woman Is the Nigger of the World; New
York City; John Sinclair; Come Together; Hound Dog; Mind Games;
Aisumasen (I'm Sorry); One Day (At a Time); Intuition; Out of the Blue;
Whatever Gets You thru the Night; Going Down on Love; Old Dirt Road;
Bless You; Scared; #9 Dream; Surprise Surprise (Sweet Bird Of Paradox);
Steel and Glass; Nobody Loves You (When You're Down and Out); Stand By
Me; Ain't That a Shame; Do You Want to Dance; Sweet Little Sixteen; Slip-
pin' and Slidin'; Angel Baby; Just Because; Whatever Gets You thru the

Night (live version); Lucy in the Sky with Diamonds; I Saw Her Standing There; (Just Like) Starting Over; Cleanup Time; I'm Losing You; Beautiful Boy (Darling Boy); Watching the Wheels; Woman; Dear Yoko; I'm Steppin' Out; I Don't Wanna Face It; Nobody Told Me; Borrowed Time; (Forgive Me) My Little Flower Princess; Every Man Has a Woman Who Loves Him; Grow Old with Me.
(EMI/Capitol, 1990)

Lennon Legend: Imagine; Instant Karma!; Mother (single edit); Jealous Guy; Power to the People; Cold Turkey; Love; Mind Games; Whatever Gets You thru the Night; #9 Dream; Stand by Me; (Just Like) Starting Over; Woman.
(Parlophone, 1997)

Lennon with The Beatles

Please Please Me: I Saw Her Standing There; Misery; Anna (Go to Him); Chains; Boys; Ask Me Why; Please Please Me; Love Me Do; P.S. I Love You; Baby It's You; Do You Want to Know a Secret; A Taste of Honey; There's a Place; Twist and Shout.
(Parlophone, 1963)

With the Beatles: It Won't Be Long; All I've Got to Do; All My Loving; Don't Bother Me; Little Child; Till There Was You; Please Mr. Postman; Roll Over Beethoven; Hold Me Tight; You Really Got a Hold on Me; I Wanna Be Your Man; Devil in Her Heart; Not a Second Time; Money.
(Parlophone, 1963)

A Hard Day's Night: A Hard Day's Night; I Should Have Known Better; If I Fell; I'm Happy Just to Dance with You; And I Love Her; Tell Me Why; Can't Buy Me Love; Any Time at All; I'll Cry Instead; Things We Said Today; When I Get Home; You Can't Do That; I'll Be Back.
(Parlophone, 1964)

Beatles for Sale: No Reply; I'm a Loser; Baby's in Black; Rock and Roll Music; I'll Follow the Sun; Mr. Moonlight; Kansas City; Eight Days a Week; Words of Love; Honey Don't; Every Little Thing; I Don't Want to Spoil the Party; What You're Doing; Everybody's Trying to Be My Baby.
(Parlophone, 1964)

Help!: Help!; The Night Before; You've Got to Hide Your Love Away; I Need You; Another Girl; You're Going to Lose That Girl; Ticket to Ride; Act Naturally; It's Only Love; You Like Me Too Much; Tell Me What You See; I've Just Seen a Face; Yesterday; Dizzy Miss Lizzy.
(Parlophone, 1965)

Rubber Soul: Drive My Car; Norwegian Wood (This Bird Has Flown); You Won't See Me; Nowhere Man; Think for Yourself; The Word; Michelle; What Goes On; Girl; I'm Looking through You; In My Life; Wait; If I Needed Someone; Run for Your Life.
(Parlophone, 1965)

Revolver: Taxman; Eleanor Rigby; I'm Only Sleeping; Love You Too; Here, There and Everywhere; Yellow Submarine; She Said She Said; Good Day Sunshine; And Your Bird Can Sing; For No One; Doctor Robert; I Want to Tell You; Got to Get You into My Life; Tomorrow Never Knows.
(Parlophone, 1966)

A Collection of Beatles' Oldies (But Goldies): She Loves You; From Me to You; We Can Work It Out; Help!; Michelle; Yesterday; I Feel Fine; Yellow Submarine; Can't Buy Me Love; Bad Boy; Day Tripper; A Hard Day's Night; Ticket to Ride; Paperback Writer; Eleanor Rigby; I Want to Hold Your Hand. (Parlophone, 1966)

Sgt. Pepper's Lonely Hearts Club Band: Sgt. Pepper's Lonely Hearts Club Band; With a Little Help from My Friends; Lucy in the Sky with Diamonds; Getting Better; Fixing a Hole; She's Leaving Home; Being for the Benefit of Mr. Kite; Within You Without You; When I'm Sixty-four; Lovely Rita; Good Morning Good Morning; Sgt. Pepper's Lonely Hearts Club Band; A Day in the Life.
(Parlophone, 1967)

Magical Mystery Tour: Magical Mystery Tour; The Fool on the Hill; Flying; Blue Jay Way; Your Mother Should Know; I Am the Walrus; Hello Goodbye; Strawberry Fields Forever; Penny Lane; Baby You're a Rich Man; All You Need Is Love.
(EMI, 1967)

The Beatles ("The White Album"): Back in the USSR; Dear Prudence; Glass Onion; Ob-La-Di, Ob-La-Da; Wild Honey Pie; The Continuing Story of Bungalow Bill; While My Guitar Gently Weeps; Happiness Is a Warm Gun; Martha My Dear; I'm So Tired; Blackbird; Piggies; Rocky Raccoon; Don't Pass Me By; Why Don't We Do It in the Road; I Will; Julia; Birthday; Yer Blues; Mother Nature's Son; Everybody's Got Something to Hide except for Me and My Monkey; Sexy Sadie; Helter Skelter; Long Long Long; Revolution 1; Honey Pie; Savoy Truffle; Cry Baby Cry; Revolution 9; Good Night.
(Apple, 1968)

Yellow Submarine: Yellow Submarine; Only a Northern Song; All Together Now; Hey Bulldog; It's All Too Much; All You Need Is Love; Film Score Composed and Orchestrated by George Martin.
(Apple, 1969)

Abbey Road: Come Together; Something; Maxwell's Silver Hammer; Oh! Darling; Octopus's Garden; I Want You (She's So Heavy); Here Comes the Sun; Because; You Never Give Me Your Money; Sun King; Mean Mr. Mustard; Polythene Pam; She Came in through the Bathroom Window; Golden Slumbers; Carry That Weight; The End; Her Majesty.
(Apple, 1969)

Let It Be: Two of Us; Dig a Pony; Across the Universe; I Me Mine; Dig It; Let It Be; Maggie Mae; I've Got a Feeling; One after 909; The Long and Winding Road; For You Blue; Get Back.
(Apple 1970)

The Beatles Live at the BBC: Beatle Greetings; From Us to You; Riding on a Bus; I Got a Woman; Too Much Monkey Business; Keep Your Hands off My Baby; I'll Be on My Way; Young Blood; A Shot of Rhythm and Blues; Sure to Fall (In Love with You); Some Other Guy; Thank You Girl; Sha la la la la!; Baby It's You; That's All Right (Mama); Carol; Soldier of Love; A Little Rhyme; Clarabella; I'm Gonna Sit Right Down and Cry (Over You); Crying, Waiting, Hoping; Dear Wack!; You Really Got a Hold on Me; To Know Her Is to Love Her; A Taste of Honey; Long Tall Sally; I Saw Her Standing There; The Honeymoon Song; Johnny B Goode; Memphis, Tennessee; Lucille; Can't Buy Me Love; From Fluff to You; Till There Was You; Crinsk Dee Night; A Hard Day's Night; Have a Banana!; I Wanna Be Your Man; Just a Rumour; Roll Over Beethoven; All My Loving; Things We Said Today; She's a Woman; Sweet Little Sixteen; 1822!; Lonesome Tears in My Eyes; Nothin' Shakin'; The Hippy Hippy Shake; Glad All Over; I Just Don't Understand; So How Come (No One Loves Me); I Feel Fine; I'm a Loser; Everybody's Trying to Be My Baby; Rock and Roll Music; Ticket to Ride; Dizzy Miss Lizzy; Medley: Kansas City/Hey-Hey-Hey-Hey!; Set Fire to That Lot!; Matchbox; I Forgot to Remember to Forget; Love These Goons Shows!; I Got to Find My Baby; Ooh! My Soul; Ooh! My Arms; Don't Ever Change; Slow Down; Honey Don't; Love Me Do.
(Apple, 1994)

The Beatles Anthology 1: Free as a Bird; Speech: John Lennon; That'll Be the Day; In Spite of All the Danger; Speech: Paul McCartney; Hallelujah, I Love Her So; You'll Be Mine; Cayenne; Speech: Paul; My Bonnie; Ain't She Sweet; Cry for a Shadow; Speech: John; Speech: Brian Epstein; Searchin'; Three Cool Cats; The Sheik of Araby; Like Dreamers Do; Hello Little Girl; Speech: Brian Epstein; Besame Mucho; Love Me Do; How Do You Do It; Please Please Me;

One after 909 (Sequence); One after 909; Lend Me Your Comb; I'll Get You; Speech: John; I Saw Her Standing There; From Me to You; Money (That's What I Want); You Really Got a Hold on Me; Roll Over Beethoven; She Loves You; Till There Was You; Twist and Shout; This Boy; I Want to Hold Your Hand; Speech: Eric Morecambe and Ernie Wise; Moonlight Bay; Can't Buy Me Love; All My Loving; You Can't Do That; And I Love Her; A Hard Day's Night; I Wanna Be Your Man; Long Tall Sally; Boys; Shout; I'll Be Back (Take 2); I'll Be Back (Take 3); You Know What to Do; No Reply (Demo); Mr. Moonlight; Leave My Kitten Alone; No Reply; Eight Days a Week (Sequence); Eight Days a Week (Complete); Kansas City/Hey-Hey-Hey-Hey! (Apple, 1995)

The Beatles Anthology 2: Real Love; Yes It Is; I'm Down; You've Got to Hide Your Love Away; If You've Got Trouble; That Means a Lot; Yesterday; It's Only Love; I Feel Fine; Ticket to Ride; Yesterday; Help!; Everybody's Trying to Be My Baby; Norwegian Wood (This Bird Has Flown); I'm Looking through You; 12-Bar Original; Tomorrow Never Knows; Got to Get You into My Life; And Your Bird Can Sing; Taxman; Eleanor Rigby (Strings Only); I'm Only Sleeping (Rehearsal); I'm Only Sleeping (Take 1); Rock and Roll Music; She's a Woman; Strawberry Fields Forever (Demo Sequence); Strawberry Fields Forever (Take 1); Strawberry Fields Forever (Take 7 & Edit Piece); Penny Lane; A Day in the Life; Good Morning Good Morning; Only a Northern Song; Being for the Benefit of Mr. Kite! (Take 7); Lucy in the Sky with Diamonds; Within You Without You (Instrumental); Sgt. Pepper's Lonely Hearts Club Band (Reprise); You Know My Name (Look Up the Number); I Am the Walrus; The Fool on the Hill (Demo); Your Mother Should Know; The Fool on the Hill (Take 4); Hello, Goodbye; Lady Madonna; Across the Universe. (Apple, 1996)

The Beatles Anthology 3: A Beginning; Happiness Is a Warm Gun; Helter Skelter; Mean Mr. Mustard; Polythene Pam; Glass Onion; Junk; Piggies; Honey Pie; Don't Pass Me By; Ob-La-Di, Ob-La-Da; Good Night; Cry Baby Cry; Blackbird; Sexy Sadie; While My Guitar Gently Weeps; Hey Jude; Not Guilty; Mother Nature's Son; Glass Onion; Rocky Raccoon; What's the New Mary Jane; Step inside Love/Los Paranois; I'm So Tired; I Will; Why Don't We Do It in the Road; Julia; I've Got a Feeling; She Came in through the Bathroom Window; Dig a Pony; Two of Us; For You Blue; Teddy Boy; Medley: Rip It Up/Shake, Rattle and Roll/Blue Suede Shoes; The Long and Winding Road; Oh! Darling; All Things Must Pass; Mailman, Bring Me No More Blues; Get Back; Old Brown Shoe; Octopus's Garden; Maxwell's Silver Hammer; Something; Come Together; Come and Get It; Ain't She Sweet; Because; Let It Be; I Me Mine; The End. (Apple, 1996).

Index

Compositor:	Impressions Book and Journal Services, Inc.
Text:	11/13.5 New Caledonia
Display:	New Caledonia
Printer:	Edwards Brothers, Inc.
Binder:	Edwards Brothers, Inc.